RIGHT TO RIDE

THE JOHN HOPE FRANKLIN SERIES

IN AFRICAN AMERICAN HISTORY AND CULTURE

Waldo E. Martin Jr. and Patricia Sullivan, editors

RIGHT TO RIDE

STREETCAR BOYCOTTS AND AFRICAN AMERICAN
CITIZENSHIP IN THE ERA OF *PLESSY V. FERGUSON*

Blair L. M. Kelley   The University of North Carolina Press Chapel Hill

All rights reserved. Designed by Courtney Leigh Baker and set in Merlo and Serifa by
Keystone Typesetting, Inc. Manufactured in the United States of America. The paper in
this book meets the guidelines for permanence and durability of the Committee on Pro-
duction Guidelines for Book Longevity of the Council on Library Resources. The University of North Carolina Press has been a member of the Green Press Initiative since 2003.

Library of Congress Cataloging-in-Publication Data
Kelley, Blair Murphy, 1973–
Right to ride : streetcar boycotts and African American citizenship in the
era of Plessy v. Ferguson / Blair L. M. Kelley. — 1st ed.
p. cm. — (John Hope Franklin series in African American history and culture)
Includes bibliographical references and index.
ISBN 978-0-8078-3354-4 (cloth : alk. paper) — ISBN 978-0-8078-7101-0 (pbk. : alk. paper)
1. African Americans—Civil rights—History. 2. Civil rights movements—United
States—History. 3. Segregation in transportation—United States—History.
4. Boycotts—United States—History. 5. United States—Race relations—
History. 6. New Orleans (La.)—Race relations—History. 7. Richmond (Va.)—
Race relations—History. 8. Savannah (Ga.)—Race relations—History. I. Title.
E185.61.K355 2010
323.1196'073—dc22
2009050000

CLOTH 14 13 12 11 10   5 4 3 2 1
PAPER 14 13 12 11 10   5 4 3 2 1

FOR JULIA

CONTENTS

A section of illustrations appears after p. 115.

ACKNOWLEDGMENTS

Acknowledgments are a moment when an author is able to acknowledge that most of what often felt like a very solitary enterprise is actually the result of thousands of pages read by friends, mentors, and colleagues and hundreds of moments of kindness and critique, arguments and heart-felt conversations. I was nervous about writing my own, worried about accurately sharing my gratitude with those who have helped along the way. It is my hope that these few pages will begin to express the debt that I owe to so many people who believed in my efforts.

Throughout this project I have received research support. I am grateful to the institutions that provided financial support, including the Duke Endowment Fellowship; the Anne Firor Scott Award from Women's Studies at Duke University; the University of Notre Dame's Erskine Peters Dissertation Year Fellowship; a fellowship from the National Endowment of the Humanities, which designated Right to Ride a We the People project; and research funding from the College of Humanities and Social Sciences at North Carolina State University. I owe a debt of gratitude to many of my colleagues in the Department of History at North Carolina State University for their support. In particular, I thank Gail O'Brien for her close reading of the manuscript early in the process. I am especially thankful to the community of scholars who participated in the National Endowment for the Humanities Institute on African American Civil Rights Struggles in the Twentieth Century, hosted by the Department of African and African American Studies at Harvard University in the summer of 2006.

I thank all the people who have read chapters of the manuscript at different points during the process. My colleagues Hasan K. Jeffries and Dionne Danns read chapters during the National Endowment for the Humanities workshop in Cambridge and gave helpful criticisms. My department head and mentor at North Carolina State University, Jonathan Ocko, helped review the manuscript before my initial submission. Three North Carolina State colleagues—David Ambaras, David Gilmartin, and Craig Friend—read the manuscript and offered encouragement and suggestions. I also thank Kathleen Mellen Charron for her advice, assistance, and encouragement about the process of publishing. I thank Suzanne Lebsock, who reviewed the manuscript in such a caring and exhaustive manner. I believe her suggestions have strengthened the book in important ways.

I think I was raised to be a historian. My parents, Leroy Murphy and Frances Duncan Murphy, are not professional storytellers, but they constantly told stories as a way to frame the meanings of their lives and the lives of their forebears. Mundane acts would serve as reminders of the past. From my family, I learned that the historical moments that shaped African American life could be understood as personal: the Great Migration, North Philadelphia, World War II, the death of FDR, Howard University in 1956, the air force in the first throes of desegregation—all came filtered through their own rich narratives. My parents taught me that to understand history, you have to understand how individuals experienced it. For their lessons and their constant support, I am forever grateful.

Reginald Butler and Patricia Sullivan, who taught me as an undergraduate at the University of Virginia, were the first to encourage my desire to forgo law school and pursue history. Butler's classes in African American history were eye-opening experiences—they showed me that history could speak volumes about the present. Sullivan nurtured my newfound interest with profound kindness and generosity, and she still serves as my most generous mentor. Thanks for always getting it when I was trying to find my way. You have been such a selfless teacher, and I am proud to be your student.

The rich community of scholars at Duke University was a wonderful training ground. The members of my dissertation committee—William Chafe, Peter Wood, Barry Gaspar, Wahneema Lubiano, and chair Raymond Gavins—helped clear a path so that I could explore this history. I thank emeritus professor Anne Firor Scott for supporting my work at a moment when I needed a boost and for reminding me recently to "just get the book out." My inquiry was enriched by the community of scholars working on the Behind the Veil project, including faculty investigators William Chafe, Raymond Gavins, and Robert Korstad; student workers, particularly Alex Byrd and Paul Ortiz; and fellow field investigators Keisha T. Turner and Mausiki Scales. Thank you to my friends in the Duke campus community who offered moral support and mentorship—in particular, Lois Deloatch and Mazella Hall. I thank my colleague and friend, Paul Ortiz, for his incredible generosity. Paul read both my dissertation proposal and years later my manuscript with incredible patience, insightful criticism, and uplifting support. My debt to you is enormous.

I have a wonderful family that has always been supportive of my goals. Your prayers have kept me going. I thank my parents for always allowing me to pursue my goals, no matter how unusual they seemed at the time. Your support is immeasurable. I thank my extended family, particularly my aunts and uncles, Ernestine and Clifford Carty, Ethel Robinson, Shirley Downes, Eloise and Donald McMichael, Nathaniel and Iris Murphy, and Brian and Sonia Duncan. Thanks for all your cards, calls, advice, and years of loving support. My cousins are too numerous to name here, but I thank Stephen Minus for always offering a respite from my work as a student.

I have incredible friends who have always offered love and support. I thank Pamela Mebane for putting up with all of my research trips to Washington, D.C., and always allowing me to stay even on shockingly short notice. Your belief in me from way back has meant so much. Thanks to Nikki Barnett for always sweeping in to dust me off and make me feel better. Your style and grace always make me feel at ease. Thanks to Nicole Waligora-Davis for always being my scholarly sister-friend. Your tremendous skills as a researcher, writer, and theorist have made my work much stronger. Your laughter and commiseration always remind me that I am not alone. Thank you to Hilary Jones, my Peters Fellowship officemate and friend. I have learned not only from your rich scholarship on the diaspora but also from your patience and gentle manner. Thanks to Kelly Richmond Pope for being such a steady phone-a-friend, always willing to listen to any gripe and cheer every victory.

I THANK MELISSA HARRIS-LACEWELL for being my best friend. Never did I imagine that I would have a friend so brilliant, funny, loyal, and generous, all in one package. Thank you for the research trips, thank you for reading the manuscript over and over and over. Thanks for being both a brilliant cheerleader and an insightful critic. Thanks for constantly helping me make the "to do" lists that help me reenergize and restart. Thanks for filling in every gap, putting up with every bout of self-doubt, and thanks most of all for making this journey so much fun. Without you, this book would not exist.

Thank you most of all to Patrick and Julia Blair Kelley. Patrick, your patience with my quest has been endless. From the moment I met you, you never let me quit, and you always reminded me that this was possible. Thanks for blending your life with mine. I can think of no better person to share the journey. Finally, thank you to Julia for putting up with my turned back and diverted eyes as I worked on this book. Thanks for all the drawings and notes you wrote on my drafts and thanks for making me occasionally stop to play. I hope that when you are able to read this book, you will enjoy it, because it is dedicated to you. But for now, let's just say, "Mommy's done."

RIGHT TO RIDE

INTRODUCTION

In February 1956, Dr. Martin Luther King Jr. and eighty-eight other leaders
of the Montgomery Improvement Association (MIA) willingly turned themselves in for arrest.[1] A grand jury had indicted King for violating an Alabama
antiboycott law. The protest leaders knew that segregationists, led by the
state chapter of the White Citizens' Council, would stop at nothing to halt
their protests, but King and the MIA did not know that they were not the
first to organize boycotts to protest segregation in their state. Indeed, the
law the MIA leaders were charged with violating had originally been designed to crush black efforts to boycott segregated city streetcars in Montgomery in 1900 and Mobile in 1902.[2] The original 1903 law prohibited
"boycotting, . . . picketing or other interference with . . . lawful business,"
just the kind of protests that had been launched by Rosa Parks's December
1955 refusal to give up her seat and the collective efforts to avoid segregated
buses in the city. The law criminalized any organized efforts to protest,
prohibiting the distribution of leaflets and buttons and making it "unlaw-
ful to print or circulate any notice of boycott, boycott cards, stickers."
Police could charge boycotters with vagrancy as they waited for alternative
rides. It was even illegal for local black newspapers to publicize the protest;
in an almost exasperated tone, the law forbade "publishing or declaring
that a boycott . . . exists or has existed or is contemplated." Protest leaders
could be punished with a high fine or months of hard labor. Although
unaware of this long history, Parks, King, and the other indicted protest
organizers were reviving a protest fifty-five years old, connecting them to

the southern streetcar boycott movement that began at the turn of the twentieth century. Protest had deep roots.[3]

The 1903 law unintentionally bears witness to the character of these early protests; we can imagine black men and women picketing segregated streetcars, posting signs, and handing out buttons to participants. The law's commands about loitering help us envision laundresses and day laborers waiting for rides to work from African American hackmen using mule-driven wagons in support of the boycott. Prohibitions on publicizing protests hint at the headlines in black newspapers advertising mass meetings and inspiring readers to press on. No black newspapers from turn-of-the-century Montgomery exist today, but much can be discerned about the character of the protests from the text of the law. One bit of evidence that does survive reports that the Montgomery Street Railway Company lost more than fourteen hundred dollars in revenue during the first twenty-five days of the boycott.[4]

Despite the protests' financial impact, black Montgomery was not completely united in resisting segregation in 1900, just as there were black residents of Montgomery who doubted the wisdom of the bus boycott in the 1950s. The Reverend Titus Atticus Weathington, one of the city's leading black Methodist ministers, endorsed the segregation law and refused to participate in the boycott. The Reverend A. N. McEwen, a Baptist minister and newspaper editor from Montgomery's sister city, Mobile, argued that Weathington betrayed the protest cause for his own advancement: "It is a great pity that so many Negro preachers and school teachers throughout the country are making asses of themselves by trying to cater to white prejudices in order to be called a 'good nigger.'" McEwen saw no middle ground: "Discrimination on public conveyances after charging all the same price is wrong."[5]

McEwen would apply the lessons of the Montgomery streetcar boycott when he led the boycotts in Mobile in 1902. Having served from 1885 to 1891 as the pastor of Dexter Avenue Baptist Church—the Montgomery church where Martin Luther King Jr. would become pastor and boycott leader more than sixty years later—McEwen committed to protecting racial justice in Montgomery even after taking a pastorate in Mobile.[6] In Mobile, his leadership helped make the boycott a brief success, even causing streetcar officials to desegregate the cars in violation of the Jim Crow law.[7]

Thus, the passage of the 1903 antiboycott law was an effort to shut down protests in Montgomery and Mobile and silence their leaders. Within months of the law's passage, collective resistance to segregated transportation in Alabama was effectively crushed. McEwen had insisted that African Americans in Alabama were "going to fight and contend for equal rights and justice to all men in all parts of the South, and we will not despair until the sad news comes to us that God is dead." However, in the face of legal and perhaps extralegal pressure, McEwen ceased publishing weekly accounts of protests and instead asked readers for their feedback on a "Church Edition" of the *Southern Watchman* focused solely on events in local and regional congregations. Like many others, the once outspoken leader was silenced.[8]

The passage of the 1903 law may have stunted protests by threatening boycott leaders with time on the chain gang, but the law reflects more than the vengeance of segregationist legislators. It also reflects the complexity of African American turn-of-the-century protest. Between 1900 and 1907, the leaders of black Montgomery, Mobile, and at least twenty-three other southern cities posed a serious challenge to the progress of Jim Crow segregation. The Alabama law itself was emblematic of the challenges faced by black southerners struggling to maintain their citizenship in the face of difficult circumstances and their willingness to organize vibrant, collective opposition.

Right to Ride is about this forgotten generation of black southerners, who, like African Americans in Montgomery, organized in opposition to the passage of laws segregating southern trains and streetcars at the turn of the twentieth century. But it begins with a reminder that southern segregation policies and protests were not the first in the nation. Segregation began in the North in the 1840s and 1850s as an effort to control gradually emancipated former slaves. Policies segregated African American passengers on trains and forced black streetcar riders to stand on outdoor platforms even when the cars were not full. But fledgling communities of emancipated black Americans and abolitionists of all colors protested vigorously, ending the segregation of public conveyances in the North by the end of the Civil War. But Jim Crow trains and streetcars were reimagined and revived in the postbellum South, and the politics of racial separation reached its greatest complexity and virulence in the American South at the turn of the twentieth century.

Historians have called this time the age of accommodation. African Americans were painted with the brush of their most politic leader, Booker T. Washington, an educator who compromised on the question of black citizenship and maintained public silence in the face of white supremacist atrocities. Washington did not publicly oppose policies of racial separation, accepting segregation as the price of economic advancement. Washington was the most influential black political figure of his day, and much of the black elite were beholden to him. However, no one man can define an age.

Black citizens in the 1890s and 1900s lived in an America where black men, women, and children were hunted like sport. The targets were lynched, often with the complicity of local law enforcement officials. Beaten or charred corpses were displayed like trophies of the chase, while the hunters smiled in the pictures. These murders were considered an acceptable control on black people, so much so that the pictures were turned into postcards that were forwarded by the U.S. Postal Service with captions like "This is the way we do them down here."[9] The terror of lynching reached its high point just as disfranchisement and segregation became law in every southern state. White supremacist legislators plotted how best to permanently strip African Americans of their right to vote, after continual fraud proved unreliable. National leaders turned blind eyes when state politicians held unconstitutional conventions, rewriting state laws to disfranchise and segregate black populations.

Thus, to speak at all was admirable. In the decades following the close of federal Reconstruction, most moderate whites in the North and South abandoned the defense of African American citizenship in favor of national reconciliation. In a time of such stark brutality, agitation of any kind was dangerous. But African Americans in this age were not silent; they stood against injustice, risking their lives to report on lynching and battling to protect the innocent, fighting a losing effort to maintain their right to vote, and contesting the stigma of segregation and second-class citizenship. Because their protests ultimately failed, their efforts have not been well remembered. Even as their struggle faltered, however, participants in these lawsuits and boycotts learned to navigate communities circumscribed by Jim Crow segregation, doing their best to avoid the harshest insults and most dangerous situations. Few recorded their history of thwarted resistance. Still, the protests remind us that many black southerners did not simply view segregation as inevitable; they grudgingly took the back seats or rode in smoke-filled Jim Crow cars only after a fierce effort to dissent. Black citizens faced down this fearful challenge, refusing to acquiesce without a fight. As W. E. B. Du Bois noted of his generation, "Whenever we submit to humiliation and oppression it is because of superior brute force; and even when bending to the inevitable we bend with unabated protest."[10] The protests of the nadir were a valiant, popular fight to defend black citizenship and protect the dignity of everyday life.

African Americans' efforts to stop the segregation of trains and street-cars, the organizations created to contest Jim Crow laws, and segregation-ists' attempts to silence the protests all provide rich testimony to the spirit of agitation present even in this bleak time in American history. Historians August Meier and Elliott Rudwick rediscovered these protests in the 1960s. Their groundbreaking "The Boycott Movement against Jim Crow Street-cars" was followed by a series of articles chronicling these early protests in notable cities and states. Yet only a few contemporary local historians have done exhaustive work on African American dissent against segregated con-veyances beyond the Meier and Rudwick framework.[11] Few extended stud-ies have examined these remarkable protests, and none have connected an assessment of *Plessy v. Ferguson* (1896) to an examination of African Ameri-can life and political culture in the age of segregation and protest.[12]

Until this study, the work of Meier and Rudwick has stood as the inter-pretation of the history of resistance to segregated conveyances. Most broad histories of the Jim Crow South that mention the movement simply cite Meier and Rudwick. Their work set the standard because they were masterful chroniclers of African American history. Beginning in the 1950s, they had set out to trace the African American experience in the Jim Crow South. In article after article, they cataloged the broad sweep of the African American experience, with their most notable work examining the influence of Booker T. Washington and the little-known streetcar boycott movement, which echoed through the recent Montgomery Bus Boycott. "The Boycott Movement" was an informative, detailed account, tracing protests in multi-ple cities, identifying extant sources, and tallying up twenty-five cities of dissent. In part because their study was so exhaustive, Meier and Rudwick's article and approach have been taken as a given. With a few notable excep-tions, most contemporary accounts adopt not only the facts of the article but its judgments about the character of the movement as well.

While Meier and Rudwick were spot-on in accounting for the facts, their analysis of the scope and meaning of this movement, judged through the lens of the civil rights revolution that occurred in their midst, was blurred. Meier and Rudwick judged the earlier protest movement to be conservative and accommodationist, stilted by the class biases of many of its leaders, and shaped in Washington's image. Without probing the details that may have fleshed out the character and meaning of these protests, they compared this "conservative" streetcar movement to the "radical" Montgomery Bus Boy-cott. Lost in their analysis was a clear sense of the context in which the earlier movement's leaders made claims for inclusion.

In the face of violent white supremacy, African American boycott leaders in the 1900s couched their protest in the terms they hoped would be most acceptable to white lawmakers and streetcar managers. However, the language of the leaders—which often blamed the poor for racial tensions—could not mask the fact that most black southerners saw streetcar segregation as part of a three-pronged attack on their citizenship. Even if Meier and Rudwick correctly assumed that the boycott was a conservative, class-driven movement, their analysis failed to move beyond the language of the leadership and account for the high levels of working-class participation.

No comprehensive work on the streetcar boycott movement was completed after the Meier and Rudwick study. Some local histories of the urban South have done more to chart the movement, but *Right to Ride* is the first book-length examination and the first study that explicitly connects the history of organizing in the antebellum North, the legal efforts against segregated rails in New Orleans, and the streetcar boycotts. Efforts to defeat segregation took place not only in the public sphere of ideas and arguments in the press, the courts, and the legislatures but also in the physical struggle for seats on trains and streetcars. By connecting the black middle-class debate over the meanings of citizenship in an age of segregation to the everyday black working-class contests for physical space and social recognition, this book throws into question the very notion of accommodation, reminding us that dissent also ruled the day.

MOST ACCOUNTS of turn-of-the-twentieth-century black political thought center on the conservative educator Booker T. Washington and the young agitator W. E. B. Du Bois. Although they were two of the foremost "race men" of their day, this book does not focus on these formidable figures. Although both Washington and Du Bois contested segregated conveyances, neither man stood at the forefront of public protests against transportation segregation. The silence of the two preeminent black men of this age has perhaps been taken as assent.

Washington disagreed with policies segregating southern rails. Although he personally experienced few difficulties with discrimination during his travels, beginning in the 1880s he disapproved of discriminatory railroad practices on the economic principle that black riders who paid full first-class fare deserved first-class accommodations. Over time, Washington became more surreptitiously active in the fight against segregated trains and streetcars, penning anonymous editorials, lending behind-the-scenes support to boycotts, and secretly sponsoring suits against discriminatory railroads, including a case on behalf of Du Bois.[13] But Washington did not speak publicly in support of train litigants or streetcar protesters.[14]

Du Bois's most eloquent and influential work, *The Souls of Black Folk* (1903), adamantly declared that the color line would define the century. Indeed, at the birth of the century, African Americans battled against one of the color line's most demeaning dimensions, public transportation. In a variety of ways, Du Bois was a pathbreaker, one of the best-educated men of his day, trained first at Fisk in Tennessee and then going on to Harvard, where he received a doctorate in 1898. He sought to be an activist-scholar, using his scholarship to reveal the problems of race in America to the nation and the world. As a young man, he hoped that racist ignorance could be shed if whites better understood the history of slavery and race and the conditions of contemporary black life. His frustration with Washington's leadership led him to organize the Niagara Movement, a collection of black men and women willing to agitate. He eventually became a founding member of the National Association for the Advancement of Colored People, which led efforts to end all forms of discrimination against African Americans.

Du Bois vehemently opposed segregation on trains and streetcars. He called railroad segregation "the most annoying sort of race discrimination." His opposition to segregation began at age seventeen, when he moved from his childhood home in Great Barrington, Massachusetts, to Nashville, Tennessee, to attend Fisk. Growing up, the bright and handsome Du Bois had experienced race as an ambiguous stigma, a mark of difference, but one that had not limited his imagination or prevented people in his family or mostly white community from supporting his efforts to be well educated. As Du Bois moved south, he experienced race in a hard and punitive manner. Blacks in the South had been marked by slavery; he explained the experience in two of his most famous and poignant metaphors—as a heavy veil that separated black from white and obscured the vision and possibilities for the race and as a hard and fast color line that divided black from white, cutting away possibilities for black humanity.

There was no better example of the color line than the southern railroad. Du Bois explained that the car would stop "out beyond the covering in the rain or sun or dust," and boarding was usually difficult because there was "no step to help one climb on." Rather than separate but equal facilities, the colored car was just "a smoker cut in two," just "a half or a quarter or an eighth of the oldest car in service on the road." Cars set aside for black passengers were rarely cleaned; "the old plush . . . caked with dirt, the floor gummy and the windows dirty." Black passengers rode alongside the "white train crew," whose members used the colored car "to lounge in and perform their toilet." The conductor rode in the car but offered no courtesy or directions. No class lines existed in the colored cars; genteel black women and their children sat beside prisoners serving on chain gangs.[15]

As the foremost scholar of the race, Du Bois remained vigilant in his efforts to dedicate his work as a historian, sociologist, and author to trace the historical and contemporary contours of African American life and to delineate the "the problem of the color line." Du Bois deplored the practices of the Jim Crow South and avoided using segregated trains and streetcars whenever possible. He actively contested the inequitable treatment he received when forced to travel by train and in 1900 pressed a claim with the Interstate Commerce Commission, the federal body charged with arbitrating train segregation. His suit was never resolved.[16] The Niagara Movement supported suits against separate and unequal conditions on trains in Virginia, but these protests had little impact. Despite his leadership, Du Bois made no public comment specifically in support of the wave of streetcar boycotts that African Americans initiated throughout the urban South in the 1900s, an odd stance given the many ways that the popular movement would have dovetailed with his cause.[17]

Although Washington was the most influential black man in America and Du Bois was certainly the most visionary race man of his day, this book is not about either man. The men and women who led the fight to stop the segregation of southern trains and streetcars were not as well known as Washington and Du Bois, but their leadership was just as complicated. Male and female black businesspeople, journalists, ministers, and community and labor organizers from Louisville, New Orleans, Atlanta, Savannah, Richmond, Nashville, and Washington, D.C., help us better map black political thought. The leadership of the fight was diverse, adopting various tactics and distinct agendas in the effort to contest segregation. The figures outlined in this project do not fit neat categories of "accommodation" and "protest." The writers, entrepreneurs, ministers, and social advocates who led had complex, even messy approaches to the battle against segregated conveyances. They adopted diverse ideologies from nationalism to feminism; some were advocates of integration, others of separatism; some were ardent advocates of capitalism, while others were populist labor leaders.

What we believed we knew about this generation is that the majority of black southerners acquiesced—receded behind the veil, grudgingly accommodated the policies of segregation, and retreated into all-black institutions. The contemporary blooming of black mutual societies, businesses, churches, schools, trade unions, and social orders is seen as evidence of black acceptance of the inevitability of segregation. Intracommunity institutional development is characterized as evidence of the age of accommodation, when black southerners, led by Washingtonian compromise, deemphasized the quest for civil rights in favor of economic advancement and community building. Historians have accurately outlined the ways in which black communities turned within, seeking to develop a separate institutional life— what Earl Lewis aptly calls the "home sphere"—to counter racial segregation and to enrich life within the black community.[18] But as black southerners sought to strengthen their resources within the bounds of the community, they did not disengage from the defense of their citizenship. These same community-based institutions fueled the movement to contest lynching, disfranchisement, and the daily humiliations of segregation on trains and streetcars.[19]

Black organizational life provided a crucial base for launching collective responses to the passage and enforcement of unjust laws. Members of the Prince Hall Masons, the United Order of True Reformers, the Independent Order of Saint Luke, the Knights of Pythias, the Odd Fellows, and even Booker T. Washington's National Negro Business League and Afro-American Council supported protests in their cities, publicized their causes, and provided support for dissent throughout the South. New committees, umbrella groups, and associations formed to respond to the passage of train and streetcar segregation laws. While some ministers were reluctant dissenters, many church edifices served as meeting places, and church members provided the networks necessary to fuel protests. The support of black businesses and banks propelled dissent as well; most of the cities that waged effective boycotts were also home to at least one black-owned bank.[20] Labor unions—particularly dockworkers unions, which had gained strength since Reconstruction—also led the protest charge, offering leadership and knowledge about the power of opting out, either through strikes or in the form of a boycott. The enterprise and independence fostered by African American churches, black colleges, fraternal orders, clubs, benevolent societies, financial institutions, and labor unions nourished the spirit of protest, provided cohesion, and developed the leadership necessary to guide the movement.

Right to Ride also grapples with the contested meanings of class within African American communities. The tone of Meier and Rudwick's study has caused some historians to dismiss the suits, boycotts, and organizations of this time as futile middle-class efforts at inclusion.[21] Consequently, much of the historiography of the Jim Crow South that discusses train protests and particularly the streetcar boycott movement classifies this wave of contestation as the failed effort of a small and select privileged class of black southerners to gain inclusion in a cross-racial middle class. Indeed, the efforts to contest segregation were led by an emerging black middle class. But this project demonstrates that segregation recognized no class divides. As railroads and electric streetcar systems were expanded and modernized, people from all walks of life could afford to ride. As cities expanded and opportunities multiplied, more people came to depend on trains and streetcars for travel to work, school, and recreation. For the nickels they paid to ride, black southerners wanted dignity along with a seat.

As the technology improved, segregationists devised increasingly formal and complicated ways to decrease equal access along racial lines. Segregation laws resonated with the dehumanization of slavery. Southern blacks remembered that bondage robbed their forebears of not only their labor but also their mobility, self-determination, and personal dignity. The prosperous and the poor alike resented the humiliation of racial separations, connecting acts of racial degradation to the larger attack on black citizenship. Hundreds of black rail passengers avoided Jim Crow cars, and thousands of southern blacks resisted streetcar segregation, affirming that slavery was over or, as one boycott leader often asserted, that "the day of the time-server is past."[22] Efforts to contest segregation became notable precisely because African Americans from all walks of life participated. The individual and collective protests of African Americans were not simply class-based attempts at bourgeois respectability; protesters recognized that segregation was not only a daily inconvenience and public humiliation but also part of a focused attack on the citizenship of all black southerners.

Class consciousness did, however, color the ways African Americans viewed one another and the appropriate paths to protest. This book traces the ways in which the shrinking possibilities available to southern blacks sometimes distorted their vision of one another. The striving middle class often blamed impoverished and poorly behaved blacks for their compromised condition. In a country and culture that cited material prosperity as evidence of innate ability and Westernized social progress as a mark of civilization, the glaring poverty, disease, and despair among the urban South's working poor made them scapegoats and created a climate of judgment and blame. A desire to reshape these conditions motivated others toward uplift. The distance between the rising middle class and the working poor sometimes misshaped protest and may have stymied the movement.

The movement's full potential was realized only when both women and men participated in the fight to defend black citizenship. On trains and streetcars, middle-class and working-class black women argued for their right to be seated. From antebellum black New Yorker Elizabeth Jennings and Virginia clubwoman Maggie Lena Walker to the nameless black laundresses and domestic workers who rode streetcars to and from work each day, black women's participation made the movement possible. Women served as some of the most articulate spokespeople against Jim Crow. Their lawsuits against segregated rails and their rallying cries against segregated streetcars offered poignant reminders that black women were also at the forefront of defending their rights as ladies and citizens. As Walker explained, "Our self-respect demands that we walk."[23]

Women's presence laid bare the irrationality of segregation. As domestic workers, black women were allowed to sit with the white children and elderly in their care; as passengers, however, they were assaulted for sitting in those same seats. When women challenged the color line, they often faced vicious attacks just as violent as those waged against men. But the excuses used to justify attacks on men formed around the mythical image of the black male rapist. Black male passengers were said to pose a sexual threat to genteel white women. However, such false images could not be stretched far enough to apply to black women. So when African American women were excluded, beaten, and thrown from moving streetcars; physically dragged out of their seats in ladies' rail cars; or made to stand on the outdoor platforms of moving trains, such acts of brutality revealed that segregation was about not separation and protection but violence and stigma. Black women protesters left segregationists nowhere to hide. Shaped by this gendered dynamic, women became some of the most effective leaders and protesters in the fight for full citizenship and dignity.

While the generation of blacks that lodged protest in the era of *Plessy* were not the first to contest segregation, their legacy offers a unique opportunity to understand popular black thought at the turn of the twentieth century. We now know that Du Bois's often quoted insight that the problem of the twentieth century would be the problem of the color line was shockingly true. But what was the outlook of the masses of black Americans as the new century dawned? Collective efforts to stop the legal segregation of trains and streetcars show that African Americans were not united in outlook or approach. They did not agree on how to define the problem facing black America. Black leaders disagreed about how white supremacy could best be challenged. Some communities insisted that independent black institutions would give black southerners new opportunities and shield them from the barbs of race prejudice. Other communities clung to the legacies of inclusion first forged by interracial abolitionism and Reconstruction Republicanism. Many African Americans believed that exemplary black behavior was the solution to the problem. Only when the poor and poorly behaved improved through thrift, piety, and education could white southerners recognize black southerners' potential. Could African Americans simply improve themselves in education and attainment to prove their worth to the nation? Was black success the solution or the problem? How could black men and women best face down the specter of racial violence and second-class citizenship? Was protest the answer? Should men or women be at the forefront of the challenge to southern segregation? This study seeks to better understand the variety of approaches that characterized black political thought as expressed in the protests against segregated trains and streetcars. The movement united the prosperous and the poor, men and women, educated and illiterate, and gave them all an opportunity to use their voices, to contest, in the courts or with their feet, the injustice of second-class citizenship. The fight for the right to ride demonstrates the depth of black anger and desire to be recognized as citizens even in the age of accommodation.

This story, then, connects two dissonant themes: the collective nature of the struggle against the segregation of trains and streetcars and the tensions that existed within black communities. In a movement where success would have required complete solidarity, intracommunity tensions of class, color, culture, and gender existed. In a movement where loyalty was essential to success, instances of trickery and betrayal occurred. In a movement where the participants needed unflagging bravery, many great advocates were understandably quieted by fear. In a movement that required the physical discipline of walking or adopting alternate means of transportation, many participants grew tired. And of course some members of each community did not choose to contest segregation or disagreed with the tactics. These many shortcomings, generated by internal and external pressures, help us to understand the everyday costs of protest, revealing what citizenship meant to those engaged in a fervent struggle to defend it. A recognition of tension and difference helps to begin an outline of the difficulties present in every struggle for justice.

In spite of the challenges implicit in this forgotten movement, this story reminds us that the age of "accommodation" was simultaneously a time of resistance. African Americans from all walks of life took risks and made sacrifices to fight the passage and enforcement of segregation laws. And while the leaders were middle class, participants from the working class were just as concerned about the character of their citizenship. But in this broad-based movement, class division weakened the participants in the midst of a formidable fight. Finally, the book forces a reassessment of the meaning of failure and forgetfulness in African American history. The movement for full and equitable inclusion in American society did not reach its goals in these difficult decades. But the effort to contest the everyday insults of segregation on southern trains and streetcars can now take its place as a valiant part of a longer struggle for civil rights and the recognition of black citizenship.

1 NEW YORK

The Antebellum Roots of Segregation and Dissent

The most iconic decision in the history of segregation in America is *Plessy v. Ferguson* (1896). The Supreme Court institutionalized legal segregation, making the phrase "separate but equal" the new standard. Indeed, *Plessy* opened the floodgates of southern segregation. *Plessy*'s prominence, however, has left many people with the mistaken notion that segregation began at that moment and that it was really just a southern problem. Lost is the collective understanding that Jim Crow segregation began long before *Plessy* and far from the trains of New Orleans.

This chapter traces the roots of segregation and resistance, outlining one of the earliest collective movements of black citizens against segregated streetcars.[1] In New York City, the heart of urban America in 1854, Elizabeth Jennings, a young schoolteacher and church organist, was ejected from a white car on her way to church. Her suit against the Third Avenue Railway Company and the movement that it spurred reverberate with the challenges faced by the black southerners who tried to halt de jure segregation fifty years later. Black opposition to segregation began at the same moment that segregation itself began: free black people throughout the urban North sought to establish their rights as passengers on public conveyances. That this generation of abolitionists, still fighting to end the enslavement of millions, also contested segregation tells us a great deal about the importance of mobility, dignity, and the freedom from public violence. This story stands as a reminder that African Americans in all parts of the nation found segregation abhorrent.

Their legacy of dissent would be remembered when sympathetic law-makers sought to shape the law to protect black public citizenship after the Civil War. However, this history also served as a template for the next generation of African Americans crafting their own meanings of freedom, citizenship, and equality in the postwar South. Black northerners were the first emancipated citizens—that is, the first former slaves to try to map out the meanings of freedom. Northern segregation taught African Americans that freedom was not the same as equality. And it was this generation that would serve as examples for the next when black northerners, along with their institutions and outlook, traveled South after the Civil War.

Antebellum African American passengers who fought for full and equitable inclusion did not seek special treatment or unusual protection but instead desired equitable recognition of their personhood, an extension of their work as antislavery advocates. Equal access to trains, streetcars, and ferryboats went beyond travel; it became fundamental, a test of the quality and character of black citizenship. If black urbanites did not belong on public conveyances, then not only was their mobility limited physically, but they were symbolically blocked from the social mobility promised by American life. Segregation was a mark of race slavery, a public signifier that stigmatized black people both slave and free. Their willingness to protest segregation in that moment was significant. Even when standing at the margins of American citizenship, battling for the right to vote, and seeking decent housing and education for their children, all while working to end slavery and aid the enslaved, they saw their equal right to ride as a crucial question. They were willing to gather their meager funds and sue, to risk their safety to sit in spaces set aside for whites, and organize to make change. Their dignity was not expendable. When black Americans fought for seats on trains and streetcars, they fought for public recognition of their citizenship. Decades before *Plessy v. Ferguson*, segregation and protest had a long and tangled history, highlighting the meanings of race, citizenship, and urban life throughout the nation.

SEGREGATION WAS NOT a southern invention. It belonged to no one region; it was an American phenomenon. The name "Jim Crow" became synonymous with the inferior, racially segregated train cars designated for black passengers, first in the antebellum North and later in the postwar South. As the black-faced minstrel character played by the white performer Thomas "Daddy" Rice, Jim Crow was an uncouth, uncultured, humorously danger-ous runaway slave, insistent on barging in on the white world. Jim Crow was a traveler; in Rice's performances, Jim Crow could frequently be found riding in otherwise elegant trains, streetcars, and steamboats. Dressed in tattered traveling clothes, Jim Crow imagined himself escorting his wife in the ladies' car of a train: he sang "I tink I see myself on a Rail Road, wid a wife upon my arm, an to foller up de fashum, dare sure can be no harm."[2]

White audiences made Rice's minstrel performances enormously popular in the 1830s, marking the consciousness of America with the image of the black intruder. The racial segregation of public conveyances in the 1840s was designed to prevent these sorts of transgressions of the social order. The Jim Crow car was the place to shunt black passengers, a place where the "uncivilized negro" of white imaginations could be prevented from mingling with whites.

The early attempts to segregate or exclude black passengers met with dissent from black Americans across the nation. Not only were free blacks in the cities of the antebellum South regularly ejected from streetcars and omnibuses, but black abolitionists traveling in northern states were also thrown from railcars and cabins set aside for white passengers.[3] Massachusetts was the first state where the term "Jim Crow" was used to describe segregated cars in the 1840s. With the support of antislavery activists, black abolitionists David Ruggles and Frederick Douglass vigorously protested these segregated cars. Douglass, in fact, began his political life as a leading opponent of segregation. Calling the Jim Crow car a "custom . . . fostering the spirit of caste," Douglass described his physical battle for change on the railways of New England in his second autobiography, *My Bondage and My Freedom* (1855).

When traveling, Douglass insisted on sitting in the first-class car even though he was "often dragged out of my seat, beaten, and severely bruised, by conductors and brakemen." He once so thoroughly resisted being moved, weaving his hands and arms into the upholstery of his seat, that when he was grabbed by several men on the "head, neck, and shoulders" and ripped from his place on the train, it "must have cost the company twenty-five or thirty dollars, for I tore up seats and all." After years of individual and collective protest New England railcars were desegregated.[4] Douglass, who fought for freedom from slavery on the Underground Railroad, also had to battle to ride the public rails.[5] In the next decade, the fight against policies would take on a more collective tone on New York City's mule-drawn omnibuses, or streetcars.

On 16 July 1854, a Sunday, the twenty-five-year-old Elizabeth Jennings, and her friend, Sarah E. Adams, attempted to ride the Third Avenue streetcar to the First Colored American Congregational Church on Sixth Street in Manhattan. Company policy directed black passengers to ride on the dangerous outside platforms, although African Americans were occasionally allowed on board if no white passengers objected. This particular line also had cars for the use of black riders, which bore signs that read, "Colored people allowed in this car," but they filled quickly with black passengers uninterested in paying for rides on the dangerous outside platform.[6] Jennings was well dressed and well behaved and considered herself a lady and a member of the city's educated black middle class. She was accustomed to riding inside the cars on the Third Avenue line without trouble, but that afternoon, she encountered a conductor who insisted on removing her.

Jennings was not the first black woman to be treated violently on the city cars; a black woman had been violently ejected from a Harlem Railroad streetcar just one year earlier.[7] However, Jennings was the first to sue the streetcar company and win. Fortuitous circumstances brought Jennings and her successful lawsuit to the forefront of protest led by black New Yorkers and the interracial abolitionist community.[8] The incident and legal case pitted Jennings against a vague and discriminatory policy that privileged the preferences of white conductors over the rights of African American riders.

After hailing one streetcar, Jennings, who was late for an engagement at the church, was told that there was no more room on the car and that she would need to get off and "wait for the next car," which had been set aside for black use. When she looked inside the first car, however, she saw only eight passengers, leaving more than enough room for Jennings and Adams. Jennings informed the conductor that because she was in a hurry, she wished to ride on the car that was available. When the conductor explained that "the other car had [her] people in it," Jennings replied that she "had no people" and was not traveling with any party, intentionally ignoring the conductor's assumption that she should ride with other black passengers. Jennings explained to the conductor, "I wished to go to church as I had been going for the last six months, and I did not wish to be detained." The car had available space and no white passengers had voiced any complaint. Jennings waited inside the car, ignoring the conductor, who continued to insist that she get off and wait on the curb.[9]

When the "colored" car arrived, the second driver told Jennings there was no room. The first conductor nevertheless continued to insist that he would not leave until Jennings and Adams exited. Growing angry, the conductor warned Jennings that if any white passenger complained about her presence, he would put her out. Jennings responded that she was within her rights, asserting her citizenship while questioning that of the conductor: "I answered again and told him I was a respectable person, born and raised in New York, did not know where he was born, that I had never been insulted before while going to church, and that he was a good for nothing impudent fellow for insulting decent persons while on their way to church." Jennings continued, "When I told the conductor I did not know where he was born, he answered, 'I was born in Ireland.' I made answer it made no difference where a man was born, that he was none the worse or the better for that, provided he behaved himself and did not insult genteel persons."[10]

Jennings was a third-generation New Yorker. *Frederick Douglass' Paper* described her as coming from "a good old New York stock."[11] Her grandfather was Jacob Cartwright, an African slave turned Revolutionary War patriot, and her father was Thomas L. Jennings, a tailor, a boardinghouse operator, and one of the founders of the New York African Society for Mutual Relief.[12] Grounded in an understanding of her family history, personal achievement, and contributions to her community, Jennings saw herself not as a second-class citizen stigmatized by slavery but as a respectable member of her community and her city. Evoking the memory of her grandfather as a soldier and patriot, Jennings made her status as a "native" New Yorker and her heritage of citizenship the basis for her dissent.

In the weeks following the incident, Jennings's defenders also framed their arguments in terms of citizenship and respectability. Stories detailing her case highlighted her status as a lady, describing her as a young Christian woman traveling to church and contrasting her gentility with the "ruffianly Irish driver."[13] The abolitionist daily *New York Tribune* asserted, "It is high time the rights of [respectable colored] citizens were ascertained, and that it should be known whether they are to be thrust from our public conveyances, while German or Irish women, with a quarter of mutton or a load of codfish, can be admitted."[14] By emphasizing her status, they hinted that segregation along the color line was ridiculous when no segregation along class lines was enforced.

This argument did little to advocate for poor or working-class black women carrying their own loads on the same cars. Working-class women, who often traveled great distances in the city for their work, would have benefited from fair use of the cars as well. An anonymous letter to the *New York Daily Times* reported that the author's black housekeeper walked several miles from Brooklyn to Manhattan and back again to travel to and from work in the heat and cold. When her employer asked "why she did not ride in the cars or omnibus she said she did not like to do it, for 'they made such a fuss about colored folks riding in them.'" The writer described the house-keeper as a "worthy citizen" and a "tax-payer" and insisted that women like her also ought to be able to use the cars in comfort and dignity.[15] While Jennings's status as a lady provided one rationale for resisting segregation, working-class black women had no such cover. Only a complete revision of the discriminatory policies, without regard for class, would allow them to find seats as well.

Fed up, the conductor violently removed Adams and then attempted to eject Jennings from the car, dragging her by the feet across the platform while she "screamed murder with all [her] voice." Jennings resisted until the conductor flagged down a passing policeman, who booted her without asking what had happened. When Jennings protested, the policeman told her to "seek redress if she could."[16] Using family, professional, and civic connections, Jennings did just that, garnering support from sympathetic whites and the abolitionist community.

A meeting was called at the First Colored American Congregational Church to discuss the incident. Jennings's detailed account of the assault on the car was read aloud to the congregants because her injuries prevented her from attending the meeting. Those in attendance resolved to sue on her behalf and to "demand . . . as colored citizens, the equal right to the accom-modation of 'transit' in the cars." Jennings had a strong case; not only was she a dignified woman whom employees of the rail line had brutally attacked, but also her side of the story would be bolstered by the testimony of a white onlooker who witnessed the incident from the street, a German immigrant who worked as a bookseller in the neighborhood. He followed Jennings after the assault and offered support if she carried her case to the courts.[17] The testimony of a neutral white observer backed up Jennings's statements and demonstrated that some white passengers had no problem sharing the cars. But her greatest moral support came from black people who had suffered similar insults. A letter came from as far away as California, where the Young Men's Association of San Francisco resolved that "even from the distant shores of the Pacific, that we, with them, do, and will ever protest against this [injustice], and resist it by all proper means, by appealing to justice and importuning public sentiment, until we secure our rights."[18]

In the effort to organize a test case, Thomas L. Jennings, Elizabeth's father, penned an "appeal to the citizens of color, male and female of the city and state of New York." The elder Jennings spoke not only as an aggrieved father but also as a citizen interested in exposing an unfair policy that did not carry the force of law. He argued that he was "not aware of any difference in the law of this State in relation to persons of color, except the elective franchise." He hoped that the case would clarify black rights: "What we want to know is, what our legal rights are in this matter, not only by hearsay, but by the decision of the Supreme Court of the State of New York. . . . What is law is law, and by its decision we must all be governed." But Thomas Jennings did not want to continue to bend to exclusion: "I, for one, am not willing to submit and I hope that you all feel the same. The assault, though a very aggravated case, is only secondary in our view, to the rights of our people." Emphasizing African Americans' collective strength, the senior Jennings called for donations to cover the cost of legal fees: "Our opponents are rich and influential, we are the reverse, but our cause is just and we do not fear them. A willing mind with many hands makes light work."[19]

Jennings's case came to trial in February 1855 in the Brooklyn Circuit of the New York State Supreme Court. According to Chester A. Arthur, Jennings's attorney and a future U.S. president, the case was simple.[20] Citing a New York state law that made common carriers liable for the actions of their employees, Arthur insisted that the employees had overstepped the bounds of custom by assaulting Jennings. Arthur asked that she be awarded damages of five hundred dollars and court costs. The *Tribune* reported that Judge William Rockwell charged the jury forcefully, informing them, "The Company was liable for the acts of their agents, whether committed carelessly and negligently, or willfully and maliciously. . . . They were common carriers, and as such bound to carry all respectable persons; *that colored persons, if sober and well-behaved, and free from disease*, had the same rights as others; and could neither be excluded by *any rules of the Company, nor by force or violence*; and in case of such expulsion, the Company was liable."[21]

Jennings won a $225 settlement, less than half of what she had requested. More importantly, however, she received assurances from the Third Avenue Rail Company that respectable blacks would be admitted without discrimination.[22] Although the judge's charge was encouraging, clearly outlining the duty of common carriers to serve people of all races, the final decision did not call for the desegregation of any of New York City's or Brooklyn's myriad other streetcar or omnibus lines.

Frederick Douglass now urged others to press for change; in an article in his weekly newspaper, he encouraged black New Yorkers to put the decision into action. Douglass hoped that the victory would have a wider effect and encouraged city residents to assert their right to ride inside the streetcars. While praising the court victory, the editor played on Jennings's status as woman and leader, warning that "New York City gentlemen" were "responsible for carrying out this decision into practice by putting an end to their exclusion from cars and omnibuses; they must be craven indeed if they fail to follow the lead of a woman."[23]

Indeed, black women were at the forefront of the movement for change; the same day Douglass issued his challenge to the gentlemen, another black woman insisted on her right to ride on a different streetcar line. A "decent-looking colored woman" boarded an Eighth Avenue streetcar at Canal Street. The conductor ordered her to leave even though, as in Jennings's case, no white passengers had objected to her presence. The unnamed rider refused, telling the conductor that she wished to ride and had a right to do so as a recent judicial decision in Brooklyn had established. The conductor and the driver nevertheless forcibly removed her.[24] Despite the streetcar lines' unwillingness to put new policies of desegregation in place, black New Yorkers saw the Jennings victory as precedent setting and broadly applicable.

Abolitionist circles heralded the victory with stories in the *New York Daily Tribune*, the *National Anti-Slavery Standard*, and *Frederick Douglass' Paper*, although white dailies ignored both the initial incident and the court victory.[25] However, the *New York Daily Times* did take note of the wave of protests on streetcars that came in the wake of Jennings's victory. Over the next few months, a cadre of black men led by Thomas Jennings and the Reverend James W. C. Pennington, pastor of the First Colored Presbyterian Church (later renamed Shiloh), organized the Legal Rights Association and continued to challenge segregation and exclusion on public conveyances around the city. Pennington was an established antislavery advocate and saw the fight against segregated conveyances as crucial in the quest for full citizenship.

Pennington was an escaped slave who became a leading educator, abolitionist, and Presbyterian minister. As an activist, Pennington had many passionate crusades. He used his formidable determination to educate himself, learning to read clandestinely as a slave, attending Sunday schools, hiring private tutors as a free man, and even auditing a full course of study for the ministry at Yale's School of Divinity after he was denied formal admission on the basis of race. He turned his battle for education into a broad defense of the need for excellent institutions for black children. Although Pennington was an integrationist, he believed that black communities had to fill in the gaps left by a racially biased society. As long as public schools were nonexistent or seriously underfunded, Pennington insisted that black people had to found institutions of their own.[26]

For a fugitive working to maintain his freedom and liberate his family, the movement to abolish slavery was urgent and personal. Pennington's work for the Underground Railroad and the New York Vigilance Committee stood at the center of his political efforts, demonstrating his faith in the transformative power of peaceful protest grounded in Christian morality. While advocating abolitionism abroad, Pennington published his memoir, *The Fugitive Blacksmith*, and was lauded for his antislavery lectures in Great Britain. While on a speaking tour in Europe, he received an honorary doctorate from the University of Heidelberg; Pennington accepted the degree "in trust for my people, and as an encouragement to the Sons of Ham to rise."[27] But Pennington was just as concerned about the quality of everyday black life as he was about abolitionism. He fervently believed that the quality of free black life was a barometer for all of black humanity. Proving black capability for achievement and success was central to his argument against slavery. Only if free African Americans were allowed to prove themselves to be educable, hardworking contributors to the greater society could they show the world the full horror of slavery. For Pennington and many others, free black success served as proof positive that slavery was wrong.[28] The descendants of slaves deserved dignity and inclusion in the cities of the North, just as their southern brethren deserved liberty.

Taking this approach to antislavery, Pennington was a leading voice of the black convention movement; he believed in African American unity, arguing that local, regional, and national meetings that called on representatives from African American communities and civic organizations were necessary to strengthen black citizenship. To Pennington, access to public schools, the right to vote, and the end of segregation and discrimination were inextricably tied to the battle to end slavery. Colored convention meetings would help to "inspire our people with proper feelings of self-respect, independence, and moral courage." Pennington believed that free black people suffered in part because of their own fears: "We are cheated out of some precious privileges, only because we have not courage to demand them."[29]

Pennington had utilized the abolitionist press for a variety of causes, including the fight against segregation. For *Frederick Douglass' Paper*, he wrote a fictionalized account of a black minister riding on an omnibus. The story depicted black New Yorkers as paying customers and contributing members of the larger society, arguing that "in that 'Bus were ladies, gentlemen, lawyers, merchants, physicians and mechanics. Each of them was going about his or her own business, or to their home. What had they to do with the color of any man's skin?—Nothing at all." Pennington concluded "All they wanted was to reach their homes or business in season. The real object of all public conveyances is to keep to this single object."[30] Such harmony was rarely replicated on the cars in Pennington's day-to-day experience, however. Although he had long encouraged a color-blind policy on public conveyances, Pennington's courage was tested when he suffered discrimination on the Fulton Ferry Boat.

For decades, Pennington traveled regularly on the ferry from his home to his church. But an 1854 change in ferry policy prevented black men from entering the ladies' cabin, even just to pass through after the ferry had docked and the car emptied. An outraged witness wrote to the *New York Daily Times* to report that Pennington "was rudely ordered out of the ladies' cabin by the Captain of the boat . . . because he is a colored man." The author went on: "And who is he? Rev. Dr. Pennington, a pastor in this City . . . ministering to . . . a large number of men and women. . . . Yet this worthy and good clergyman may not sit nor stand in the ladies' cabin of a ferry-boat, which is the common carrier of all men, sober and otherwise." Pennington was confined to "gentlemen's cabin," a space that was "not a suitable place for a gentleman, whether he be white or black. The cabin is filled with smoke and smokers, and the floor is often wet with the juice of the *weed*." The witness went on to explain that the ladies' car was open to "'vermin-dropping beggars,' low rowdies, the worst characters with white skin," and even dogs but remained forbidden to all black men. "If a decent man with a colored skin only wishes to walk through the cabin, he is clutched by the throat and sent reeling." The writer reminded readers that black passengers suffered discrimination on all forms of transportation in the city: "Dr. Pennington cannot ride in a car or in an omnibus, in this City, unless the driver will condescend to let him sit or stand by his side. How long will the citizens of this great and noble City allow such men . . . to be treated worse than the canine species?"[31]

Pennington verified the witness's report in the next week's *Times*, explaining that he had resorted to bringing his wife on the ferry with him each day to accompany her into the ladies' cabin and avoid the smoke-filled gentlemen's cabin. He did so "simply to avoid insult and annoyance, but the matter cannot rest here. I do this for peace's sake, but under protest."[32] Pennington's treatment was the norm for the city's free black population.

Like many African American New Yorkers, Pennington hoped that Jennings's win would signal the beginning of the end of segregated public conveyances.[33] Free people of color in New York had long been interested in challenging segregated cars and omnibuses. In 1840, he served as a representative to the Jamaica Queens convention, a body that resolved that "colored citizens [should] obtain redress" for a number of forms of discrimination. African Americans were disfranchised, debarred from schools, and "wronged and insulted by the proprietors of public conveyances, in denying us those accommodations which they promise travelers, in considerations of their money." The Queens convention saw such segregation as an outrage, "a system of public caste, which reigns through all orders of the community."[34] In the wake of the Jennings victory, *Frederick Douglass' Paper* published a notice from the reverend to visitors to New York City "that all our public carrier-conveyances are now open to them upon equal terms" and that "if any driver, or conductor molests you by laying the weight of his finger upon your person, have him arrested." The notice concluded with an encouragement: "Don't let them frighten you with words; the law is right, and so is the public sentiment."[35] The affirmative court decision offered African Americans the opportunity to challenge a system of segregation that had degraded them for decades.

In early May 1855, Pennington also spoke out from his pulpit about the need for black passengers to challenge racial separation on the streetcars. At the conclusion of his sermon, he laid out his case for action. The pastor informed his congregation that "colored people could no longer be excluded." Pennington believed that the *Jennings* decision had "placed the matter of public conveyances in the hands of the colored people themselves, and they would be to blame if they long continued subject to the great disadvantages involved by the proscriptions of conductors and drivers of cars and omnibuses." He insisted that the desegregation of the cars was a matter of principle: "nothing short of the utmost tameness and unjustifiable . . . cowardice would induce colored men and women . . . to surrender the privilege of common transit." On the streetcars, black residents could take a stand, if not for themselves then as a lesson to the coming generation. "Colored people [should] show a bold front in this and other . . . matters of equal importance, so that the coming age might know the value of perseverance."[36]

Black New Yorkers acted that very day. A conductor on the Sixth Avenue Railway violently ejected Sidney McFarland, a black passenger, when he disembarked from a "Colored People's Car" and boarded a car designated for white passengers. McFarland reportedly stated that he "meant to test the question whether persons of his shade could ride on the white folks' car or not." The conductor of the car set aside for whites threw him out. McFarland attempted to file assault and battery charges against the conductor, but the case was thrown out by a police court justice, who insisted that "the conductor did not use more force or violence than was necessary to eject the obnoxious passenger." Black supporters went to the court to voice their collective outrage. The *Times* reported that "the affair has created some considerable excitement, and a large concourse of people visited the court-room to learn the result."[37] Despite the dismissal, McFarland took his case to Kings County, the jurisdiction where the *Jennings* case had been tried. Several other black passengers also attempted to ride the white cars on the Sixth Avenue line, and they too were forcibly ejected.[38]

Finally, Pennington joined his congregants in protest and was thrown out of a Sixth Avenue car on 24 May. But Pennington refused to leave and instead grabbed the back of the streetcar, attempted to chase the moving car, and was finally dragged behind for several blocks. The reverend held on until he spotted a policeman and then insisted that the officer arrest the conductor. The police insisted that he drop the issue, but Pennington argued and was arrested for disturbing the peace.[39]

Officials from the Sixth Avenue streetcar company disagreed with Pennington's interpretation of the *Jennings* decision and attacked him and his campaign to end segregation. Streetcar official T. Bailey Myers argued that black passengers' only "right" was to ride in the colored cars set aside for their use. Black passengers should appreciate the "service," Myers complained; the colored cars were a costly courtesy to black passengers at the request of the "trustees of the Colored Half-Orphan Asylum . . . and of the more respectable portion of the colored people." He wrote, "We hold that this is doing more than is required for their convenience—far more than their census ratio entitles them to." The Sixth Avenue line had no intention of honoring the *Jennings* decision. Myers insisted that "as to their right to ride in our cars other than those specially assigned to them, we cannot admit it, and shall not until a legal decision to that effect virtually instructs *to take off our colored cars*."[40]

More than company rights, however, Myers insisted that segregation was appropriate and universal: "Of all the roads in the Union, we know of no other that does as much. Besides this colored people are allowed to stand on the front platform of any of our cars." He asserted that Pennington "certainly must know that a great many people do object to riding next to a colored man; and many other to allowing the ladies of their families to mingle with them in public conveyances." Myers mocked Pennington's honorary degree, asserting that "even the metaphysical air of Heidelberg, where he took his degree, is not free from prejudices, if not those of color, and that many in this more practical country, who are willing to recognize a black in the abstract, as a man and a brother, are not quite prepared to carry it into practice in our cars." Moreover, black passengers should not go where they were not wanted: "Even if [Pennington] had a legal right, he would be wise to waive it, if he desires to live down a prejudice, than to force himself in where a large majority do not wish him and where his feelings would be more wounded by success than failure." Myers characterized Pennington as violent, offensive, and out of control, claiming that a white "gentleman of the highest respectability" had been offended by Pennington's presence and had "indignantly demanded the return of his fare and refused to ride with him." Myers claimed that after repeated requests to leave the car, Pennington "refused and resisted, and conducted himself so violently as to cause his arrest by a policeman of his own accord, and his severe censure . . . for breach of the peace." Myers insisted that the whole experience had made him more sympathetic to the cause of southern slave owners: "Personally, I may say . . . that my present experience is almost enough to change any Free-Soil proclivities into those of a Northern man with Southern principles."[41]

Although Myers and other streetcar officials insisted that the presence of any black person was offensive enough to turn white passengers into proponents of slavery, white abolitionists disagreed and were quick to point out the hypocrisy of racial segregation. The New York Tribune reminded its readers that "the pretext . . . of a natural repugnance on the part of the Whites toward being brought into proximity to Blacks is a most transparent lie." Black barbers, waiters, housekeepers, and nannies were close to whites in all parts of the city. "In several of our best hotels, and in many of our most sumptuous dwellings, the only servants are blacks. . . . [T]here is not a Negro-hater among us who will object to the company of Negroes at his dinner, provided that they stand behind his chair." The Tribune clarified, "It is not . . . the fact that Negroes ride in the same cars that gives offense; it is their riding there on terms of equality with Whites."[42] The insult of riding with black passengers may have had much more to do with black striving than with the poverty or degradation of black passengers.[43]

Seeking a clear determination of black rights on public conveyances, Pennington and the Legal Rights Association brought a civil suit against the Sixth Avenue line. At a protest forum in September, the reverend asked, "Is it right that a respectable colored citizen shall not have the same privileges in public conveyances that white citizens have? The laws of the state give to every person the right to travel in conveyances. . . . [I]f it is the right of colored persons to ride without being insulted or abused, let us maintain our right." Pennington tied his current battle with Sixth Avenue to his history of struggle against discrimination and violence on the ferry. He promised to carry the case as far as he could, from court to court and even to the "ballot-box." Praising the *Jennings* victory as a turning point, the association members called on black residents to register their outrage and support the Pennington suit. Insulting treatment on the cars made life more difficult for blacks of all walks of life; black residents hoped that this suit might set a universal standard for dignity and fairness on the cars. The association continued to meet throughout the fall in support of the case.[44]

But even as black residents continued to test their rights on conveyances, public sentiment outside of the abolitionist community was not terribly sympathetic.[45] The *New York Daily Times* cautioned against change in an editorial, "The War of Colors." The article mocked Pennington's protest and compared the former slave to the mules pulling the car: "The other day he might have been seen hatless with horizontal coat-tails streaming after a Sixth-avenue car . . . affording a fair test of the comparative speed of a pair of Western jackasses, and the clergyman in single harness, weighted with all the dignity of a Heidelberg degree." Suggesting that "those of the obnoxious color" should tone down their demands for change, the editorial preached, "We are creatures of prejudice; and right or wrong prejudice is a very Sebastopol of resistance against deliberate attacks. It is in their failure to recognize this fact, that our colored population go wrong." The more blacks dissented, the more the white public would turn against them. Warning that "petty skirmishes," "weekly meetings," and "agitation" only hardened sentiment against their cause, the *Times* counseled patience: "Prejudices cannot be conquered. To contend with them is to render them inveterate. They must wear out, by patient and consistent contradiction to them—the contradiction of manners, habits, and daily behaviour—they may be gradually weakened, and at last eliminated;—but by the assertion of a clamorous and arrogant claim—a claim unsupported by that quiet dignity of carriage, that refinement of culture, and enlargement of information, to which all social barriers give way, no concession is at all likely to be obtained. To get the better of a deep-rooted antipathy, something more than adverse, but abstract right must be set up."

Black citizens had no right to ride public conveyances; according to the

Times, African Americans were not really citizens, just people who must be tolerated, an inferior and degraded people who had refused the invitation to "return to Africa." Given that blacks remained unwelcome guests, they had to "accept the terms of [their] choice with all possible patience." The editor insisted that any demands for citizenship and rights were inappropriate and untimely. "Leaving then, the present litigious and vexatious plans, by which social prejudices will be strengthened rather than weakened, we recommend to all colored men the better way of self-elevation, by moral and educational means." The *Times* cautioned that only through improvement would change eventually occur.

Such a standard of perfection was required only of black passengers; poor whites were excused. Attacks such as those launched in the *Times* blamed black people who did not meet standards of civilized ladies and gentlemen. Blaming the poor and the poorly behaved was a tantalizing distraction but a distraction nonetheless from the fact that black achievement itself was the greatest threat. Black New Yorkers were not deterred by race-baiting arguments that suggested that black citizens would have to wait patiently for their rights. Resistance to unequal conditions on Sixth Avenue cars continued.[46]

Undeterred, Pennington presented a compromise. The minister hoped to appeal to state lawmakers to pass a color-blind law barring unruly passengers "whether white or colored" and imposing a $250 or $500 penalty on companies whose employees ousted or assaulted "orderly and decent persons." The Legal Rights Association planned to put forth "a respectful, but earnest, and persevering petition" calling for class- rather than race-based exclusion from cars in hopes of a having "a uniform law" governing the cars throughout the state. Pennington published his plan in a note to the "stockholders of the Sixth-Avenue Railroad," hoping that their concerns about the financial health of the railroad would sway them to stop the "many serious outrages . . . committed on [the] road upon . . . respectable colored persons."[47] No such law was enacted.

As the Legal Rights Association awaited the outcome of Pennington's case, brutal treatment continued. On 16 December 1856, five men beat the treasurer of the Legal Rights Association, Peter S. Porter, after he refused to leave the Eighth Avenue streetcar. After boarding with his wife and four of her female friends, Porter rode unmolested for a few blocks. Even though no passengers complained about Porter or the women, the conductor suddenly insisted that he leave the inside of the car. When Porter stayed in his seat, the conductor had the driver stop the car while he found other men to help eject Porter. The conductor, the driver, a conductor from a nearby Sixth Avenue streetcar, and two passersby "beat, kicked, and banged him about most ferociously," tearing Porter's clothing from his body and breaking his pocket watch. When Porter's wife objected, one of the men "caught her by the throat and shook her." Severely injured, Porter was bedridden from his injuries. The Porters believed that they had been deliberately targeted because of his outspoken role in the Legal Rights Association. They decided to sue.[48]

The case of *Pennington v. Sixth Avenue Railroad Company* was finally tried in Superior Court just few days after the assault on the Porters. Pennington and the Legal Rights Association found esteemed legal council in Frederick A. Tallmadge, conservative Whig, former congressman, and New York City recorder. Pennington sought one thousand dollars in damages but stated that he simply wanted "to test the question whether in this country, a colored man can or cannot ride in these public conveyances." Tallmadge highlighted the class standing of his client, describing Pennington as "respectable," "a taxpayer," and a man who "moves in good society, and is deemed by the religious world as a fit person to teach others." But Tallmadge reminded the court that the case was really quite simple and did not require a broad revision of the racial order. Pennington and the association had expressed no desire to force themselves into the social lives of whites, Tallmadge explained. Black New Yorkers "do not expect to be invited to sit at their tables, or share their beds." But "the right of passage" was more fundamental; if railroads and steamboats were chartered by the state to serve the public, they had a duty to accommodate all decent and respectable people, regardless of color. Tallmadge closed his statement with a question: "Is not this man [as] entitled to be a passenger as any one? . . . He is a citizen."[49]

Despite the clear-cut argument, the Superior Court jury found in favor of the Sixth Avenue line. The jurors' decision stated that the streetcar had the right to restrict the passage of anyone deemed offensive by the majority of the passengers; desegregated cars would be so offensive to white passengers that most would avoid riding, causing the company to lose revenue.[50] The decision was a disappointing defeat to an already faltering movement. The Legal Rights Association had lost some steam months earlier when it was revealed that Pennington suffered from alcoholism and had been asked to leave Shiloh's pastorate. In a community deeply shaped by the temperance movement and a belief in spiritual and moral self-control, the faltering Pennington was a compromised leader. The failure of his legal case shortchanged the potential of the New York City protest and stifled the momentum of the *Jennings* decision. One success was not enough to end patterns of prejudice on the cars.

The Porters had a better outcome in the courts. In February 1858, the New York State Supreme Court found in their favor and asserted the equal rights of African Americans on the cars. But much like the *Jennings* decision, the legal finding did not change conditions. Conductors continued to eject black passengers, even without the force of law. Black New Yorkers were not deterred; they continued to hold spontaneous protests on the streetcars and formal protests in the courts, fighting back against violent conductors and random policies of segregation on city streetcars until the Civil War.[51]

The *Jennings* decision is nearly forgotten in the history of black resistance to Jim Crow. But the case highlights a central challenge in the battle for black citizenship. Jennings's efforts to simply sit inside a streetcar as a paying passenger remind us of the difficulties of stigma in a postemancipation society. Just thirty years after the majority of New York's slaves had been freed by law and just six years after the slow process of gradual emancipation had finally ended in the state, a stigma still stunted the possibilities of black life.[52] Even in a locality that voluntarily agreed to gradually free its slaves, the majority of whites were less than sympathetic to the conditions facing free people and refused to treat black citizens as equals in schools, at the ballot box, or on the railcar. Race slavery was not just an oppressive means of extracting labor from a trapped population; it also trapped their descendants in a framework of policies that assumed inferiority. Such beliefs, undergirded with the force of law and the courts, were hard to overcome. Even when blacks were accomplishing a great deal of personal and collective success—contributing to their community as educators, ministers, and business owners—the stamp of inferiority and difference remained. And this was in a community that largely believed that slavery was morally or at least economically wrong. The battle for inclusion in a hostile postemancipation South would be even more difficult.

In the wake of a flurry of organization, Jennings and Pennington receded from the forefront. Jennings married, built a successful career as an educator, and continued serving as an organist for black congregations throughout the city. Pennington was less fortunate, suffering recriminations because of his alcoholism. He recovered and became one of hundreds of free black northerners who heard the call to travel south and serve the cause of the freedpeople. Although he was no longer prominent, church organizations were eager to have him serve, first in Natchez, Mississippi, and then in Jacksonville, Florida.[53] Although Pennington had been less than successful in desegregating the Sixth Street line, he and hundreds of others brought their own perceptions of what citizenship should mean to the emancipated South. Although there is no evidence of northerners encouraging protests on trains and streetcars in the South, they were part of the community of ideas exchanged among African Americans North and South who found new hope in the promise of a free black South.

2 THE COLOR LINE AND THE LADIES' CAR

Segregation on Southern Rails before Plessy

"Liberty came . . . not in mercy, but in wrath. . . . The very manner of their emancipation invited to the heads of the freedmen the bitterest hostility of race and class."
—FREDERICK DOUGLASS, "Speech on West Indies Emancipation"

In the nineteenth century, the evolution of train service reshaped the
American landscape. Both people and products moved more efficiently to
more diverse locations. Interstate lines connected disparate communities
and became the pathways by which new cities took shape and new fortunes
were formed. As railroads expanded after the Civil War, passenger service
grew more elaborate. First-class cars were inlaid with ornate woods such as
walnut, cherry, and mahogany. Clerestory roofs—raised ceilings that provided additional light and ventilation—ornamentation, and oil lamp chan-
deliers replaced simple curved ceilings. Passengers reclining in plush velvet
seats were made more comfortable by adjusting the breezes from windows
and blocking the light with built-in shades. First-class ladies' cars, decorated with sofas for reclining, provided ice water for women and their
gentleman companions. Long-distance trains began to feature sleeping
cars, made famous by the Pullman Company, which changed daytime seating into comfortable sleeping berths. Dining cars serving elaborate and
formal meals became a standard in interstate travel by the 1870s and 1880s.[1]

But the quality that made American trains truly distinctive was their
emphasis on "accessibility." One account of American railroads asserted
that "the ever-surging spirit of democracy [was] rampant on the railroads.

There, no class structure, no social caste applied—only pure, raw, down-to-earth democracy was evident." Unlike their European counterparts, American railroads did not establish elaborate distinctions between first-, second-, and third-class cars. Most white passengers had access to comfortable coach seating. One train historian has argued that "the rail car was one of America's greatest economic and social levelers."[2]

Indeed, trains helped shape the social fabric of the postwar South. A railroad boom between 1870 and 1890 created moving societies open to any person who purchased a ticket. Trains represented the pulse of expanding southern urbanity, connecting the residents of growing cities with the inhabitants of rural towns and counties. By 1890, 90 percent of southerners lived in counties serviced by the rails. First-class passengers from both cosmopolitan urban areas and rural outposts enjoyed elegant meals, plush seating, and generous sleeping quarters.[3] But the presence of black travelers, particularly elite and middle-class patrons, threatened the stability of the racial order in an increasingly fluid society.

Prior to the Civil War, most black riders, predominantly slaves, were relegated to "combination cars," spaces divided into both luggage and passenger compartments attached behind the engine. These impromptu cars, where black passengers paid half fare, were developed explicitly for black riders. But not all people of color were forced to ride in the small compartments. Travelers' accounts reported that, in places in the South with substantial populations of free people of color, well-to-do freemen could purchase full-fare coach seating and ride with white passengers.[4]

In the immediate aftermath of the war, most southern rail lines were segregated. The Republican Congress, recalling the struggle to desegregate northern rails, overturned these restrictions and eventually established constitutionally guaranteed black citizenship rights. Despite these legislative changes, however, the majority of white southerners were unwilling to treat former slaves as citizens. Even without segregation laws in place, the random denial of service to black passengers was widespread throughout the South and even in the Midwest and West. Black passengers, no matter how prominent, were frequently denied admission to first-class cars. In a time when most women were not smokers, abolitionist Sojourner Truth commented in 1867 that she "has been sent into the smoking-car so often she smoked in self-defense—she would rather swallow her own smoke than another's."[5] White conductors in Louisiana even denied service to the state's African American lieutenant governor, Oscar J. Dunn, in 1869.[6]

African Americans could not predict whether they would encounter discrimination on any given journey on the rails or streetcars. Even passage of the federal Civil Rights Act of 1875, which forbade racia ination in "accommodations, advantages, facilities, and privilege public conveyances on land or water, theaters, and other places amusement," chaos and confusion confronted black travelers in the south. Those who could afford first-class tickets were not always properly accommodated. Conductors might choose to enforce the color line at their own discretion, moving black passengers to smoking cars or even ejecting African Americans from trains well before they had arrived at their destination. With no regard for federal law, rules and regulations varied from state to state and even on different lines within states.

The Supreme Court's 1883 nullification of the Civil Rights Act of 1875 opened the floodgates of both formal and informal discriminatory policies, making African Americans' legal standing even more tenuous. School-teacher, journalist, and frequent rail passenger Ida B. Wells was startled when she was asked to get up and move to the smoker in the fall of 1883. She had regularly traveled the same route and had always been permitted to ride with whites. Wells fought hard to stay in the car, biting the conductor's hand and holding onto her seat for dear life just as Frederick Douglass had done forty years earlier. Despite her vigorous resistance, a conductor and three white male passengers forcibly removed her from the first-class car. She recalled that "ever since the repeal of the Civil Rights Bill . . . there had been efforts all over the South to draw the color line on the railroads."[8] But like Wells, many black passengers resisted unequal treatment and pressed suits challenging inequitable racial practices. Inspired by such suits, Wells twice sued the Chesapeake, Ohio, and Southwestern Railroad when it denied her first-class seating.[9] The increase in the number of suits brought by offended black passengers suggests that informal segregation was becoming more common.[10] But on the whole, such suits were uncommon; while thousands of black passengers experienced insult and injury, very few could afford the time, expense, and risk of suing offending railroads. In the decade before the *Plessy* decision, most African Americans were forced to tolerate unpredictable policies.

Conditions varied dramatically depending on the line, state, and number of passengers on trains. Passengers could purchase first- or second-class tickets at railroad stations. The number of cars on trains varied, but all lines included an engine; a luggage car or compartment; a smoking car for passengers who wanted to use tobacco during the journey; and the "ladies' car," a first-class car with plush seating and clean and smoke-free air, as far away from the foul coal-burning engine as possible. More elaborate or long-distance routes might also have a dining car and a luxury sleeping car. Some lines included a bare-boned colored car, but most often black riders prevented from entering first-class cars were shoved behind a partition in the smoker or luggage car or seated in the smoking car.

Blacks were usually permitted to purchase either first- or second-class tickets; however, the seating they received for their money was always in doubt.[11] Those who had purchased second-class tickets sat in the smoking car. On some lines, the color line in first-class cars was somewhat porous. Some railroads seated passengers along class lines and allowed black riders holding first-class tickets to be seated in the ladies' cars. Men and women of color sometimes gained entrance to first-class accommodations if they were well dressed and well behaved, according to the standards of individual conductors. Some conductors would avoid disturbing white passengers in the effort to unseat black passengers, so if black women and their male companions could quickly find seats, they were often allowed to stay for the entire journey.[12] George Washington Cable, a white southerner sympathetic to the difficulties faced by black rail travelers, noted in 1885, "In railway travel the colored people's rights are tossed from pillar to post with an ever-varying and therefore more utterly indefensible and intolerable capriciousness." Law, custom, and practice varied from state to state:

In Virginia [black passengers] may ride exactly as white people do and in the same cars. In a neighboring state, a white man may ride in the ladies' car, while a colored man of exactly the same dress and manners—nay, his wife or daughter—must ride in the notorious "Jim Crow car," unprotected from smokers and dram drinkers and lovers of vile language. "In South Carolina," says the Charleston *News and Courier*, on the other hand, "respectable colored persons who buy first-class tickets on any railroad ride in the first-class cars as a right, and their presence excites no comment on the part of their white fellow-passengers. It is a great deal pleasanter to travel with respectable and well-behaved colored people than with unmannerly and ruffianly white men." In Alabama the majority of the people have not made this discovery, at least if we are to believe their newspapers. In Tennessee the law *requires* the separation of all first-class passengers by race with equal accommodations for both.[13]

In a society deeply marked by race, the presence of black passengers in first-class cars increasingly threatened white supremacy. Where passage was purchased, elite and middle-class black riders who could afford first-class tickets would have had better seats than poor white passengers who rode in smokers. In response, railroads officially sought to walk the line of law, comfort, class, and custom by seating some black riders. If white passengers complained, threatened by the notion of riding with African Americans of any class, railroads would refuse African Americans first-class passage. Even when black passengers held first-class tickets purchased at a higher price, they could suddenly be forced into the second-class car.

Companies would shift their policies based on the whims of white passengers and usually displayed little concern about pleasing black passengers. If railroads had been interested in creating a balanced separate but equal system, however, they could have run two first-class cars and two smokers. But the railroads wanted to avoid the expense of creating separate black cars. The high costs ensured that railroads never ran expensive first-class cars exclusively for black use.[14]

Although the ladies' car was often the only first-class seating available for both men and women travelers, the conductor retained the discretion to bar men or women of "questionable character"—those who did not behave in a "genteel" manner.[15] Second-class seating was available in the plainly appointed smoking car. The car's usual positioning as the first passenger car behind the engine made it hot, loud, and uncomfortable. The social conditions were also coarse. Indeed, in the antebellum South, the smoking car had originated as a space where white men could smoke, drink, gamble, and chew tobacco without offending the sensibilities of women.[16] After the war, the smoking car remained a space where bawdy behavior was acceptable. Cable described smoking cars as "the most uncomfortable, uncleanest, and unsafest place." When first-class African American passengers were forced into these spaces, Cable asserted, the "discomfort of most of these places are a shame to any community pretending to practice public justice."[17]

Segregation, however, did not truly separate the races; black male workers could be found in nearly every part of the train. Historically, the labor of black men made train travel possible: hired slaves and slaves purchased by southern railroad companies had laid the majority of the first railroad tracks in the South when Irish workers had proved "less reliable."[18] After the Civil War, railroad companies worked with state lawmakers to arrange leases of black convict laborers to repair and maintain rail lines damaged during the war. Many black men forced to work on these gangs died from exhaustion, brutality, and disease. Southern railroad companies relied primarily on convict labor through the 1880s.[19] Despite the treatment of convicts, free black men sought work on the rails, which provided a better living than sharecropping in tough times and offered a degree of mobility. In sharp contrast with agricultural work, wage labor provided black men with the flexibility to earn a certain amount and then move on.

African American men also predominated as workers serving on the cars. George Mortimer Pullman, owner of the largest line of sleeping berths in the nation, hired only black men to serve as porters on his cars, believing that southern black men were superior servants.[20] Black men also held most positions as waiters and cooks in the dining cars. However, black men were never permitted to work in the supervisory positions of conductors and stewards, who supervised dining cars, which paid more and were considered white men's work.[21] Racial divisions of labor mimicked the divide of the cars, allowing working-class whites to feel superior to their black counterparts.

The presence of black male workers on all cars of the train made drawing the color line particularly ridiculous. Pullman porters worked in close quarters with white male and female passengers, preparing their beds, providing water, and shining shoes. Dining car workers heated and served meals to white men, women, and children. White travelers could share space with black men only if they were smiling servants. Black men who were equal to white passengers in education and attainment posed a threat, while the presence of black servants reassured white passengers about their respective places in society. Segregation did not provide physical distance; rather, it reaffirmed social distance.

The complaint brought by the Reverend William H. Heard, a resident of Charleston, South Carolina, against the Georgia Railroad Company in 1888 gives detailed insight into such conditions. Heard, a minister in the African Methodist Episcopal Church, brought a claim before the Interstate Commerce Commission to contest unequal provisions for black passengers. On the final leg of a journey from Cincinnati to Charleston, conductors had ejected Heard from first-class accommodations despite the fact that he had ridden undisturbed as far as Atlanta.[22]

On the Georgia Railroad Company train where Heard was a passenger, the "colored car" was a poorly partitioned section of the smoking car separated by a wooden divider that stopped one foot short of the ceiling. Smoke poured into the side designated for black riders. In addition, segregated riders had only one bathroom for both men and women, and no ice water was provided for the cramped, hot compartment. "The seats were not upholstered, and there was no carpet on the floor." Heard testified that the car was "dusty and dirty." The compartment also carried "train hands and laborers with their tools," who sat among well-dressed black men and women passengers. Although the Georgia Railroad conductors avidly policed the color line in the first-class car, white men were allowed to enter the "colored compartment" "with whisky" and were allowed to use "rude and profane language" in front of black women. The smoking car was a lurid, public space in which the standard social order was confused and African American women and children were exposed to white men behaving in a rough and uncultured manner. Only when Heard protested did the conductor ask the white men to leave.

Increasing numbers of black passengers were prevented from using the first-class facilities, but no one sought to bar white men from colored compartments. While many hinted at the sexual nature of white male forays into Jim Crow cars, James Weldon Johnson explicitly explained, "It was— and in many parts still is—the custom for white men to go into that car whenever they felt like doing things that would not be allowed in the 'white' car. They went there to smoke, to drink, and often to gamble. At times the object was to pick an acquaintance with some likely-looking Negro girl."[23] If white men frequented the car for the purpose of soliciting black women for sex, the racial and sexual mores of the day meant that black women risked their safety when resisting or rejecting such advances.

Heard took his case to the Interstate Commerce Commission (ICC), a federal board organized to monitor domestic commerce and transportation under the Interstate Commerce Act of 1887. The commission found that "educated and reputable colored persons . . . have reason . . . for complaining under such conditions." Black passengers were "not furnished the just and equal accommodations for which they pay and to which they are entitled under the Law." Although the commission did not find that segregation was a violation of the law, they encouraged dividing the cars by class rather than color so that "persons of both colors may purchase tickets for and ride in either class of car according to their inclination or ability to pay." Although the commission ordered the Georgia Railroad to cease and desist, the ICC had little power to enforce its decision. Railroad executives knew that most African American patrons could not afford attorneys or have their cases heard by the ICC and continued to pursue demeaning practices.

However, railroad officials were not always the catalyst for the ejection of African American passengers; disgruntled whites often demanded that blacks be put out of the first-class cars. Johnson remembered that on a ride from Atlanta University to his home in Jacksonville, Florida, prior to the passage of a Jim Crow law in Georgia, he and a group of students were asked to move to the colored car but told the conductor that they "were comfortable and preferred to stay where we were" because they had purchased first-class tickets and were traveling in the company of a young woman schoolmate. The conductor dropped the matter, but white passengers ejected the students: "A murmur started in the car, and grew until it became a hubbub. The conductor was called upon to put us out; but doubtless his instructions were to stay on the safe side of the law in such cases and he took no action."[24]

Then, according to Johnson, "the remarks in the car . . . became open and loud. Threats began to reach our ears." A white passenger whispered a warning for them to move; passengers had sent a telegram to the small town of Baxley, Georgia, to organize a mob to remove them at the next stop. Johnson recalled reading in the *Atlanta Constitution* that at Baxley, a group of black preachers had been pulled from a train and made to "dance" as a flurry of bullets were fired at their feet. A black porter confirmed the story, warning that a mob had been organized to injure if not murder them. Johnson and his companions reluctantly moved to the colored car as passengers in the first-class car taunted and cheered. Johnson wrote, "If their satisfaction rose from any idea that I was having a sense of my inferiority impressed upon me, they were sadly in error; indeed, my sensation was the direct opposite; I felt that I was being humiliated." As the train passed Baxley, Johnson saw "a crowd, but no indications of a mob," and he thought that the "colored porter had merely been made a tool of by the white passengers." He regretted having willingly moved.[25]

However urbane black travelers might have been, the train itself moved through a variety of cities, towns, and small communities. No one could predict how white passengers might react to the sight of well-dressed, sophisticated black riders. The mob mentality that could terrorize black southerners with the threat of lynching and race riots could also be found on rail cars. The genteel conditions of the cars did not prevent passengers from behaving rudely or even violently toward African American passengers.

On a journey on the Western and Atlantic Railroad Company from Chattanooga, Tennessee, to Atlanta, the Reverend William H. Council, an African Methodist Episcopal minister and the principal of the State Colored Normal and Industrial School at Huntsville, Alabama, was attacked by white passengers in an attempt to oust him from his first-class seat. After Council ignored a passenger who told the minister to leave the ladies' car, a brakeman repeated the order. Since the brakeman had not seen Council's first-class ticket, he responded that he would wait for the conductor to take his ticket and would move if the conductor directed him to leave. Violence quickly ensued.[26]

The employee and two male passengers assaulted Council. One of the passengers struck the minister repeatedly with a train lantern taken from the flagman, causing Council to fall out of his seat and cut his head badly on the broken lantern glass. Although Council cried out for help, neither the conductor nor any other train employee came to his defense. The men then pushed the injured minister into what they described as "the darkies' car," a second-class compartment that was "filthy and full of smoke." White passengers clearly had tremendous authority to govern racial conditions in first-class cars. Railroad employees sought to ensure the comfort of white passengers and made no effort to ensure the safety of black riders.

Council also took his grievances before the ICC. The commissioners were sympathetic, describing Council as "an intelligent colored man, well dressed, self possessed and of good address." Both Council and Heard were well-established African Methodist Episcopal ministers traveling on church business, yet their prominent place in the African American community could not purchase first-class privilege or even physical safety. "Proper" education, manners, and attire did not necessarily improve a person's status on the train, just as improvements in class standing did not improve black chances toward full and equitable inclusion in southern society.

The commission issued a report that represented a bungled attempt to argue for a fairer segregated system. The ICC did not find that segregation itself was an injustice but did find that the conditions in the colored car were unacceptable. The car set aside for blacks was "a half car, half lighted, in which men and women were huddled together, and where men, white and black, smoked at pleasure." The ICC insisted that the railroad would need to run a separate first-class colored car to serve black passengers who had purchased first-class tickets and declared the railroad in violation of the law: "There was in the train no car furnishing the accommodations for which the complainant had paid and was entitled to have, other than the one from which he was removed." They ordered the railroad to "cease and desist from subjecting colored persons to undue and unreasonable prejudice and disadvantage" but upheld the railroad's right to segregate by race.

The ICC did, however, hint at what commissioners believed was a weakness in Council's claim. Under the rules of the railroad, men traveling alone—that is, not escorting women—could always be excluded from first-class ladies' cars. The commission found that the "rules providing separate cars for ladies, and for gentlemen accompanied by ladies" were unquestionable, and "a man, white or colored, excluded from the ladies' car by such a rule could hardly claim successfully . . . that he had been subjected to unjust discrimination." Black men could find no legal protection on the cars.

Given the gendered divisions on rail lines, African American women could make more thorough claims for fair inclusion on southern rail lines that ran first-class ladies' cars. Black women were leaders in the fight against railroads; the majority of published state and federal court cases lodged by black litigants against the railroads between 1870 and 1889 were brought by women.[27] Black women who complained about inequity risked verbal and physical attack from whites unhappy with any lack of deference on the part of African Americans. In addition to the physical dangers, the expense of pressing a legal suit against a rail company meant that only women of strong financial means would risk the cost of a legal case with an uncertain outcome. Willing to risk their safety, reputation, and livelihood, these black women litigants must have dearly valued civic recognition, inclusion, and equality.

The ladies' car was not just a first-class convention but was understood as a necessary social buffer. Railcars for women mimicked the private sphere of the idealized American home and were established to keep women from being forced to socialize "with strange men."[28] But the private sphere of the ladies' railcar also replicated racial divides, re-creating a domestic sphere where black women were accepted only in a servile capacity. Black women serving as nurses to white children or caring for the elderly were never barred from ladies' cars. As Ida B. Wells explained, "The dislike of the South is not to the Negroes as laborers or servants, but to the recognition of them as citizens. As a servant a Negro may enter places from which, whatever her wealth, intellect, education or refinement, she is still ruthlessly excluded as a citizen."[29]

African American women's roles as mothers and protectors of children were disregarded on southern railways. George Washington Cable told the story of a dignified young black mother and child riding the segregated railroads in Alabama. Although they were "neatly dressed" and "very still and quiet," they were forced to sit in a car with nineteen "penitentiary convicts" clothed in "filthy rags, with vile odors." Throughout the train ride, the mother and child listened to "the clanking of shackles and chains" in the crowded and dirty car even though there was "plenty of room" in the first-class ladies' car where Cable rode. Neither her status as a mother nor their respectable demeanor could gain the pair entry to the train's first-class car. In fact, their respectability made them more of a problem. Cable reminded his readers that the woman and child were "refused . . . admission elsewhere because they were of African blood, and not because the mother was, but because she was *not*, engaged at the moment in menial service. Had the child been white, and the mother not its natural but its hired guardian, she could have sat anywhere in the train, and no one would have ventured to object."[30] If the black woman and child had been servants tending to white passengers, they would have received better treatment.

Black girls also faced mistreatment on railcars. Memphis-born activist Mary Church Terrell remembered "having the Race Problem brought directly home" when she was five years old and her father left her alone sitting in the first-class coach. The conductor "glared . . . and asked who I was and what I was doing in that car." Unhappy with the little girl's answer, the conductor yanked her out of her seat and "turned to the man sitting across the aisle and said, 'Whose little nigger is this?'" Although Terrell's father defended his daughter's right to ride in first-class accommodations, Terrell never forgot that although she was "behaving like a little lady," the conductor had singled her out for attack and tried to remove her. The logic of white supremacy dictated that even young children did not deserve protection.[31]

African American women suffered from the stigmas of both race and gender on southern railroads. The limitations on rights of white women that marked society also had shaped rail travel; trains were first segregated by sex prior to Emancipation, building on the notion that fragile women needed protection from the crude world of men. During a time when gender distinctions were an understood part of American citizenship, women were granted the promise of social protection in lieu of political rights. If citizenship for women was not grounded in political rights such as suffrage, jury participation, and the right to seek political office, it was instead expressed through the social allowances unique to women. In this context, inclusion on the ladies' car became an expression of right.[32]

Black women were allowed neither the comfort nor protection normally afforded to ladies. Slave women had been just as exploited as black men, with little regard for their needs for dignity, privacy, or protection. In addition, they had suffered the stigma of sex, and the larger society characterized them as wantonly sexual; in fact, slavery apologists would argue that black women were so indiscriminate about their sexual partners that they could not be raped. In the post-Emancipation era, these same stereotypes continued to plague black women, who were depicted as immoral, unladylike, and undeserving of protection. In this context, black women suffered a unique double burden of race prejudice and denial of the protection of womanhood—what black feminist author and activist Anna Julia Cooper aptly described as "slighted womanhood."[33] In such context, black women's attempts to demand equitable treatment represented a question not only of privilege but also of "social rights." Segregation involved not only publicly shaming, degrading, and controlling a rising black middle class but also reaffirming the myths of white supremacy. Black women's insistence that they be treated as ladies worthy of first-class treatment provided a very striking challenge to the strictures of segregation.

The gender dynamic on railcars mirrored the sexualized anxiety of the larger society. In the 1890s, a decade after Wells sued the Chesapeake Railroad, she became a noted author and antilynching advocate. Wells's work was a potent analysis of the myths that undergirded southern lynch law. While Wells was working as a journalist and editor of the *Free Speech and Headlight*, a leading black Memphis newspaper, three black men, Thomas Moss, Calvin McDowell, and Henry Stewart, owners of the successful People's Grocery Company, were lynched by white business competitors. The killers justified the atrocity by arguing that local white women found the men sexually threatening. Wells published a scathing editorial that pointed out that justifications for lynching were most often grounded in the myth of the black male rapist—a notion that most black men were sexually wild and uncontrollable beasts poised to harm innocent white women. Southern apologists for lynching argued that in this context, violence was a justified and civilized response. Lynching was said to be a means to restore the honor of white womanhood. Wells believed that this myth masked two important facts. First, lynching victims were often successful farmers, educators, or businesspeople who challenged whites economically, not sexually. Second, the hyperbolic myth of protecting white women from black men required a simultaneous denial of the victimization of black women at the hands of white men. Wells was one of the first analysts to outline the violent irony of the mythology surrounding lynching, exposing the continuing legacy of abuses committed by white men against black women. Wells's plainspoken criticism made her a target. She fled to Chicago, while an angry white mob burned down the offices of the *Free Speech and Headlight*.

Wells's sharp analysis of lynching must have been honed in part by her experiences in the segregated ladies' car, which was demonstrative of the racial and sexual dynamics of lynching in the American South. The sexual dynamics aptly described by Wells were physically acted out in the gender- and race-based segregation of the railcars. Highlighting the history of black women's victimization at the hands of white men, black women litigants demanded respectability, arguing that they too required protection from "strange men."

To challenge segregation on the trains, African American women had to confront myths about black women's sexuality, but bringing these myths to the forefront harkened back to a painful collective history. Slavery apologists had argued that black women slaves were loose and immoral and therefore could not be sexually violated. Freedom and citizenship for black women also required black women to try to challenge this myth. In an 1888 essay, Wells outlined the characteristics of the "noble" yet "typical" black woman: "She counts no sacrifice too great for the preservation of honor. She knows that our people, as a whole, are charged with immorality and vice; that it depends largely on the woman of to-day to refute such charges by her stainless life."[34] Historian Darlene Clark Hine has called this pursuit of a "stainless life" the "culture of dissemblance," the attempt to refute the myths about sexuality with hypervigilance. Black women advocates hoped that living a chaste life would prove that race slavery had been grounded in a lie. Black women who sought to better their stature believed that proper ladylike behavior could undermine racist notions about immorality and impurity. Thus, the culture of dissemblance complicated African American women's resistance to segregation, which implicitly required them to acknowledge this history of victimization and the need for protection.[35]

While black travelers became targets for exclusion or inequitable treatment to shield white women from "inappropriate contact," conductors ignored black women's need for protection. The Reverend G. H. Flowers, who testified as a witness on Wells's behalf in 1883, stated that when she was forcibly removed from the first-class car and forced into the smoker, "there were no white ladies in there, but there were white men and colored men and women." Flowers described the people in the second-class smoker as "very rough, they were smoking, talking and drinking, very rough. It was not fit place for a Lady."[36] In this context, protest against segregation on trains was a question not just of elite black women seeking "first-class" treatment but of affording black women the same protection given to white women regardless of class.

Although African American women could make stronger legal claims than black men in cases of exclusion, they suffered the same violent treatment when they resisted ejection. In 1890, a passenger, Alice Williams, sued after being brutally assaulted in a ladies' car by the conductor when she tried to retain her seat on a journey through Florida. Williams, "decently and becomingly dressed, and behaving in a modest, decent, and lady-like manner," was traveling alone. She had purchased a first-class ticket and found a seat in the car "set apart for the use of ladies and gentlemen traveling on the railroad." But the conductor ordered her to go to a car "set apart for negroes and persons of color" that was "inferior, less comfortable and less decent"—"a second-class car." When Williams refused to move, she was thrown out of the seat and onto the floor. The conductor and another train employee then grabbed her feet, sending her skirt up around her waist, and dragged Williams on her back down the aisle, out the door, across the platform, and into the second-class car. Williams and her husband sued the railroad for damages for the pain she suffered and medical expenses she incurred.[37]

Lola Houck, a schoolteacher from rural Texas, sued after suffering a miscarriage when she was blocked from entering the first-class rear car of a Southern Pacific Railroad train. Houck had purchased a first-class ticket for the ninety-mile journey from Victoria to Rosenberg, Texas. Because she was very light-skinned and had only "some degree of Negro blood in her veins," she had customarily passed for white and traveled in the first-class cabin. But in her everyday life, Houck was a respectable member of Victoria's small African American community and had been educated at a local colored teachers college.[38] An African American bootblack at the train station who knew Houck exposed her identity to the train's conductor. Angered by Houck's ability to fool him about her race in the past, the offended conductor locked Houck out of the first-class car.[39]

Houck refused to enter the car designated for blacks; throughout the journey, she stood on the platform between the cars while trying to regain entrance to the first-class car. At each train stop, she went around to the other end of the car, where the conductor was blocking the door, leaving the woman outside when the train left the station. The brakeman mocked Houck, who feared the loud black and white men in the smoking car. Although it was cold and rainy, at each stop she tried to enter the first-class car. At one stop, the conductor shoved her away from the door, causing her to fall against the wheel of the brake and almost tumble off the moving platform. Houck, who was visibly pregnant, got no sympathy from the aggressive conductor.

In state court, Houck received a favorable judgment and was awarded two thousand dollars in punitive damages for her injuries. The dynamic that caused her to stand, both literally and figuratively, between the black and white spaces provides an especially useful window into the linkages between race, class, and skin color. Passing was a weapon retained by a few light-skinned African Americans to battle the strictures of segregation. But the practice was a double-edged sword, functioning both as a victory over the narrow and punitive system of racial classification and as an acquiescence to the rules of white privilege. Passing for white must have been difficult, both as an individual choice and a performance observed by other black Americans. The African American man who exposed Houck's racial identity may have perceived her behavior as a betrayal that had to be exposed. Or perhaps he was simply trying to curry favor with the conductor. In either case, his behavior hints at the precarious position of those who chose to pass for white to receive equitable treatment on the rails.

Houck's case highlights the question of class and color divisions within the African American community. How did people who were unable to pass or could not afford to purchase first-class passage feel about those who did? The majority of African American southerners did not travel the rails regularly; they may have traveled occasionally to visit family or attend church gatherings, but many could not afford the expense of a first-class ticket or time away from their jobs and family obligations. Most frequent travelers were part of the professional class: teachers, politicians, educators, business leaders, and ministers. Conditions on southern rails were not a central issue to many who did not travel regularly.

Many observers would assert that the struggles of the black middle class were marginal to the majority of black southerners. But the traveling patterns of working-class African Americans also reveal a desire for protection and shielding from hostile whites, even in colored cars. It is reasonable to assume that poorer black women who could not afford first-class tickets were equally concerned with protecting themselves from the advances of strange white men. In the post-Emancipation era, many black men sought to protect their wives and daughters by sheltering them from wage labor under the direct supervision of white male employers. Even black women who had to work outside of the home attempted to avoid work that left them vulnerable to attacks from white men, rejecting employment as live-in domestics in white households, for example. Given this evidence, we can reasonably assume that poor women also took measures to make themselves less vulnerable in smoking cars.[40]

One of the ways that working-class African Americans may have sought to protect themselves was the tradition of excursions. Beginning in the Reconstruction era, black churches, social clubs, societies, and entrepreneurs sponsored affordable recreational trips to southern cities or vacation areas. Many of these group trips were very large, often including one or two thousand passengers on specially chartered trains. Some middle-class blacks complained about the character of excursion group behavior, claiming that boisterous, bawdy, and loud blacks drew too much attention to themselves on trains, undercutting the respectability of the black community as a whole. One writer commented, "No man who cares for the morals and welfare of our people will lead them into such demoralizing excursions as are so often given by our people."[41] Such critics labeled excursions at best a waste of precious resources and at worst dangerous diversions and, counseling black people to "give excursions a wide berth and save your earnings."[42]

Some excursions may have been too large and attracted a violent element, leading to arguments and fights on trains. However, most trips involved smaller groups. Families, groups of friends, or churches would sponsor homecoming trips to visit, attend conventions, or enjoy fellowship with sister church congregations.[43] This kind of collective travel bolstered community networks and reinforced family ties stretched by migration. However, excursions may have also served as a racial buffer for poorer blacks who wanted to travel the rails.

Black passengers, particularly women, could find greater safety traveling in large, boisterous groups that filled up the second-class cars. Many black women chose to limit their social and sexual vulnerability by traveling in groups or with male escorts. The familiarity of large, community-based groups increased the comfort and safety of black women, who normally rode in second-class accommodations. Black excursions probably warded off hostile whites, creating moveable safe havens for black passengers who could not otherwise afford to ride in first-class cars. Loud talk could have served as a defensive tool to prevent whites from bothering black riders. Also, these groups provided no threat to the social order because their behavior melded with stereotypes: poor blacks laughing, smiling, and entertaining one another in their proper place, the second-class car. White expectations melded with the behavior of blacks on excursions; thus, few whites would complain. Despite the poor conditions in these forward cars, black passengers could take comfort in the fact that they had safety in numbers. Excursions were much less likely to provoke the anger or attention of white passengers or railroad workers than were middle-class black passengers fighting for seats in the first-class car.[44]

While coping strategies may have helped the working class avoid the rough edges of segregation in the first-class cars of southern trains and suits pressed by middle-class black riders challenged the legality of racial separation, the rising tide of segregation would soon prove unavoidable. Against these tough odds, African Americans continued to contest assaults on their citizenship. The protest against segregated rails would reach its peak in New Orleans, where it was put forth by one of the most idiosyncratic African American communities in the American South.

3 OUR PEOPLE, OUR PROBLEM?

Plessy and Divided New Orleans

When Homer Plessy boarded the East Louisiana Railroad in June 1892, he set into motion one of the most important legal challenges by black citizens in the Jim Crow era. The lawsuit that followed his arrest represents not only the legal benchmark for Jim Crow legislation but also the culmination of the battle waged by southern blacks to establish and maintain their public rights as citizens in the post–Civil War South. *Plessy v. Ferguson* was African American citizens' first collective effort to challenge the legality of Jim Crow cars through a test case brought before the U.S. Supreme Court. Although the *Plessy* case would eventually shape the lives of all African Americans, it emerged from a community like no other in the American South. African American New Orleans was divided by differences in culture and separated by distinct histories.

WHEN MULE-DRAWN streetcar service began in New Orleans in the 1820s, companies initially instituted policies that barred all African Americans— both free and slave—from riding. After people of color protested, some companies initiated the "star cars," a system of cars marked with large stars, to accommodate passengers of color. Free Creoles of color demanding integration vigorously resisted being forced onto special cars. The star car system was revived in 1862 in an effort to control the burgeoning population of freed slaves in Union-occupied New Orleans. Paul Trevigne, the leader of the call for universal black male suffrage and editor of the Creole of color newspaper *L'Union*, demanded that the cars be integrated and suggested that African Americans conduct sit-ins on streetcars until they were seated on an equal basis. In a bitter five-year battle, protesters boarded whites-only streetcars, physically fought white passengers and drivers who attacked and ejected them, and lodged formal complaints with military government authorities. One protester, Joseph Guillaume, fought off a conductor who had tried to eject him, threw the conductor out of the car, and drove off with the vehicle.[1]

The fight against segregation involved not only black residents but also African American soldiers, including the young future legislator P. B. S. Pinchback, who had come from Ohio to join the Union cause. Some black militiamen used their military authority to order white drivers to pick up black passengers. The military government under the authority of General Philip T. Sheridan eventually agreed that the streetcars needed to be desegregated, and the star cars were abolished.[2]

As a legislator, Pinchback and his colleagues of color were at the forefront of innovative legislation that challenged attempts to segregate rails in Louisiana. Instead of fighting segregation on a case-by-case basis, African American lawmakers of the early 1870s pushed successfully to include prohibitions against racial discrimination in railroad charters. Attempts to segregate blacks in Louisiana were met not only with damage suits but also with reviews of offending railroads' charters. Pinchback sued the Jackson railroad when his wife was denied admission to the Pullman berth and threatened to put the railroad out of business. Under pressure, the Jackson railroad, along with the other railroads in Louisiana, had a policy honoring first-class tickets purchased by all patrons throughout the 1870s.[3] New Orleans's African Americans, both those of Creole descent and Americanized freedpeople, had united in their efforts to crush segregation at the close of the Civil War.[4] However, shared leadership did not imply a shared history.

Histories of the city's antebellum Creole of color community emphasize its distinctive in-between status. Indeed, Afro-Creoles emerged from a legacy marked by differences of culture, color, and language.[5] The cosmopolitan and racially diverse city had once been home to alternatives to strict racial segregation. French-speaking descendants of mixed-race freed slaves (*gens de couleur libres*) were a unique community. The Creoles of color originated during the French and Spanish colonial era in the late eighteenth century, when colonists were permitted to free and educate their children born to black slave women. As a result, Louisiana was home to thousands of free descendants of mixed unions. Some free people descended from African slaves or slaves of African and Native American descent who had purchased their freedom in the decades before the Louisiana Purchase and southern emancipation. These racially mixed freed slaves, along with free émigrés of color from Haiti and Cuba, gained a degree of social and political liberty.

During the antebellum period, free people of color maintained an economic and social foothold. Many became the skilled tradesmen whose intricate ironwork, carpentry, and masonry distinguished New Orleans architecture. Others became part of the city's vibrant working class, finding employment as longshoremen, draymen, and factory workers. Many purchased homes and raised families in the Faubourg Tremé, a mixed-race community just north of the French Quarter. Some Creoles of color became wealthy and elite, residing in the French Quarter, purchasing both land and slaves, and seeking a classical education for their children at home and abroad in Europe. Most white Creoles (mixed French and Spanish descendants of white colonists) chose not to identify racially with their colored counterparts, particularly as American conceptions of race held increasing sway in the nineteenth century. However, colored and white Creoles shared a common Creolized French language and helped to make New Orleans a Creole society with racially integrated neighborhoods and Catholic churches and schools. Free people of color created a distinct niche that allowed for greater autonomy and freedom than that available to black slaves.[6]

Although Creoles of color enjoyed the privileges of liberty, their freedom was increasingly circumscribed after Louisiana became part of the United States in 1803. Theaters were the first public accommodations to be legally segregated in 1816, followed by jails in the 1830s. Privileged Creoles of color had been educated in private schools but were officially barred from the New Orleans public school system when it was initiated in the 1840s. Creole of color political leaders turned philanthropists such as Thomy Lafon and Aristide Mary founded and funded a number of private institutions, providing increased opportunities for education to both poor and wealthy Afro-Creoles. But Creoles of color always resisted racial separations and whenever possible sought to slip past the city's color lines through artful persuasion or silently passing for white.[7]

Afro-Creoles existed in the murky middle between free white society and enslaved blacks and suffered a severe erosion of their citizenship rights as fears of slave insurrections led by free people of color peaked in the mid-nineteenth century. But despite obstacles, Creoles of color enjoyed a more liberated existence than did black slaves and other free black people in the

American South. From this second tier, Afro-Creoles built a society rich in culture and relatively sheltered from most of the barbs of race prejudice and violence that circumscribed the lives of the majority of slaves and rural free blacks. Upon emancipation, many Creoles of color assumed political leadership of the race, based on the belief that they were best equipped to craft the meanings of freedom in postwar New Orleans. Some served as reluctant "leaders" of the "less fortunate" former slaves, while others partnered with the freed slaves and worked as outspoken advocates for all African Americans. But identity in New Orleans remained distinctively marked, divided by color, language, and heritage.[8]

After the Civil War, Afro-Creole legislators, guided by French ideals of universal liberty, led the fight to dissolve the color line, passing laws desegregating public schools and accommodations during the Constitutional Convention of 1867–68. Indeed, in the postwar period, Creoles of color took full advantage of their newly affirmed rights as citizens, participating in public life in the city. New Orleans's people of color not only gained a foothold on citizenship but also attempted to become more fully entrenched in a network of racial integration. They continued to attend Catholic mass with white congregants; lived in racially integrated neighborhoods on the Creole side of Canal Street; attended Carnival festivities, public plays, and sporting events; and rode freely on public conveyances. Their community was a cosmopolitan hub for mixed-race people in the Caribbean. Many residents also traveled to study in Europe or visit family abroad. This is not to suggest that the lives of Creoles of color were free from discrimination and oppression; race remained a tremendous barrier to even the most successful. After the Reconstruction had ended, moreover, their wartime loyalty to the Union forces and their effort to institute universal male suffrage made them targets for vengeful whites determined to reestablish power.[9]

Unless they chose to separate from families, friends, and communities to pass for white, Afro-Creoles in New Orleans could not escape the larger social reality of race.[10] Some light-skinned Creoles of color desired the privileges usually connected with white skin and deeply resented their invisible connection to blackness. In 1877, an angry Creole of color wrote anonymously about his social discomfort, believing that there was no racial middle ground, even for those who appeared to be white. He complained that "a person having a few drops of african blood in his veins, no matter how white he may be[,] is considered a nigger." Pressing the viewpoint of the Afro-Creoles who had decided to pass permanently as white citizens, he continued, "I think that man has a right to choose for himself, weather [sic] he will be a white man or a nigger. So it is, the mortal suffering of a man having a little Negro blood in his veins is something terrible—for he is always in hot water."[11] Some descendants of free people of color felt enslaved by their black heritage and sought ways to distance themselves not only from other African Americans but also from black identity.

But the majority of Afro-Creoles were not bitter about their racial status. Not all Creoles of color were pale-skinned enough to pass for white, but more importantly, most did not want to break with their rich legacy of family, friends, culture, and community. Furthermore, Creole of color folklore suggests that those who tried to hide or disguise their color paid social costs. Any efforts to pass might fool white society, but passing Creoles could not fool their own people.[12] Most Afro-Creoles did not want to be considered white or black. They wanted to be themselves and sought alliances with those who recognized their unique, in-between status. To Afro-Creoles, the eroding conditions on the trains exemplified the irrational nature of racial segregation. After all, they believed, it was cheaper for the railroad to seat the few first-class respectable passengers of color among white riders than to establish and run entirely separate colored cars.

New Orleans resident George Washington Cable argued just such a case; he believed that "neither race . . . wants to see the civil rewards of decency in dress and behavior usurped by the common herd of clowns and ragamuffins." Instead, Cable asserted, elite African Americans, particularly Afro-Creoles, had earned the "rights of gentility by the simple act of being genteel."[13] Although Cable was heralded for his historical fiction about the city's people, he may have hinted at the silent conviction held by some whites who had grown accustomed to a few elite Creoles of color in their midst. Cable saw no harm in allowing these privileged few to flourish, arguing that educated and propertied Afro-Creoles should be respected because they had over time earned class-based civil privileges.

Cable wanted a class-based hierarchy in southern society and rejected racial segregation as an illogical divider, asserting, "These distinctions on the line of color are really made not from any necessity, but simply for their own sake—to preserve the old arbitrary supremacy of the master class over the menial without regard to the decency or indecency of appearance or manners in either the white individual or the colored." Cable believed that racial segregation fostered "the confusion it pretends to prevent" by waiving "all strict demands for painstaking in either manners or dress of either master or menial." To explain his beliefs, Cable used the example of the railcar, suggesting that racial segregation made "the average Southern railway coach more uncomfortable than the average railway coaches elsewhere" and forcing the "average Southern white passenger to find less offense in the presence of a profane, boisterous, or unclean white person than in that of a quiet, well-behaved colored man or woman."[14] Cable fervently believed that other white southerners shared his belief that class sometimes trumped race. However, Cable was one of just a handful of whites who were willing to argue on behalf of respectable citizens. When segregation law and popular white opinion turned against the rights of black railcar patrons, few white southerners supported flexible racial policies. When the statute requiring separate railcars was introduced in the Louisiana state legislature, it threatened the tenuous compromise that had been established in New Orleans. The quiet concessions of the earlier decade were increasingly confronted with white supremacist notions asserting that any form of racial integration would lead to race mixing or "social equality." Lawmakers argued that access, even for an elite few, would threaten the sanctity of white womanhood.

Although much of the historical record focuses on the elite leaders, Creoles of color as a group were also divided along lines of wealth, employment, and privilege. The majority of the light-skinned Creoles of color were not wealthy and propertied; most lived in circumstances similar to those of Homer Plessy. Most New Orleans Afro-Creoles were literate skilled laborers employed as metal workers, brick masons, or cigar rollers. Born into a family of skilled working men, Plessy held a variety of jobs during his working life: he was employed as a clerk, a warehouse laborer, and an insurance collector. When litigation began in 1892, Plessy's occupation was listed as shoemaker; by 1902, the city directory listed him as a laborer, a revealing change given W. E. B. Du Bois's argument that segregation deskilled the black working class.

The occupations of working-class Creoles distinguished them from both the elite Afro-Creole professional class and the masses of unskilled black workers. And although working-class Creoles of color lived in integrated neighborhoods along with the elite downtown on the French side of Canal Street, they generally did not reside in the more exclusive Seventh Ward but in the Tremé section. Plessy and his wife lived in the Tremé in a rented house on North Claiborne Avenue, near the city's famed Congregation Hall.[15] Plessy's Creole status and light skin may have allowed him some intracommunity privilege, but he was far from elite.

Although the twenty-nine-year-old Plessy was judged to be the proper person to lodge the test case by leading members of his community, he lived a life very different from the Creole of color doctors, lawyers, politicians, and property owners who led the fight against segregation. In fact, Plessy was never an official member of the Citizens' Committee, the organization that pressed the test case. In *Our People and Our History* (1911), published by prominent committee member Rodolphe Desdunes, the only mention of Plessy reports that "the Committee engaged Mr. Homere Plessy as its representative." In a detailed account of the work of the Citizens' Committee, Desdunes offered no details about Plessy's life or praise for his willingness to press the case. None of the extant correspondence between the members of the Citizens' Committee and their lawyer includes any personal, political, or professional reference to Plessy.[16] But this does not mean that the silent litigant did not engage in his own political work. Plessy was a registered voter and participant in community-based activism. Working-class Creoles of color were also concerned with contesting segregation, maintaining the franchise, and uplifting the needy through mutual aid and benevolent societies.[17]

Homer Plessy was part of a community of color with a distinctive approach to questions of race. The majority of Creoles of color had battled hard to break down the color line and valued color-blind inclusion in the city of their birth. They approached the fight against turn-of-the-century Jim Crow laws with their belief in the value of an integrated society. But opportunities for African Americans of both Creole and American descent began shrinking in the 1890s with the advent of formal laws barring blacks from public accommodations. Afro-Creoles united with newly freed blacks to contest segregation. But these two separate communities had different origins and maintained divergent outlooks on the problem of segregation.

The descendants of the freed slaves who had resided in New Orleans or migrated there faced more difficult circumstances than the Creoles of color. After Emancipation, freed slaves were attracted to the port city, seeking work and the relative security of an urban setting. This migration continued in the decades after the close of federal Reconstruction. Between 1880 and 1900, more than twenty thousand new black migrants moved to the expanding city from the rural counties of Louisiana and Mississippi. Nearly half of the black population of New Orleans was illiterate in 1890. Lynching and racial violence increasingly threatened the black populace, as did dismal urban living conditions. By the turn of the century, the hot and often-flooded city still had no adequate sewage system, so sickness and disease plagued the poorest residents.[18] In 1902, it was flippantly suggested that pneumonia and tuberculosis was so rampant among black residents that mortality would "solve the negro problem."[19] But the poor and working class gained a strong grip on citizenship during Reconstruction and the decades that followed, working to improve living conditions in their communities, maintain their right to vote, and seek fair representation in every aspect of public life.[20]

Black residents of New Orleans had continued to progress only because of their efforts to improve their communities. By 1890, black illiteracy had dropped dramatically, in part because black educators supplemented the poor system of public education through black churches and mutual aid societies. Black communities established church schools to meet the tremendous demand for education. Care for the physical health of poor black residents also improved. Community efforts to organize black hospitals and benevolent societies, often led by prominent black women, helped to improve public health. Numerous middle-class and poor African Americans made valiant attempts to address the needs of their communities.[21]

Blacks in New Orleans also built coalitions with white residents. Many notable politicians who emerged as leaders in the Republican Party were not part of the Creole elite. During Reconstruction, blacks worked alongside white politicians for more than fifteen years. Before 1880, the black electorate's support of the Republican Party held back the tide of white supremacy and violence. African Americans in New Orleans also united with whites in the interracial Methodist Episcopal Church. Many northern whites who moved to New Orleans to aid the free people after the war were motivated by their Methodism, building new churches and schools that promoted interracial brotherhood. Although whites and blacks worshiped separately, the Methodist Episcopal church created a dialogue between freed slaves and a sympathetic community of white Christians at crucial time. Coalition building also temporarily buttressed the city's working class. Interracial unionism among dockworkers dramatically improved conditions for black and white longshoremen. During the General Strike of 1892, more than twenty thousand longshoremen and dockworkers of both races united to improve pay and working conditions.[22]

But most of the progress black people experienced grew out of autonomous effort. In the closing decades of the nineteenth century, a black middle class slowly emerged from the population of former slaves and their children. A class of educators, preachers, merchants, and businesspeople nurtured by black churches and schools grew prominent and more successful and served as community leaders for blacks who lived outside of the Vieux Carré (French Quarter). Thus, over time, New Orleans developed a divided black leadership class, one Creole and one non-Creole. While such a distinction might appear minor, it did have political meaning. These two communities maintained not only separate societies but also distinctly different approaches to the question of race, equality, and integration. Creoles of color had an exclusive identity; their sense of self was fixed in the past, drawn from their French ancestors and their forebears' free status in the age of slavery. Leading Creoles of color looked back at their history as a guide to shape their identity and political outlook. By contrast, the majority of the former slaves were stripped of direct knowledge of their heritage and the accomplishments of their ancestors. Their identities were rooted in their quest to improve the future.

The Methodist Episcopal newspaper, the *Southwestern Christian Advocate*, reflected the maturation of New Orleans's non-Creole black middle class. Funded and governed by the church and guided by a series of black editors, the *Advocate* served as a bridge between these two worlds. The paper's content was a testament to the strides black New Orleans had made since Emancipation with the assistance of northern whites and the growing independence of a black leadership class. The paper featured weekly columns by prominent black Methodist ministers, Sunday school lessons, suggestions for Bible study at home, and serial Christian stories for African American readers. Even the advertisements were interspersed with updates from Methodist Episcopal churches and recommendations for suitable Christian publications. The pages of the *Advocate* also touched on the social world of the budding black middle class, publishing marriage announcements, reporting on the educational advancements of the city's black Methodists, advertising excursions sponsored by local mutual aid societies and professional groups, and reporting the yearly celebration of Emancipation Day. The *Advocate* promoted social uplift and encouraged middle-class respectability in a column, "The Household."

However, the *Advocate* was also a political newspaper that closely followed the rise of white supremacy in the 1890s. The *Advocate* became explicitly political under the leadership of A. P. E. Albert, a black Methodist minister who took charge of the weekly in the 1890s. The *Advocate* provided news about the status of African Americans in the South, faithfully reporting changes in the law and the encroachment of segregation on New Orleans as well as city, state, and national political news. The *Advocate* warned black men to do all they could to hold onto their right to vote, stressing that the "importance of a vote can scarcely be overestimated." The *Advocate* regularly published stories that highlighted southern elections where black voters held the margin of victory. While reporting in a frank manner on the crimes of Louisiana lynch mobs, the paper reminded readers that the noose was used not to stop rape but to eliminate prominent and successful black leaders. The *Advocate* led the charge to organize a response to racial violence and inequity by becoming one of the major voices of the Colored Convention Movement in Louisiana and the American Citizens' Equal Rights Association (ACERA), both of which represented progressive black leadership during troubled times.[23]

As much as the paper reflected New Orleans's non-Creole black leadership, Albert empathized with the concerns of the Creole of color community, constantly trying to connect the two African American groups. He frequently reported on the achievements of "our people of French extraction." Although the black middle class and the Creoles of color saw themselves as distinct communities, their political concerns connected them as crucial allies. Albert's parentage provided a link: his father was a working-class Frenchman, and his mother was a slave. Although Albert spoke French and had a white parent, he did not consider himself part of the Creole of color community; he and his mother had broken with the Catholic Church because of an incident of discrimination when he was a child. Also, he had not been born free. Among Creoles of color, his background and faith may have made his status dubious; among Americanized blacks, his talent made him a leader.[24]

Albert's slave past, not his French name, seemed to frame some of his most important work at the *Advocate*. Albert published a collection of slave narratives gathered by his wife, Octavia Victoria Rodgers Albert, first as a serial story in the *Advocate* and later as a book, *The House of Bondage; or, Charlotte Brooks and Other Slaves* (1890). The enormously popular slave narratives recounted in *The House of Bondage* resonated with a readership that was still mourning its slave past. Some twenty-five years after Emancipation, the "Lost Friends" column was printed monthly, offering readers the opportunity to publish inquiries about family and friends separated during slavery. Ministers read the notices to their congregations, so that those who could not read or afford the paper might still be able to hear from missing loved ones. The majority of subscribers were descendants of slaves, striving toward literacy and education in a hostile society.[25]

Despite or perhaps because of the progress made by African Americans of all classes in New Orleans, Louisiana's white legislators renewed their attacks on black citizenship rights in the 1890s. African American leaders quickly responded to the threats. In 1889, under the leadership of Louis Martinet, New Orleans's Afro-Creole community founded the weekly *Crusader* specifically to counter the rising tide of hostility toward citizens of color. Describing the newspaper as an "organ of justice and equal rights, the enemy of wrong and injustice, the friend and defender of right and justice," Martinet, along with Rodolphe Desdunes, an Afro-Creole writer of Caribbean descent, promoted civic equality in a progressive, fiery style that reflected the unique political heritage of Creole *liberté*.

Although both Creoles of color and Americanized blacks were concerned about their future as citizens, Afro-Creoles were nevertheless unwilling to identify as Negro. Following a *New Orleans Times-Democrat* article that described the *Crusader* as a "Negro paper," Desdunes vehemently rejected such a notion. Challenging traditional assumptions about race, Desdunes asserted that Martinet was "as white as the editor of the *Times-Democrat*, as any who will see both together can judge." Questioning his critics' racial "purity," Desdunes provocatively asserted that the *Crusader*'s "proprietors are men of as pure Caucasian blood as any, and perhaps purer than some on the T-D staff." Although Desdunes made proprietary claims of whiteness, his arguments targeted what he believed were false dichotomies between black and white. Although they wanted to avoid being stigmatized by blackness, Desdunes and others in the Afro-Creole community did not want to become white. Rather, they sought to embody the literal meaning of Creole—a complicated blend of historic cultures and communities that emerged from a unique legacy.[26]

The weekly *Crusader* served as the voice of politically engaged Creoles of color, presenting not only a unique vision of race but also an emphasis on egalitarian principles and a deep belief in the racial integration of institutions such as Catholic schools and churches. The pages of the *Crusader* reveal that Afro-Creoles sought to preserve their antebellum status, seeking to maintain a role in an integrated civic world. The community of Creoles of color opposed segregation of every sort, even the establishment of all-black colleges and churches that most non-Creole African Americans favored. Creoles of color had become invested in a lifestyle that allowed them to participate in many of New Orleans's institutions of public life. Segregated facilities, even when encouraged by black American leaders or founded to further black education and independence, were anathema to the Afro-Creoles. As a community, they rejected any changes that would have placed them alongside the black masses. They hoped that within an egalitarian and integrated New Orleans, they might be able to maintain their distinct identity.[27] The *Crusader* provides a glimpse at the ways leaders of the Creole of color community danced the line between maintaining an independent identity and fighting for the rights of all.

Non-Creole black Americans in New Orleans also closely monitored the growth of segregation law, particularly restrictions on access to public conveyances. Reporting on the U.S. Supreme Court's decision in *Louisville, New Orleans, and Texas Railroad v. Mississippi*, which reversed earlier trends and declared interstate segregation constitutional, Albert bemoaned, "One by one all the results of the war secured at such tremendous cost in life and property, are being frittered away by the Supreme Court." Local white segregationists hoped to make hay of the new opportunity, and Albert reported, "This last decision moves the *Daily States* of this city to see 'a chance for the introduction of star cars.'"[28]

White advocates of racial segregation viewed integrated trains and streetcars as a symbol of "Negro rule" and the legacy of federal Reconstruction that had to be undone. The *Louisville, New Orleans, and Texas* decision emboldened New Orleans's segregationists: the local Democratic newspaper, the *Daily States*, began a campaign targeting "Carrollton Negroes" as especially "offensive to white ladies," accusing black laborers who rode the Carrollton line streetcars down St. Charles Avenue to work each morning and home each evening of traveling while dirty from their day's labor and crowding the cars. The paper warned "the Negroes that if they do not cease making themselves offensive that prompt steps will be taken to set apart cars for them which they will be compelled to ride."[29]

The *Advocate* responded that white workers used streetcars in the same manner and were equally dirty: "Has it come to this that the laborer is thus to be abhorred because he is a laborer?" Hinting at the power of the black electorate, the weekly cautioned the members of the city council that they had been "put into power by Negro votes" and concluded that the segregationists' approach could not have been representative of "the spirit of white people . . . of this city." Yet the *Advocate* overestimated the staying power of the black franchise as well as the fair intentions of white legislators.[30]

In response to the changing racial climate, African Americans, under the leadership of P. B. S. Pinchback, organized a state branch of the American Citizens' Equal Rights Association (ACERA) in February 1890. Although the association took a cautious approach to the race problem, it sought to make a statement that African Americans would not accept the legal and extralegal deterioration of their citizenship. A founding document argued, "After years of oppression and injustice, the colored citizens of this country finding that their constitutional rights continue to be most violently trampled upon and that a relentless organized public sentiment continues . . . to rob them of every constitutional [right] have determined to organize."[31]

Pinchback explained that ACERA would "demand protection" for all African Americans "because we are American citizens." Although Pinchback was a very fair-complexioned descendant of a free black mother and a white father, he was from Ohio and hence not a Creole of color.[32] But the new organization bridged the Canal Street divide attracting Creole and non-Creole leadership and members. Albert became ACERA's president, the non-Creole J. Lewis and Creole William J. Rudolphe served as the organization's vice presidents, and Pinchback and Martinet served as ex-officio members of the group's board. Although Creoles of color may have sought to maintain a distinct identity throughout the post-Emancipation period and into the 1890s, some Creoles initially respected the experience of political elders such as Pinchback and of new voices such as Albert who shared similar approaches to working for the benefit of people of color. Albert was even welcomed as a board member of the Crusader Publishing Company.[33]

Segregationists were not concerned with the unique history of Creoles of color in New Orleans. These proposed laws made no exceptions; everyone with a drop of Negro blood would be excluded.[34] Creoles and Americanized blacks had united to defeat the star cars thirty years earlier and would come together again to contest this new wave of segregation. Adversity in a city where white segregationists cared little about the different origins of people of color drew together embattled communities. Even if Afro-Creoles and the black Americanized middle class did not share birth languages, members of both groups were familiar with the language of disfranchisement and race-based segregation.

While ACERA's leaders bridged New Orleans's cultural divide, they realized that organizing across the state would pose an even greater challenge. In an increasingly dangerous climate, the leaders were wary of the possibility of violence, particularly while organizing in rural Louisiana. Early on they warned voters "in communities where lawlessness exists [to] abstain from any participation in politics."[35] This may have been sound advice in a state where the massacre of more than one hundred black voters in rural Colfax in 1873 went unpunished. In dismissing the conviction of the Colfax murderers in *United States v. Cruikshank et al.* (1876), the U.S. Supreme Court ruled that it was up to the states, not the federal government, to make voting a functioning right. The Fifteenth Amendment to the U.S. Constitution had given the freedmen the right to vote; the Supreme Court ruled that the amendment had simply removed the barrier and did not imply federal enforcement of the right to vote, abandoning black citizens in small rural areas like the parishes of Louisiana to the will of local authorities.[36] ACERA counseled its members that voting rights might be more safely pursued in cities, where safety in numbers usually implied a modicum of protection.

Arguing that blacks wanted to organize not in secrecy or out of vengeance but rather to "act in concert in intelligent and dispassionate agitation . . . against every injustice," Albert explained that the association was "non-political and non-partisan." Although the majority of members had once been active supporters of the Republican Party, local and national moves toward "lily white" Republicanism created a bit more ambivalence about the usefulness of party identity. The fledgling ACERA also hoped to avoid reprisals from whites fearful of black political organizations. But in the eyes of segregationists, even the most dispassionate and apolitical approach was still radical. A few months after the association's launch, the *Advocate* reported that Raymond Carter, a Leland University–educated schoolteacher, had been lynched in Avoyelles Parish for speaking in favor of organizing a local branch of ACERA. Although the paper later printed a correction—the schoolteacher had in truth not been killed—the account of violence must have had reverberations. Lynching rumors may not have helped to grow ACERA. Even a nonpartisan organization that suggested that blacks should refrain from voting in lawless areas was radical in Louisiana.[37]

ACERA also promoted African American uplift; leaders agreed that education, thrift, and virtuous behavior were the best rejoinders to white arguments about the inferiority of the African race. Believing that hard work was the path to change, Albert cautioned his readers, "Let us have less show and feathers, and more comfortable homes, nice churches, and substantial schools," much like what Afro-Creoles had already established for themselves.[38] Pinchback asserted that black political power depended on black behavior. "To secure civil equality and political influence," African Americans needed to increase their "wealth by frugal industry . . . intelligence by study . . . moral force by fidelity to truth and to principle." Through self-improvement, they would become model citizens; "instead of seeking recognition it will seek us, and . . . parties will court our support after first according our rights. We must do not only well for ourselves, but rely on ourselves."[39] But self-help may have come too late; popular white opinion had already turned against any defense of black rights.

In 1890, in response to mounting local pressure and the federal decision condoning racial segregation on the rails, the Louisiana General Assembly proposed a law that required separate accommodations for black passengers on railroads, similar to the Mississippi law that had been upheld by the

Supreme Court.[40] ACERA immediately organized a campaign against the bill, forming a committee of Creole and non-Creole leaders "to draw up protests against the proposed class legislation now pending before the Legislature." The association composed a written protest for a black legislator to present to the assembly and sent a delegation "to visit Baton Rouge and exert all influence" to defeat the law. Albert was "selected to address the Legislature in behalf of the Association."[41]

The campaign to stop the passage of the separate car proposal spurred ACERA's growth. "Branch Associations are springing up in every ward," reported the *Advocate*, "and the meetings continue to grow in attendance and interest. Petitions are being circulated throughout the State." New members worked to halt what they called class legislation—that is, the notion that all African Americans were worthy of second-class citizenship.[42]

Although ACERA's all-male leadership implies that women held secondary roles, the organization's literature argued that women's presence was still valued as part of the membership. The association styled itself as an open organization that sought to recruit members from various parts of the African American community. Women were officially welcomed into the ranks. ACERA's literature stated that women would be "an effective element of success in this grand movement to secure equality of Citizens' Rights for the Colored American." Women were advised to form auxiliaries if they were not interested in membership in the main body. ACERA cultivated broad support, suggesting that the cause "be constantly agitated in the family circle, in public meetings, in the pulpits, and in the press" in the hope that all African Americans would organize "against the organized lawlessness, that prevails especially in the southern states, where our people are constantly outraged and murdered for attempting to exercise their rights as American Citizens." Women members could support the cause by encouraging their husbands, brothers, and sons to vote as well as by pushing for ACERA's mission in their churches, social clubs, and benevolent societies. Black men remained registered voters in 1890, and although their votes were often subject to manipulation and fraud, the state legislature remained somewhat accountable to black citizens. For women, however political encouragement was not a seat at the table, although their concerns were central to the fight against segregation. The organization's approach to the question of the ladies' car was complex and seemed to reflect a keen understanding of the challenges women faced in segregated railcars. Even as ACERA faltered on the importance of women's leadership, the group's analysis of the difficulties black women faced in the Jim Crow car was spot-on.[43]

Seeking to protect the black citizens they believed were most victimized by segregation, the all-male ACERA delegation pleaded the case of African American women and children. Through African American state legislator T. T. Allain, the association submitted its protest to the Louisiana assembly, insisting that "the immediate effects of such legislation would be free license to the evilly-disposed [to] insult, humiliate and . . . maltreat inoffensive persons . . . especially women and children who should happen to have a dark skin." They deserved to be protected from the company of unknown men, the pollution of smoke, and cursing and spitting in the smoking cars. ACERA recognized the legacy of black women's railcar protest and included their special circumstances in the argument against separate cars.[44]

The protest went on to decry the separate car law as "unconstitutional, un-American, unjust, dangerous and against sound public policy." Citing the Declaration of Independence and the Golden Rule, the association connected an integrated public sphere to the "American principles" that were the fundamental basis of citizenship. Segregation was not the natural organization of society but rather the expression of "unreasonable prejudice." People of color were "respectable, useful, and law-abiding" and represented "a considerable percentage of the capital and almost all the labor of the state"; they deserved better. Black Louisianans, working class and elite alike, had made profound contributions to the state and nation and should not be denied first-class citizenship: "We do not think that citizens of a darker hue should be treated by law on different lines than those of a lighter complexion. Citizenship is national and has no color." The protest letter optimistically concluded that the "best people of the South are not in favor of such legislation."[45] However, the protest delegation was aware of the hostile climate in the state and made one last stand on behalf of integrated public conveyances.

Just prior to the vote on the separate car act, Albert spoke before the Louisiana legislature, offering a variety of counterarguments. He believed that the separate car proposal "was calculated to work hardship and injustice to the humblest of our citizens" and would weaken African Americans' hold on citizenship. Albert dismissed false arguments about segregation: the separation of the races was not natural or politically neutral, and separate cars would never provide "equal accommodations." Citing the cost of operating two first-class cars, Albert argued that "colored passengers would very often be unjustly forced into compartments, one end of which would be used as smokers."[46]

The rights of African American women lay at the heart of his argument.

Albert insisted, "The Act would further subject our women and children to the brutal treatment of every rough brakesman anxious to exercise a show of brief and unrighteous authority over them." Trains had been segregated by sex to protect white ladies from male strangers. For separate to be truly equal, colored ladies' cars, separate from smoking or second-class cars, would have to be established to shield black women from male strangers on an equal basis with white women. But Albert recognized that given social perceptions about black women, truly equal accommodations would never be established. Although the association's delegation was composed entirely of men, they were genuinely concerned about the women who had suffered and battled informal limitations on their rights to first-class accommodations. Albert also hinted at the questions of sexuality and gender at the heart of railroad segregation, reminding the assembly that all segregation law "assumes certain reasons why the one race is unfit to sit in the same railway coach with the other, to [African Americans'] great mortification." Jim Crow law was a misuse of governance based in a false belief in the inferiority of blacks and the attempt to give unjust and unfair beliefs the force of law.[47]

The careful terms Albert employed to argue the association's case reflect the climate of growing hatred and violence. In contrast to his frank and unapologetic style in his weekly columns, Albert couched this argument in accommodationist terms that appealed to a shared southern history and ACERA's apolitical stance. In a state where black leaders were lynched for speaking frankly on behalf of their people, Albert insisted that ACERA was "not a black league or a political organization, bent upon the advancement of the black at the expense of . . . white . . . citizens," and did not "seek to avenge any real or imaginary wrongs." Albert tried to create rhetorical distance from the legacy of Reconstruction, which by the 1890s segregationists were reimagining as a time when black politicians lorded over whites for personal and sexual gains. Albert did not seek "Negro rule"; in his role as mouthpiece for the statewide group, Albert endeavored "to promote the moral, intellectual and material welfare of all classes of American citizens." The goal of ACERA's work was "the promotion of peace and prosperity." But he did condemn white attempts to disfranchise black voters, asserting that the association remained "mindful" and did not intend to "underrate the priceless value of [the] elective franchise."[48]

However, even in Albert's cautious address to the state legislators, his careful employment of history undercut the supremacist argument for a color line in public accommodations. In a retelling of the myths of southern history, Albert recalled the image of the loyal slave, pointing out the ways that black slaves had been faithful stewards to their white masters and mistresses even in times of great distress. This argument at first appears to be a complete capitulation to stereotypes, but embedded in Albert's argument is the reality of physical intimacy. Albert cites the slaves who nursed white children, slave women who fixed daily meals, slave men left to protect person and property when white men served in the Civil War. However debatable the wider reality of these images might have been, Albert implicitly undercut the idea that black riders on integrated railcars would fundamentally threaten white safety and comfort. His speech implied that if black women nursing white children with their own breast milk could be tolerated, then a black woman tending to her own child in first-class accommodations in proximity to white women could not be a complete violation of the sanctity of white space. Even if ladies' cars were intended to replicate the parlors of southern homes, trains were distinctly less intimate than the daily contact of house slaves and their white masters. To Albert, railcars belonged in the public realm, where equality should have been the rule. Although Albert's speech reflects the fear he must have felt while addressing the hostile legislature, his language reveals a coherent argument against the law.[49]

Despite the delegation's best effort to gain "no exclusive but common privileges," the separate car law passed in July 1890. ACERA had depended on the few remaining black state legislators and sympathetic whites to prevent the measure from being enacted, but advocates such as Desdunes believed that political deal making had diluted the effort to stop the bill. Albert's disappointment was marked in the pages of the *Advocate*. In contrast to most of the bold and large articles chronicling the association's work, the report of the law's passage was small and untitled and could easily have gone unnoticed. The paper recorded only that "the separate car bill finally passed both branches of the Legislature and has been approved by the Governor.... Our colored representatives acquitted themselves very manfully in opposing this class legislation but they were overpowered."[50] The association continued organizing throughout the fall, calling delegates from local churches and community organizations to meet concerning the improvement of black schools in New Orleans, and the group successfully pushed New Orleans to hire black teachers for African American segregated schools.[51] But never again did the association reach the level of vocal protest that it had in the fight against the separate car law.

Leadership in New Orleans changed after ACERA failed. Pinchback continued to agitate against segregation but did so from afar, as a resident of New York State.[53] Albert paid a high price for his political agitation. In 1892, despite the fact that he remained a popular leader and successful journalist, tripling the *Advocate*'s subscription rate, he faced allegations from within the Methodist Episcopal Church that his work with ACERA undercut the denomination's interracialism. Albert countered that although his political work was an effort to secure and protect black citizenship, it was not racially exclusive, and he compared his efforts to the abolitionism of a previous generation, a movement that welcomed supporters from communities of like-minded people of all colors. Although black delegates to the Methodist convention were almost unanimous in their support for reappointing Albert as editor of the *Advocate*, a majority of the white delegates voted him out, opting for a black editor with a more accommodationist tone. Albert ended his career as a journalist and began a medical practice. Although he remained engaged with his church and the cause of civil rights, he had lost the *Southwestern Christian Advocate*.[53]

Desdunes was proud of his participation in ACERA. In 1892, he credited the group with taking the "first step . . . against the passage of that infamous act." Desdunes blamed deal making within the Republican Party, part of the crooked and corrupt political style of the day, for the passage of the discriminatory act but remained hopeful that the courts were the best way to surpass party politics.[54] Martinet blamed poor leadership for ACERA's downfall, writing in 1891, "The proper men were not at the head. Its last . . . national convention was turned into a purely political resolution machine." Martinet, who had joined the organization with the aim of launching a national daily newspaper that would inform northerners about "the conditions and affairs in the South," was disturbed by what he perceived as most delegates' desire to organize without building coalitions with sympathetic whites. Martinet blamed "politicians [and] that other clan not much better —those preachers who see in their profession the means of earning a livelihood or making money only." ACERA's leadership, he went on, was concerned with nothing beyond "the honor and prestige of the moment." Believing that many African American leaders were attracted to politics for selfish gain, Martinet thought that the fight against segregation would be best served by selfless, egalitarian leaders willing to build a long-term, national, cross-racial coalition. The effort to build just such an interracial approach would be the hallmark of his effort in the Citizens' Committee.[55] Class, color, and culture shaped politics and protest. The fight against segregation forced African Americans to define what constituted their community, identify leadership, and decide which tactics would best challenge segregation. Questions of difference and solidarity lay at the center of the antisegregation struggle.

CREOLES OF COLOR continued the fight against Jim Crow. Desdunes reacted swiftly to the passage of the separate car law, writing that "Colored people have largely patronized the railroads heretofore. . . . [T]hey can withdraw the patronage from these corporations and travel only by necessity."[56] Although Desdunes's impulse to boycott was savvy in its economic approach, it was far from practical. Few African Americans rode long-distance routes regularly enough to make boycotts effective. Trains were rarely used for travel to and from work, so black riders constituted only a small percentage of daily traffic. More important, trains were the primary means of interstate travel, leaving few alternatives.[57]

The best way to challenge the Jim Crow car, therefore, would be to confront the questionable legality of segregation itself. Leading Creoles of color steered the fight against segregation into the courts. A new organization, the Citizens' Committee, came into being in 1891 to challenge segregated rails. Martinet spearheaded the group; he believed in developing an interracial coalition against segregation and blamed racial exclusiveness for ACERA's failure. Martinet argued, "The North needs to be educated as to conditions in the South and its disloyalty and rebellious tendencies. And we need to do the work soon." For the Citizens' Committee, the key to challenging Jim Crow policy was to petition the federal courts and establish a new national consensus against segregation law. If northern whites were aware of African Americans' plight in the South, Martinet argued, northerners would pressure southern legislators to protect black citizenship.[58]

The Citizens' Committee was composed almost exclusively of leading men from the Afro-Creole community and was formed with the encouragement of Aristide Mary, a Reconstruction-era Afro-Creole legislator.[59] The wealthy Mary, a philanthropist and elder statesman by the 1890s, made a sizable donation to help found the new organization.[60] Mary's conflicts with Pinchback over the founding of Southern University as a separate state-funded university for African Americans had led to an ongoing rivalry between the two leaders.[61] This disagreement over educational policy mirrored the conflicts that led Creole of color leaders to organize outside ACERA. Following the passage of the separate car law, ACERA worked to improve conditions in segregated schools, a move that Afro-Creoles opposed. The Creole of color community first and foremost sought to maintain its access to New Orleans society on an equal basis, not to improve conditions in separate facilities. Former slaves, in contrast, viewed opportunities to gain education and build religious institutions in all-black surroundings as steps to strengthen their status. Creoles of color opposed segregation in all forms and detested being lumped with the freedmen and pushed outside the white public realm. At the Colored Convention in Washington, D.C., in February 1890, Martinet tried but failed to "keep the word 'colored' out of the [ACERA] preamble." To Martinet, segregation in any form, including the exclusion of sympathetic whites from mostly black political organizations, was fundamentally wrong.[62]

The Citizens' Committee formed specifically to respond to the separate car law. Eighteen Creole of color leaders banded together to take "some definite action towards offering legal resistance" to segregation on Louisiana's rails by preparing a test case. Unlike ACERA, the committee had a single purpose and a closed membership limited to those its founders "invited" from among "a few citizens representing various interests" within the Afro-Creole community. Only three ACERA members joined the Citizens' Committee: Martinet, Desdunes, and Reconstruction politician Laurant August. The well-established weekly *Crusader* served as the voice of the newly formed organization, and the members of the committee held their first planning meeting at the newspaper's offices.[63]

The group published "an appeal, to the public" in both French and English explaining the committee's grievances and willingness to "vindicate the cause of equal rights and American manhood." The appeal insisted that the character of American citizenship was threatened if the issue of segregation was not pursued in the courts. The committee saw the Jim Crow car as part of a slippery slope toward "every manner of outrage, up to murder, without redress." Even though committee membership was exclusive, the group sought support from all people concerned with the future of the race, even writing Frederick Douglass to request his backing. The *Crusader* published Douglass's response, in which he declined because "he was opposed to making decisions and establishing precedents against his race." Douglass doubted that the courts, which had previously been unsympathetic to the question of Negro rights, would remedy the crisis of southern segregation.[64]

Early organizing centered on raising the funds necessary to hire a leading attorney and support staff to put forth a strong test case. Committee members believed that funds raised from all segments of society would serve as "proof of public sentiment and determination," but no other expressions of popular support were encouraged. On the grounds that "the obnoxious measure is the concern of all our citizens who are opposed to caste legislation and its consequent injustices and crimes," the committee wanted to raise collective funds so that the case would "not be a question as to whether one or two individuals can or ought to bear the expenses of the contest." Donations proved popular support for their cause—"a demonstration as will plainly show the temper of the people against that infamous contrivance which has been appropriately characterized as the Jim Crow Car."[65] African Americans across the South supported efforts to end train segregation.

Afro-Creole Louisiana was not the only community to campaign against segregated cars in the wake of the Mississippi decision. In 1890, a push for new segregation laws also began in Kentucky, a slave state that had not seceded during the Civil War. The state's pro-Union stance did not prevent the demand, particularly among rural white Kentuckians, to prevent blacks from riding first class on the train. In December 1891, state senator Tipton Miller from rural Calloway County proposed a new law in December 1891 resembled the 1889 Mississippi law upheld by the Supreme Court and required railroads "to furnish separate coaches or cars for the travel or transportation of the white and colored passengers."[66] It detailed an efficient and cost-effective means for dividing passengers that left blacks jammed in a smoky, uncomfortable space adjoining a polluted smoking car marked with "appropriate words in plain letters indicating the race for which it is set apart." Any black passenger who complained would face legally enforced ejection. The law gave the conductor the "right to refuse to carry such passenger on his train" and to "put such passenger off of the train." Any official who refused to comply was subject to a fine ranging from five hundred to fifteen hundred dollars for each violation. In response, a group of black educators, ministers, and businesspeople from Kentucky organized the anti-separate-coach movement.[67]

Black citizens from throughout Kentucky attempted to halt the passage of the separate coach law, organizing mass meetings, drawing up protest documents, and presenting hundreds of resolutions of protest and petitions to the governor and state legislators. Their campaign to demonstrate both their service as slaves and their progress as an emancipated people was poignant, echoing Albert's presentation to the Louisiana legislature: "Does not a race which has enriched our soil with her blood, watered it with her tears, and which has given the vigor and strength of her youth to build up our country's resources, deserve better treatment? Does not the unselfish patriotism of such a race all for true and just recognition?" Claiming their "bright record" of service to their state, movement members insisted that "a wrong has been done us. It must be righted. We have to take up the gauntlet of moral warfare, and do not intend to lay it down until victory shall be ours."[68]

The anti-separate-car movement continued after the law passed in May 1892. A case that would test the constitutionality of the new legislation emerged when an African American minister from Evansville, Indiana, the Reverend W. H. Anderson, and his wife were attacked twice on interstate journeys through Kentucky. They were roughly handled and removed from the ladies' car at the Kentucky state line on a journey from Evansville, Indiana, to Madisonville, Kentucky. On a separate journey, they were denied seating and ejected thirty miles from their destination. The couple sued. Although the couple won a substantial damage settlement in the circuit court, a test of the state law in federal court upheld Kentucky's segregation law as constitutional, despite the fact that the wooden partitions separating blacks from the smoking area were too small to seal off the space.[69]

In actuality, segregationists better understood to the national outlook, which was increasingly turning a blind eye to discriminatory southern politics. The mob mentality that had fueled assaults by white passengers against African Americans seated in first-class cars now also governed southern state legislatures. And the federal courts had demonstrated their unwillingness to make equal protection of the law a reality, arguing that to do so would be to make African Americans "the special favorite of the laws."[70] Although the majority of African Americans believed that segregation was clearly illegal, they had a difficult time gaining a sympathetic hearing for their cause in the courts.

Even as justice in the courts proved illusive, the Citizens' Committee carried popular support. Funds came from wealthy individuals and unions, benevolent societies, and civic groups throughout New Orleans. Le Silence Benevolent Association donated more than one hundred dollars. Historic organizations, such the Société des Artisans founded in 1834 by free Afro-Creole craftsmen, and labor organizations, including the cigar makers' NCR Club, the Bricklayers' Union, and the Mechanics' Social Club, supported the fight against segregation. The Creole of color chapter of the Masons also donated funds. By the end of October, the committee had raised more than fourteen hundred dollars to fund the test case.[71]

The Citizens' Committee committed to bringing on Albion Tourgée, a prominent white attorney, as lead counsel in mid-October 1891. One of the few outspoken white critics of the Republican Party's retreat from racial justice and a vocal and prolific writer on the rights of African Americans, Tourgée volunteered his services to challenge Jim Crow railroads. The involvement of Tourgée, a member of the Methodist Episcopal Church, helped to connect the Citizens' Committee with concerned northern whites. Tourgée highlighted the work of the *Crusader* and the Citizens' Committee in his column in the *Inter-Ocean*, a Republican newspaper. The cross-cultural nationwide attention boosted the *Crusader*'s circulation and helped to develop a critical consensus against segregation among sympathetic white northerners.[72]

Making sure every aspect of the arrest went perfectly would be a challenge. Because of the difficult logistics of establishing the correct situation for arrest, the Citizens' Committee had to reach a working agreement with at least one Louisiana railroad company. To craft this unholy alliance, the committee had to exploit the fact that Louisiana railroads viewed Jim Crow cars as an expensive inconvenience. In correspondence with Martinet, Tourgée encouraged the committee to work with railroad officials to coordinate the protest.

Given the difficult and unpredictable conditions of most rail cars, managing the logistics of the case was difficult. The committee had to ensure that the volunteer would be arrested in New Orleans and not simply attacked and ejected for resisting white authority. Martinet emphasized that for the case to be a test of the separate car law, the individual would "have to be refused admission into the 'white' car here before the train starts and attempt to force . . . an entrance and have himself arrested and charged under the criminal [provision] of the separate car law and not for breach of the peace." The volunteer had the risky job of ensuring that he or she was arrested for violating the particular law the committee wished to challenge. "For if the car starts first, they will simply beat and throw him out and there will be no arrest. To make this case will require some tact."[73]

The separate car law called for train officials to set up two first-class cars, a requirement that increased the daily cost of running trains in Louisiana. Railroad employees also were burdened with the awkward task of deciding if boarding passengers were white or black, an impossible proposition in a city with a large population of phenotypically white but culturally black or Afro-Creole residents. Martinet commented that if conductors "were not informed [they] would be sure to pick out the white for colored and the colored for white."[74] Although conductors had maintained informal discriminatory practices prior to 1890, their decisions now had the force of law. Conductors would fear accidentally seating light-skinned African

Americans in cars designated for white passengers, just as they would fear insulting dark-featured whites by seating them in colored cars. The risks were genuine; a streetcar company in Shreveport, Louisiana, had been held liable when a white woman passenger with dark features sued because a conductor asked, "Don't you belong over there?" in reference to the black section of the car. The court ruled that "a carrier of passengers is as much bound to protect them from humiliation and insult as from physical injury." The mere suggestion that a white person was black was judged to be as harmful as being pushed from the car.[75] Being forced to identify race in Louisiana was a multisided liability. Tourgée and the committee hoped to exploit these liabilities in building their case.

The committee's effort to work with Louisiana rail companies revealed the uneven application of the law. One railroad informed the committee that it "did not enforce the law." The company maintained "a coach for colored persons and the sign required by law." If any African American passengers did not want to be seated in the colored car, conductors were instructed "not to be violent in any way." Martinet characterized the situation on this railroad as "a victory already," yet the ambiguous situation remained unfair at best and dangerous at worst. Intimidated African American riders would be forced to sit in the colored car, while indignant riders could perhaps get a first-class seat. Such an informal policy offered no guarantees of first-class treatment and did not protect African Americans who sat in the "white" car from angry passengers. Another rail company agreed that the law was "bad" and that it "would like to get rid of it" but nevertheless enforced it.[76]

Finally, the committee reached an agreement with the Louisville and Nashville Railroad. Martinet wrote excitedly, "They are willing that we shall make the case." However, the company's willingness to allow the arrest to take place did not imply that railroad officials wanted to equalize conditions. Tourgée hoped to present photographic evidence of conditions on the Jim Crow car, but when he asked if pictures could be taken, the railroad refused, fearful of future liability given the unequal condition of colored cars.[77]

With everything in place, the committee chose a representative to be arrested on the train. Committee members did not press the case themselves. Martinet felt that he was not a good candidate because he was not a frequent target of Jim Crow policy, being "one of those whose a face complexion favors." Given that he was "well known all over the city," he was rarely excluded on the basis of race. Although he explained that "color prejudice, in this respect does not affect me," Martinet remained one of the most fervent and vocal adversaries of segregation. His status reflected the lives of elite Creoles of color, who continued to enjoy unparalleled access to New Orleans society during the 1890s even in a climate of growing hostility. But he was concerned with more than maintaining elite Creole privilege; his access to public space remained sure even after the advent of Jim Crow policy. For Martinet, segregation involved the degradation of American citizenship for both the privileged and the voiceless. Moreover, Martinet feared traveling where he was not known. Dismissing Tourgée's idea of investigating racial conditions throughout the state, Martinet stated, "I don't suppose I could travel today in the state and stop at places without becoming a *suspect* [and] run the risk of personal danger."[78] He existed in a bubble of safety in New Orleans, but outside the city limits, the same realities threatened every African American, making travel perilous.

Rodolphe Desdunes's son, Daniel, was chosen as the first test subject and was arrested on the Louisville and Nashville Railroad in February 1892. The young Desdunes was charged with violating the separate car act and pled not guilty. But the case would be dismissed in connection with a similar suit. Late in 1891, Martinet had written Tourgée regarding a Pullman sleeping car case that challenged the separate car law and wondered "if anything could be made out of this." Indeed, this unplanned and unaffiliated case paved the way for a small victory. On 26 May 1892, Martinet telegraphed Tourgée with the exciting news that "in Pullman company case . . . state Supreme Court yesterday unanimously decided separate car law [was] unconstitutional."[79] Thus, the Desdunes case never came to fruition; the Louisiana Supreme Court ruled that the separate car law as a state regulation did not apply to interstate travel and dismissed the complaint. The committee celebrated this initial decision as a victory. Martinet wrote in the *Crusader*, "Jim Crow is as dead as a doornail," leading the committee and the community to believe that the legal tide was turning in their favor.[80]

Believing that one more legal challenge might do away with Louisiana's intrastate Jim Crow cars, committee members found a new test case in Homer Plessy. Little is known about how Plessy volunteered to press the case, but his racial background made him an ideal subject in Tourgée's eyes. Like Daniel Desdunes, Plessy was phenotypically white. Tourgée insisted that a light-skinned subject would highlight the difficulty of defining race in a society where not all people of color were easily identifiable. In fact, a key part of Tourgée's argument centered on Plessy being denied his rights as a "mostly" white man simply because he had a trace of black blood. The separate car law did not define the meaning of "black" or "white." Perhaps

Tourgée believed that he could revive antebellum laws that allowed free blacks with mixed blood to be legally defined as white if they had no African ancestry for at least two generations. Plessy's status as one-eighth black meant that he had a great-grandparent with African ancestry, not a parent or grandparent.[81] Fascinated by the blurred color line in New Orleans, Tourgée wanted to exploit the light skin of Afro-Creoles to his advantage in the courtroom.

It is unclear why a woman was not chosen as a test subject. A woman might have been a more sympathetic figure, a person to whom poor treatment in a second-class car would have resulted in more dramatic ramifications. When denied entry to the car set aside for women and their gentlemen companions, a woman of color would clearly demonstrate the inherent inequality of segregated southern rails. Unless Louisiana trains began to include expensive cars for colored ladies, black women could never experience accommodations equal to those provided for white women. Martinet had made the suggestion, but Tourgée's interest in a phenotypically white litigant overshadowed the issue of gender. When Tourgée asked if a fair-skinned woman of ambiguous racial origin could be found as a test subject, Martinet responded that he believed "it would be quite difficult to have a lady *too* nearly white refused admission to a 'white' car." In the case of a woman as fair as Plessy or Desdunes, the railroad would err on the side of caution and not press her about race. Martinet argued that perhaps the test should emerge from the real-life difficulties African American women faced when trying to travel on ladies' cars. He told Tourgée of a recent case "where two colored ladies were actually forced out of the 'white' coach into the 'colored' while the train was going at the usual rate of speed." The two women "were on their way home ... from here and I don't know whether the outrage was in this state or Mississippi." Martinet concluded, "I shall write for particulars."[82] Martinet and the committee members were certainly aware of the publicized cases in which women had made pointed arguments for inclusion in ladies' cars. A man would be a less sympathetic figure; the second-class smoking car was always seen as male terrain, so the argument that riding in second-class facilities harmed them was less meaningful. Perhaps the committee feared subjecting a woman to possible violence. Perhaps because the case was politically motivated, the committee did not want to send a woman to do what was perceived as men's work.

The Citizens' Committee as a whole may not have believed it appropriate for women to enter a political realm. Perhaps they wanted to be sure their case was about race and was not complicated by questions of gender. Women were not included as members of the Citizens' Committee, and Martinet seemed critical of women activists. For example, Tourgée asked Martinet about the race of Ida B. Wells, who had recently written to Tourgée. Martinet responded, "Miss Wells is colored. She is, however, intensely devoted to the race, though I do not always agree with her views to promote its interests. Her connection with the *Free Speech* has, I am told, cost her pension in the public schools of Memphis."[83] Martinet did not write that Wells had also been a litigant in a suit against segregated rails in Tennessee, a forerunner of their own crusade. The moderate Martinet harshly judged Wells's confrontational style as well as her willingness to risk security for political work. Perhaps the men of the committee let the gender divide distract them from making a stronger case about the price of exclusion for women of color. If a woman had been chosen to protest being barred from the ladies' car, the committee would have been able to present a forceful and more dramatic case about the danger and damage of Jim Crow.

Although no women's groups spoke out against the Citizens' Committee, the organization faced challenges from other constituencies that questioned its fight and motives. Martinet was troubled by ACERA's ongoing battle against Jim Crow legislation, writing, "An attempt is being made by some politicians and preachers to revive the defunct American Citizens' Equal Rights Association, instead of . . . helping us. They are simply trying to secure notoriety." However, rather than recognizing the association's early leadership and its part in initiating the fight against the separate car law, Martinet and the committee viewed ACERA as a rival, claiming that its members "did absolutely nothing when they had the wheel . . . and cared little about this matter." Martinet perceived ACERA's work as a threat to the leadership of the Citizens' Committee, warning that "now that we have made the start [ACERA] would run the thing in the ground if they could. But they can't hurt. We'll use their move to advantage." Differences between the two organizations' approach to protest undermined their ability to work in concert.[84]

A more direct challenge to the Citizens' Committee's legitimacy came when a New Orleans minister accused it of elitism and exclusivity. In December 1891, soon after the organization was formed and began raising funds for the test case, the all-Creole committee faced complaints from black New Orleanians who felt the light-skinned leaders did not represent the race and were merely trying to remove the barriers that deprived an elite few of white privilege. Martinet warned Tourgée of "Preacher A. S. Jackson," who "charged that the people who support our movement were nearly white, or wanted to pass for white and that in 'succumbing' to our fund they did not sign their names." Martinet replied that most people donated to the cause by name, but a few were "earnest . . . but modest." Still, hurt by the accusation that his supporters were ashamed of their heritage, Martinet worried that the greatest hindrance "the race has to contend with [came from] within our ranks." Creoles of color had likely organized with one another because of their shared concerns. Afro-Creoles shared more than their pale skin tones. They also agreed on approaches to race politics differing from the beliefs of non-Creole black Americans.[85]

But perhaps the committee could have shown greater depth. The Citizens' Committee never took steps to invite local leaders from outside the Creole community to take part in planning the protest. It also failed to give ample credit to non-Creole leaders and their willingness to speak out against the discriminatory law. The committee's narrow approach did not generate mass support or build coalitions within the broader African American community. In the effort to promote their own unique approach, the members muddled the fight against segregation. The committee's effort would have been stronger had it included a broad range of viewpoints on how best to challenge Jim Crow. Division weakened the fight against segregation in New Orleans, causing African Americans to misdirect some of their political energy toward one another.

Even if they did not trust some other local leaders, the committee men had a great deal of faith in the "strong power of the courts" and remained enthusiastic in their support of Plessy after his arrest in June 1892. Few details of the arrest appear in public accounts, but his arrest on the East Louisiana Railroad had been prearranged with the rail company.[86] Plessy purchased a first-class ticket to a destination within the state and boarded the train. He found a seat in the white car, told the conductor that he was colored, and refused to move to the colored car. The committee backed Plessy as he was found guilty of violating the separate car law in both the city and state courts. But waiting for the case to be argued on the federal level in front of the Supreme Court was long and trying. As the *Plessy* case progressed through the courts, the political climate worsened, with more calls for legal disfranchisement and increasing violence.

The case finally reached the U.S. Supreme Court on appeal in 1895. As lead attorney, Tourgée argued that any limitations on Plessy's ability to purchase a first-class ticket and ride in the first-class car constituted an abridgement of his rights. Tourgée's case centered on two crucial points: first, segregation was a violation of Plessy's rights under the Thirteenth and

Fourteenth Amendments to the Constitution, which made slavery illegal and guaranteed citizenship to all persons born or naturalized in the United States. To Tourgée, the act of segregating blacks who bought first-class tickets while simultaneously allowing working black servants to travel in first-class cars affirmed that segregation law sought to maintain hierarchical racial status. Segregation was essentially about reaffirming racial divisions born in slavery and therefore violated the freedom and fundamental citizenship rights of African Americans.

Tourgée's second and more controversial argument hinged on the second part of Section 1 of the Fourteenth Amendment, which asserted that "no State shall make or enforce any law which shall abridge the privileges or immunities of citizens . . . nor . . . deprive any person of life, liberty, or property." Tourgée argued that the separate car law denied Homer Plessy "the reputation of being white." Tourgée insisted that whiteness was not simply status but also a form of property. Much like the anonymous Creole who wanted the right to choose his race, Tourgée argued that the separate car law gave Plessy's right to self-chosen identity to train conductors, who arbitrarily assigned passengers to one car or another based on personal judgment. Although Tourgée was clever to exploit New Orleans's unique, racially ambiguous population and the state's failure to define the meaning of race, he was perhaps too clever. His approach fell short of offering a more universal solution to the problem of Jim Crow. Tourgée's argument undercut the notion that African Americans, regardless of skin color, deserved protection under the banner of equitable citizenship. It undermined the claim that systematic exclusion degraded black citizenship no matter how white an individual's heritage might be.[87]

While waiting for the final decision, the Citizens' Committee encountered internal setbacks. Mary, the committee's chief benefactor, had taken his own life, a victim of dementia caused by age. Saddened by Mary's death, weary from battles within his own organization, and impatient for the outcome of the case, Martinet became discouraged with the problem of race in America. In May 1893, he asked Tourgée if they were "fighting a hopeless battle—a battle made doubly hopeless by the tyranny and cruelty of the Southern white and the Negro's own lack of appreciation, his want of energy and his submissiveness." Martinet, writing during a vacation in Chicago, a city probably much less hostile to him and his family than his home, was worn down by the climate of racial violence and the growing movement to legally destroy African American citizenship. Martinet also was discouraged by the increasing support of northern white "Negrophilists" for "the doings at Tuskegee, Ala" and what he saw as their "pander[ing] to Southern prejudices." Martinet was saddened that Booker T. Washington could not instill his students with "the spirit of true manhood, of manly courage and resistance." Those traits would not be "tolerated in the communities where they are" and would not make good copy for "accounts of the phenomenal educational and intellectual progress of the colored people . . . dished up regularly to deceive a generous philanthropy at the North."

Martinet questioned his place in the nation. His anger and frustration reflected the ways in which he felt trapped by his place between a hostile white South and a black population from which he felt estranged by culture, belief, custom, and approach to politics. The hard fight made Martinet feel divided, a bitter "twoness" that developed out of frustration.

> I feel at times as if I could tear the flag—the stars and stripes—into shreds. Yet I am not a bad citizen—as long as I live within its jurisdictions I shall be loyal to the country. . . . And yet why this feeling? I have no special love for the Negro—never perhaps had—only sympathy. As an individual I have been treated better than a great many. . . . I have always been respected by those with whom I have come in contact. . . . I do not hanker for companionship or social relations with those who do not want to associate with me, nor do'I desire unduly the personal advantages that accrue from unreserved association with one's fellow beings. I'm foolish enough to think that I am above those who view a man's worth through the glass of color prejudice. All I want is my civil rights, privileges as a citizen, and simple justice for all who are denied it. I want to *enjoy* rights and don't want to be *tolerated* merrily.

Alienated or at best angry at the failed promises of American citizenship, Martinet grew bitter about having organized on behalf of a people to whom he often felt superior, although he remained clear about his political goals and his place in society.[88]

The fight of the Citizens' Committee came to its disappointing climax in May 1896 when the majority of the Supreme Court found separate but equal accommodations to be within the bounds of the U.S. Constitution. Arguing that social equality was separate from political equality, the decision stated that the citizenship rights guaranteed by the Fourteenth Amendment did not extend to the question of public inclusion. The justices argued that separation of the races was "reasonable" given the "customs and traditions of the people." They insisted that any stigma found in separating black and white passengers occurred "solely because the colored race chooses to put that construction upon it." The *Plessy* decision was an endorsement of segregation that left African Americans alienated and their citizenship rights severely limited. As segregation grew, black southerners found no allies in the courts.

As race hardened, the space left for New Orleans's Creoles of color narrowed. A victory, even one that was unenforceable, would have slowed the tide of segregation and emboldened black southerners agitating to defend their citizenship. The loss was a blow to their community of struggle. The case that the committee had intended to reaffirm African American citizenship instead became a federal endorsement of segregationist southern policies. Although the Citizens' Committee went on to protest lynching and racial violence, its viability as an organization soon came to an end. Martinet's *Crusader* stopped publication in 1897.

LEGAL HISTORIAN MICHAEL KLARMAN has asserted that *Plessy* was not an important defeat and that *Plessy* and other similar cases reflected the "regressive racial climate of the era," which drew from "plausible interpretations of conventional legal sources." He posits that it was "unlikely that contrary rulings would have significantly alleviated the oppression of blacks: such rulings probably could not have been enforced, and, in any event, the oppression of blacks was largely the work of forces other than law."[89]

However, victory in the *Plessy* case would have been meaningful in two key ways. First, given that states clearly took their cues about what they could do from the Supreme Court, a favorable verdict might have worked to slow the passage of state laws that limited black citizenship. An examination of these laws reveals the care that states took to follow precedent and model laws that had already been upheld. Second, court cases emerged from real political struggle: the efforts of African Americans to defend existing rights and fight new laws bent on limiting black citizenship. Even in an age of terror, the force of law, even unenforceable law, would have had meaning. Throughout American history, black people had used the courts to try to secure liberty. Such appeals were a crucial component of African American resistance strategies. Just as the National Association for the Advancement of Colored People would use the courts as a wedge in the twentieth century, even small victories in the age of *Plessy* would have been meaningful to communities engaged in active defense of their citizenship.

For all its importance in American legal history, *Plessy v. Ferguson* was not considered a watershed decision in its day. After all, the Supreme Court had already overturned the guarantee of equal access to public accommodations promised in 1875 Civil Rights Act. Many African Americans had hoped for a better outcome in *Plessy*, but they were prepared for the worst. Although *Plessy* has come to symbolize the decisive defeat for inclusion in American society, most African Americans did not see it that way. For most, *Plessy* was simply yet another bad decision from a court that had done little to ensure the promises of Reconstruction; the ruling did not mean that black Americans should abandon their citizenship rights. For the boldest race advocates, it simply encouraged further agitation. For the most compliant, it was a misguided judgment that had to be tolerated.

Booker T. Washington issued a bland statement of displeasure about the decision, arguing that the "separation may be good law, but it is not good common sense." Turning the whole argument to the price of the ticket, Washington claimed, "The colored people do not complain so much of the separation, as of the fact that the accommodations, with almost no exceptions, are not equal, still the same price is charged the colored passengers as is charged the white people." Unfair charges, not the expression of full citizenship, were his stated concern. But he did call train segregation "an unjust law" that "injures the white man, and inconveniences the negro." He explained, "No race can wrong another race simply because it has the power to do so, without being permanently injured in morals, and its ideas of justice." Arguing that "it is for the white man to save himself from this degradation that I plead," Washington insisted that such unfair practices threatened the moral health of white America.[90]

For many white Americans, the *Plessy* decision was a foregone conclusion. Much of the nation had turned away from concerns about protecting the citizenship of southern blacks. The change was demonstrated best in the support of Washington's approach to race. His address to the crowds at the 1895 Atlanta Exposition called on black southerners "to cast down their bucket" in the "beloved South," the best place for blacks to prosper "by the productions of [their] hands."[91] Washington's belief that African Americans should stay in the South was not in itself groundbreaking. Frederick Douglass, for example, had attempted to dissuade African American Exodusters from moving west in 1879, arguing that "the negro . . . is preeminently a Southern man." Black southerners had invested too much time to gamble on an unknown land. The South was "best for [African Americans] as a field of labor."[92]

But unlike Washington, Douglass based his argument on black citizenship. Black southerners should not run from injustice but instead should stay and insist on the protection of their rights. In the South, they had the numbers to sway elections and channel their political power. Their history as southerners should be the basis of their demands for justice as citizens. Rather than run from violence, black southerners should stay and fight. Douglass reminded his audience that the black man "has been known to fight bravely for his liberty." Citing a global history of black resistance, Douglass continued, "He went down to Harper's Ferry with John Brown, and fought as bravely and died as nobly as any. There have been Nathaniel Turners and Denmark Veseys among them in the United States, Joseph Cinques, Madison Washingtons and [William] Tillmons on the sea, and Toussaint L'Ouvertures on land. Even his enemies, during the late war, had to confess that the Negro is a good fighter." Had he lived to see it, Douglass might have included among his pantheon of heroes the members of the black U.S. Ninth Volunteer regiment from Louisiana, who would soon fight and die valiantly for the American cause in the Spanish-American War.[93] As voters, soldiers, or rebel citizens, Douglass believed, African Americans belonged in the South. Washington's call for blacks to cast their buckets into the turbulent southern waters was not new, but coupled with his total abandonment of political rights, it was surrender.

By 1896, many white Americans saw Washington as having replaced Douglass as the arbiter of the Negro question—as the leading black man consulted in matters of politics and education. After Douglass's death in February 1895, Washington even reshaped the memory of the abolitionist's early resistance on the trains. In his autobiography, *Up from Slavery*, Washington highlighted Douglass's dignity in the face of degradation rather than his resistance. On a train ride through Pennsylvania, Washington recounted, railroad officials forced Douglass to ride sitting on cargo in the baggage car. When a white passenger tried to console Douglass for being "degraded in this manner," Washington recalled, "Mr. Douglass straightened himself up on the box upon which he was sitting, and replied: 'they cannot degrade Frederick Douglass. The soul that is within me no man can degrade.'"[94] Washington presented Douglass as compliant, not resistant. Gone was the Douglass who gritted his teeth and twisted his arms into the seat of the railcar to avoid ejection. Gone was the Douglass who had lauded Elizabeth Jennings's legal victory. Washington made no mention of Douglass's support of mass protests in Massachusetts and New York. Instead,

Washington left him stoic in the baggage car. In the wake of the *Plessy* decision, Washington wanted to leave behind the spirit of public resistance, hoping instead that work behind the scenes and economic success eventually would secure freedom for black southerners. But despite defeat, protest would continue.

4 WHERE ARE OUR FRIENDS?

Crumbling Alliances and the New Orleans Streetcar Boycott

On the street-cars, our ladies are insulted and our working men, returning from their daily toil, are treated worse than heathens by the hoodlums, while the conductors look on complacently or with a smile of approval. We simply rise in our places of humiliation and say to our friends, the yoke is galling, our manhood is despised, our spirits are being crushed, our laborers have become disturbed, our sense of security is shaken; we need your help. WHERE ARE OUR FRIENDS?—J. MAX BARBER, "Where Are Our Friends," *Voice of the Negro*, October 1906

Black southerners did not take *Plessy v. Ferguson* as a signal that they should accept Jim Crow. African Americans in New Orleans continued to contest segregation, protesting the passage of a new law calling for racial separation on city streetcars. The 1902 law divided the cars with movable screens, which surely felt like cages at the backs of the streetcars. The seating in the cars was a physical representation of ways in which segregationists not only divided blacks from whites but also tried to shame and punish blacks in the public sphere.

Large-scale boycotts to contest the segregation of city streetcars took place in nearly every state that passed such laws. Louisiana was no exception: African Americans in the Crescent City boycotted even after their political resolve was scarred by the failure of *Plessy* and the terror of a major race riot in 1900. The boycott reflected black New Orleanians' desire to stand against injustice, even at great personal risk. And unlike the Citizens' Committee, which drew its membership from a small Creole of color elite, participants from all walks of life strengthened the boycott. Working-class

African Americans, the majority of them first-generation descendants of slaves migrating from rural Mississippi and Louisiana, moved to New Orleans to find sanctuary from lynching and racial violence that confronted them daily as sharecroppers and tenant farmers. With a large in-migration after the war, New Orleans became the largest African American population south of Washington, D.C., with 89,262 black residents. And although New Orleans would be plagued by mob violence in 1900, the large community of African Americans in the city turned within for support.[1] Migrants found spiritual guidance in black churches, security from fraternal and benevolent societies, representation through labor unions, and inclusion in social clubs. In such a bleak time, the boycott became a measure of black New Orleans's collective spirit of mass protest and an ethic of self-help. Even when they found few friends, they resolved to help themselves.

THE TURN OF the twentieth century was the heyday of the trolley in New Orleans. By 1900, the Crescent City's electric streetcars, which first appeared in 1893, had completely replaced horse-drawn cars. Streetcars served all sections of the city; cars traveled past balconies in the narrow and winding streets of the French Quarter, while routes through the Americanized district above Canal Street served the city's business class. Tracks crisscrossed nearly every corner of the city, but most lines connected at Canal Street, the city's main artery. So many routes began or terminated at Canal that at rush hour, the cars appeared to be mired in a massive traffic jam. By 1900, the populous and increasingly modern city boasted the South's largest streetcar system, with more than twenty-six lines and 180 miles of track. Streetcars became the favored form of transportation; by 1902 more than 53 million journeys were taken on the streetcar every year. Streetcars were essential not only to commerce but also to culture; elaborately decorated cars took center stage in Mardi Gras celebrations.[2]

The evolution of the modern streetcar system became central to the development of twentieth-century New Orleans. Americanized city leaders saw "modern improvements and advanced ideas" such as an efficient streetcar system as a break with the city's Creole legacy. Local leaders did not want their unique cultural heritage to render the city underdeveloped and stuck "in the glories of the past." Like many New South boosters, they believed that modernization was the key to future industrial investment and economic advancement. In 1901, there were citywide efforts to expand service, revise routes for greater efficiency, and improve the conditions of tracks, while the city's largest street railway company, the New Orleans City

Railroad, purchased new, larger "Palace cars" to accommodate increasing numbers of customers. These new cars were the latest in streetcar technology. As streetcar historian E. Harper Charlton has written, "The advent of the 'Palace' cars heralded modernization of the street railways in keeping with the city wide trend."[3]

Modernization included changes in the way service was provided. The New Orleans streetcar system originally had been administered by four different private companies, but in 1902, the systems were combined to form the New Orleans Railways Company. H. H. Pearson Jr., a representative of corporate investors from Philadelphia and New York City, moved to New Orleans to reorganize the city's streetcar and power companies. The city welcomed outside help in making "the finest street railway system to be had . . . on parity with the railroads of the North." Local boosters boasted that consolidation would improve the streetcar system by "vastly increasing the facilities afforded . . . providing attractions which will increase travel on the cars, and at the same time make such traveling as comfortable as possible." An efficient system would also facilitate laborers' movement to industrial areas and business districts. Reorganization of the streetcars was part of a series of improvements. Numerous citywide expansion and development projects occurred that year, including the strengthening of levees, the updating of the city's primitive drainage and sewage systems, and the addition of water-purifying systems and paved streets.[4]

Although romantic histories of New Orleans streetcars make no mention of the advent of segregation, the shift toward modernization coincided with the passage of the state law segregating streetcars. State legislators called for the city's beautiful new Palace cars to be fitted with gates to separate the races. New, more streamlined policies governing streetcars enabled politicians to more clearly delineate the color line in New Orleans. Consolidation of the city's streetcars made segregation much easier to enforce and much more difficult to protest. A large and well-organized company could better absorb the financial impact of a protest of any kind, from striking workers to disgruntled black passengers. To state legislators, progress included a hardening of the color line. They hoped to end Reconstruction-era public liberties and give birth to a Crescent City reshaped in the image of Jim Crow.

Although Jim Crow was in reality antithetical to the meaning of the word "progress," Progressivism and segregation developed side by side in the urban South. The spirit of reform that shaped the Progressive movement— with calls for improving the social and economic well-being of the working class—served as easy cover for segregationists. Henry W. Grady, the editor of the *Atlanta Constitution*, promoted the idea of New South Progressivism in the 1880s, arguing that the South could move forward economically only if white southerners were left alone to solve the race problem. Grady interpreted white supremacy as natural and God-given and believed that clear recognition of the dominance of the white race would protect black southerners from racial violence while spurring economic development. Separation and white supremacy would make the New South grow.[5]

In the age of New South boosterism, Jim Crow was pitched as reform, designed to improve conditions for both black and white southerners. Jim Crow streetcars were seen as symbols of progress. One proponent of segregation argued that although black passengers might initially boycott segregated cars, "common sense" eventually would teach "those people that the separation of the races really defined their status and confirmed to them certain rights, which are greatly to their advantage." Segregation was simply a part of reforming and improving their cities. Other segregationists were a bit less sophisticated; one proponent of segregated streetcars in Mobile, Alabama, argued that Progressive "elevation" had turned African Americans into a problem and segregation into the solution: "If this is what education does for the negro, what will he be when a few more eastern capitalists have endowed a few more nigger schools? Is it not time . . . to call a halt on the nigger?"[6]

African Americans vigorously protested the laws that demeaned their citizenship in the name of the modern city. Black New Orleanians were defined by urban life, and like most city dwellers, they used the streetcars, which served the most populous black, white, and mixed neighborhoods. Streetcars made traveling much more comfortable; as one reporter noted, "The climate makes riding, instead of walking, a necessity." "Due to the peculiar location of the city along the banks of the river," particularly during humid summers, New Orleans was not a walking city, making "street cars more necessary."[7] During a 1902 streetcar strike, the Reverend Isaiah B. Scott, a newcomer who took the helm of the *Southwestern Christian Advocate* in 1896, commented that the uses of other forms of transportation were "novel, but . . . awfully tiresome and inconvenient for people who have to go five or six miles."[8]

Many working-class black residents relied on streetcars to travel to their jobs. Men paid the fare of a few pennies each day to travel to the city's waterfront or factories, while women employed as laundresses and domestics used streetcars to reach their employers' homes or run errands. As the *Southwestern Christian Advocate* reported, hundreds of African Americans "live anywhere from three to ten miles from their work and are compelled to use the electric cars to reach it." In the large and expanding city, working- and middle-class people used the streetcar to find employment in distant areas.[9]

In 1900, the streetcars were fluid spaces, not governed by hard-and-fast laws delineating the color line. Prior to segregation, any rider had the opportunity to find a rare open seat or to ride standing in the crowded aisles or on the outdoor running boards. And although racial etiquette made working-class blacks reluctant to find a seat next to elite whites, by law, riders were not segregated by race.

Streetcars not only served the workaday needs of African Americans but also shaped their free time. Black and Afro-Creole residents of all classes used the cars to enrich their social lives, traveling by streetcar to attend society meetings and festive events on Saturdays and to worship at church on Sundays. Black New Orleanians were among the 965,000 visitors to the city's streetcar-company-sponsored parks in 1902.[10] Churches, benevolent societies, and labor and fraternal organizations hosted annual celebrations in outlying parks and fairgrounds. African American men seeking a taste of the sporting life attended baseball games and boxing matches in the parks. And prior to 1902, the city's African American residents took pride in integrated streetcars as spaces largely free from racial tension.

The call for segregation thus disappointed many in New Orleans. Angered, unsure of why streetcars were being segregated, and tapping into a history of collective resistance, African Americans argued that as customers, they deserved better. They believed that the city should have praised the respectable comportment of African American citizens on the streetcars. Outraged at the legislature's demands that streetcar companies erect screens to divide black and white riders, local pastor E. A. Higgins stated, "Before I would ride in a screened 'Jim Crow' car I would walk my feet off." When the law went into effect in the fall of 1902, few blacks rode in the segregated compartments, and conflicts arose only when whites sat in empty seats "set apart for negroes." Black New Orleanians did not accept what they viewed as an erosion of rights the previous generation had won.[11]

African Americans had struggled against the segregation of public conveyances since horse-drawn streetcars were first introduced in New Orleans. The customs that had plagued the streetcars of New York City before the Civil War were reflected in laws in nearly every antebellum southern city. Lawmakers either banned black riders or instituted segregation as a means of controlling African Americans, both slave and free. Urban slaves often traveled within southern cities without direct supervision; restrictive race-based ordinances were attempts to control slaves' freedom of movement—that is, means of reasserting the authority that should have come from their masters. For free people, segregation was a humiliation and a brutal degradation. City ordinances in Richmond, Virginia; Savannah, Georgia; and Charleston, South Carolina, even restricted where all African Americans, slave and free, could walk. In most southern cities, people of color were forbidden to ride on streetcars driven by white male workers. In a slave society, it was unthinkable for blacks to ride while white men labored. Free people of color who violated such laws faced arrest and conviction. When a streetcar conductor discovered that a fair-skinned African American man had slipped on board a streetcar undetected in Charleston, the conductor held the man captive, driving him to the police for arrest. But antebellum free blacks continuously contested such limitations. In New Orleans, when streetcars first began operating in the 1820s, free people of color and black slaves had been barred. But the large population of free people of color demanded inclusion by both peaceful and violent means. In 1833, a group of free people of color were ejected and later arrested when they returned with pistols.[12]

A pitched battle over the segregation of the cars in New Orleans began during Reconstruction. On most streetcar lines, African Americans were either confined to separate cars or prevented from using the cars altogether. Service within this segregated system was neither equal nor separate. White passengers, particularly during peak hours, filled both the "whites only" cars and also those designated for black riders. Although carriers marked with painted stars were designated for the exclusive use of black passengers, impatient white passengers boarded the "star cars" anyway. The cars set aside for African American patrons ran infrequently and were crowded with white passengers, making streetcar travel unreliable and inconvenient for most black patrons.

Militiaman P. B. S. Pinchback and Louis and J. B. Roudanez, editors of *L'Union*, led the Reconstruction-era struggle against segregation. While federal troops occupied the city, African American street resistance to the unjust prohibitions was vigorous. Working-class men and women participated in spontaneous sit-ins on "whites only" streetcars, and physical confrontations between African American and white drivers and white passengers fed public fears of a race riot. Militant insistence finally won out in May 1867 when the streetcar company reluctantly desegregated. African American legislators attempted to enshrine their "social rights," including the right to ride public conveyances, at the constitutional convention later that fall. Comparative historian Rebecca J. Scott has directly connected the segregation of the cars and the call for social rights: "Louisiana's new Bill of Rights held that all citizens of the state should enjoy 'the same civil, political and public rights and privileges, and be subject to the same pains and penalties.' Along with the bold claim of civil and political rights, this concept of public rights was a crucial one, echoed and clarified in an explicit prohibition of racial discrimination on public conveyance and in places of 'public resort.' . . . This insistence on such public rights had its roots in a keen recognition of the shaming intent of separate streetcars, alongside a memory of multiple humiliations heaped on free people of color in the years prior to the Civil War."[13]

African Americans across the South staged dramatic spontaneous protests during Reconstruction in Richmond, Virginia; Charleston, South Carolina; Mobile, Alabama; Savannah, Georgia; Nashville, Tennessee; and Baltimore, Maryland.[14] Even after streetcars in the nation's capital had been desegregated by federal mandate in 1865, leading black abolitionist and New Yorker Sojourner Truth still waged a constant battle just to get white conductors to stop for her. On one attempt to board, Truth was dragged several yards by a conductor. On another journey, Truth had to shout, "I want to ride! *I want to ride!!* I WANT TO RIDE!!!" loudly enough to stop all passing traffic, catching the streetcar in a traffic jam. One conductor injured Truth's right arm in the effort to eject her from the car.[15] Her prominence offered no protection from Jim Crow segregation. Activist Ida B. Wells had waged her earliest political battles against segregated facilities, first in 1883 with suits against segregated railroads, and later by encouraging a streetcar boycott in Memphis in 1892. African Americans in New Orleans were part of a larger trend of contesting attempts to segregate public conveyances.

AT THE TURN OF the century, Louisiana legislators revived attempts to segregate the streetcar system. In 1900, Harry D. Wilson, a representative from Tangipahoa Parish, a rural area northeast of New Orleans in the Louisiana panhandle, proposed a bill targeting conveyances in New Orleans. Wilson explained to the legislature that he drafted the bill not in response to racial conflict on streetcars but to promote and reinforce white superiority.[16] Highlighting that the legislation had originated with an outsider and not a representative of the Crescent City, Scott asserted in the *Southwestern Christian Advocate* that outsiders resented the city's more relaxed racial mores. Although Scott had recently arrived in New Orleans from Texas, he recognized that officials such as Wilson wanted to enact laws that would create the strict racial dynamics enforced by custom and violence in rural Louisiana. State-level efforts were quickly followed by a segregation proposal by members of the New Orleans city council. Black residents of New Orleans remained confident, however, because there seemed to be little public demand for streetcar segregation. The *Advocate* reported peaceful conditions on the cars: "There may be friction here but we never see any evidence of it." Scott was sure that without the support of urban representatives and streetcar company officials, the legislation would fail.[17]

The 1900 attempt to segregate streetcars met with vigorous opposition. African American leaders saw segregation as an insult to the legacy of a Reconstruction era, when black residents had fought hard for equal access to the streetcars. Streetcar segregation would "be a source of humiliation and no little annoyance to the colored patrons of the cars." Scott called for a boycott—direct action in response to a specific offensive law and an economic response to a problem the courts had failed to remedy. Scott warned that such protests would "cause no inconsiderable loss to the companies": "There are hundreds of Negroes in this city who will not ride under such circumstances, and they have begun already to organize for the purpose of controlling the masses. Who can blame them?" Arguing that no laws separating the races were needed when the majority of black passengers consistently demonstrated appropriate behavior, Scott believed that black protest, coupled with corporate reluctance, would ensure the proposed legislation's defeat.[18]

The offices of the *Southwestern Christian Advocate* on Poydras Street, on the Americanized side of Canal Street, served as an organizing center for protesters. The editor commented that "in the midst of the agitation a large number of persons opposed to the bill visited this office and planned to do what they could to defeat it." Scott not only served as a vocal supporter on the pages of the *Advocate* but also used his skills as an educator and church leader to help the cause. He connected the local struggle to the regional movement to boycott segregated streetcars, frequently reporting on protests in Augusta, Atlanta, and Rome, Georgia.[19]

The editor supported boycott plans because he believed that segregation was part of a systematic effort to dismantle black citizenship as a whole. To Scott, it was no coincidence that segregation was coupled with disfranchisement. Since 1898, black voting rights in New Orleans had been gutted; in 1896, more than fourteen thousand African Americans were registered (23 percent of the electorate); by 1900, only around fifteen hundred black voters remained (just over 3 percent). The problems were interconnected, he argued; the 1898 disfranchisement of the majority of African American voters represented "the gateway to complete subjugation." Louisiana "has tied her colored citizen and hence has nothing to fear from his ballot. She proceeds deliberately but certainly to reduce him to what she considers his place." Segregation not only constituted "a violation of right" but opened the door for more mistreatment. Moreover, according to Scott, the city's school board had taken the "most decided step toward the Negro's consignment" by ordering "that no city public school for Negroes shall teach . . . studies more advanced than the fifth grade."[20] To Scott, the character of African American citizenship was tied not only to political strength but also to inclusion in civil society.

Much as the Citizens' Committee had argued in the previous decade, the editor also highlighted "the practical difficulties" in enforcing a streetcar segregation law in New Orleans, pointing out that riders' skin color might prevent the conductors from accurately separating passengers. He reported that "during discussions . . . of the proposed separated street car law, we were not a little interested in the various hindrances to the enforcement of such a law that were presented. Chief among these was the difficultly of determining who is white and who is colored." Scott insisted that the job of judging racial identity was too difficult in the Creole city: "The man who is given the task, by law or otherwise, of deciding this question for the citizens of New Orleans will find that he has undertaken more than he can possibly do."[21] A white resident's letter to the editor insisted that "there are, in this city, colored persons who pass for white and will ride with white people even tho the bill passes." The writer also hinted that wealthy Creoles of color maintained positions of authority in the city and would not quietly submit to a Jim Crow law: "There are colored persons of wealth in the city, some of whom have white people working for them. I am certain they own stock in the street railroads and where is the conductor who would attempt to debar them from riding in the white car?"[22]

Not only would fair-skinned people of color pass undetected, but "dark white people" might be falsely targeted for ejection. Scott recognized that "the question of determining 'which is which' is a great one here at all times" and reminded his readers of school board's difficulties in attempting to "'weed out' the 'white colored' children from the public schools for whites." Attempting to designate race by phenotype was awkward, and any mistake would stand as a tremendous insult. Scott reported that in the case of the school board members, "so great was the embarrassment that we learn they had to abandon the attempt altogether. If there is any truth at all in the reports as to how things are mixed . . . it would seem that our city should be extremely liberal on the color question."[23]

Even though he liked to hypothesize about the color question, Scott insisted that there was no middle ground for people of color who appeared to be white in the age of segregation. Both fair Creoles of color as well as light-skinned Americanized blacks might avoid segregation on the street-cars altogether by passing for white, but their passing would be temporary, an avoidance behavior that allowed them to exploit first-class conditions on the streetcars.[24] Although there were people of color with skin pale enough to be considered white, Scott did not approve of those who refused to choose a side. He suggested that the stakes of race in New Orleans were too high: "Every individual get on one side or the other and then stay there. Neither race respects that one who is first on this side and then on that. . . . [I]t is a dangerous game to play."[25] The decision to pass represented more than simply a way to get a better seat; it was a break in solidarity with other blacks. The editor believed that a unified stand was the most effective way to maintain the rights of all. But many fair-skinned Orleanians of color had chosen to pass to gain first-class treatment on trains and would surely continue to adopt similar strategies on segregated streetcars.

JUST AS PROTESTS against the divisive legislation reached a critical inten-sity in 1900, a race riot threatened black safety throughout the city. The conflict began when Robert Charles, a thirty-four-year-old African Ameri-can laborer, got into a violent confrontation with police on the evening of 23 July. While Charles was waiting for his girlfriend to end her workday at her white employer's household, police told him and a friend, Lenard Pierce, to move along. Charles argued that he was not committing any crime and wanted to be left alone. When the policemen attempted to force the two men to move, Charles fought them off, insisting that they had no reason to question or arrest him. In the gunfight that followed, both Charles and one of the officers were injured. Despite his injuries, Charles escaped, eluding capture for more than five days. When news of the police force's inability to track down the suspect became public, roving mobs of armed white men and boys organized under the pretense of finding Charles. Angered by Charles's bold stand against armed white men and embarrassed at his ability to elude police, gangs of mostly working-class white men from the city and surrounding parishes terrorized black residents for several days, hunting and attacking any African Americans they saw on the street. In the pages of the *Advocate*, Scott described the pattern of violence: "Fully armed and organized[, the mob] roamed the streets hunting Negroes. When found they were fired upon at sight; some were shot, others were beaten with clubs or cut with knives."[26]

Numerous gangs, totaling a mob of more than seven hundred white men and boys, created terror on the streets; they attacked black people without provocation, targeting black men, women, and children traveling in the city alone. Six black residents, including an elderly man and woman, were lynched, and more than fifty African Americans were badly injured. Victims included African Americans who had not heard about the riots before venturing into the downtown area and black travelers from outside the city. One gang of white men attacked Alex Ruffin, a Pullman porter arriving on a train from Chicago, when he boarded a Clay Avenue streetcar. Ruffin was beaten and shot twice before a white male bystander came to his defense, enabling him to escape with his life.[27]

Inflamed by the presence of black passengers, unruly whites attacked passing city streetcars. Mobs of men, perhaps fueled by the ongoing segregation controversy, made the conveyances a favorite target. In fact, the first African American to die in the mayhem was a Villere streetcar line passenger riding past Canal Street. Chased for blocks while dozens of rioters fired at him, the young unidentified man finally fell, was kicked and beaten, and then was repeatedly shot until he died. Attacks on the streetcars became widespread: "As a rule when they saw a Negro in a street car, they would stop the car and take him off or else shoot or club him in the car." However, at least three conductors were injured while attempting to protect black passengers. Scott described "one case where [the mob] stopped a car to get an old man" and "a white lady threw her dress skirt over him and defied them to touch him, and they didn't." Not all white residents shared the lawless sentiments of the mob.[28]

Charles eluded arrest for almost a week, and in the course of two separate standoffs with police and angry white citizens, he killed seven white men, including four police officers, and shot and injured twenty others. Charles died in a final gun battle with police and armed citizens. Although vengeful white residents took turns attacking his corpse, their anger was not satisfied. Many in the mob held all African Americans responsible for Charles's violent resistance and attempted to exact punishment on the entire community. After Charles's death, the mob murdered two more black men.[29]

Except for his remarkably bold effort to engage in a violent and direct armed struggle against white authority, Charles, whom his friends and acquaintances described as neat, quiet, and intelligent, had much in common with many working-class city residents. A migrant from nearby Copiah County, Mississippi, in 1894, he had worked as a day laborer and promoted black emigration to Africa by handing out pamphlets and selling copies of Bishop Henry McNeal Turner's *Voice of Missions*. Prior to the fateful incident, Charles had been an active participant in community life, spending time with friends and family who were also recent migrants and attending the gatherings of a black social club in his community. He also concerned himself with politics and the difficulties facing southern blacks; to his friends and family, he spoke out vehemently against lynching and disfranchisement, and he regularly expressed his belief that blacks would never have a fair chance at citizenship in the American South.[30] His willingness to confront police was exceptional, but his life and his concerns were typical.

During the week of violence, mobs proposed burning black homes, but the city's residential integration and the prevalence of highly flammable wooden houses may have quashed the idea. Instead, the gang purposely destroyed the colored Thomy Lafon School, a three-story building named in honor of a Creole of color philanthropist who in 1893 bequeathed to "the city several thousands of dollars for educational purposes." Lafon had also been a major donor to the Citizens' Committee and had supported the *Plessy* test case. Racist white critics believed that institutions such as the Lafon School produced "uppity blacks" like Charles who used their education to challenge white authority. Following this logic, black schools came under attack not only from angry mobs but also from the New Orleans School Board, which instituted plans to end public education for blacks at the fifth-grade level.[31]

The riot devastated African American life in New Orleans. Many black residents no longer felt safe. As the rising tide of lynching overwhelmed the rural South, sporadic violence had also struck the city, particularly following labor disputes in 1895, when a mob of white men murdered some black dockworkers.[32] But the scope and scale of the 1900 race riot brought the climate of violence closer to home. African American residents had lived in a bubble of relative safety. Both longtime residents and new migrants had clung to a collective sense of security in their urban community. But despite the legacy of black institution building, the burgeoning growth of a respectable black middle class, and the progressive rhetoric of city fathers, the extralegal violence that often ruled racial conditions in the rural South had come to dominate the city as well.

In the desperate weeks following the riot, African American residents of all backgrounds sought to escape by taking the train to points north, including Chicago, St. Louis, Cincinnati, and Louisville. The *Advocate* reported trains "crowded with colored passengers, many of whom have gone to stay." In one afternoon, the Illinois Central railroad ran special trains to accommodate more than fifteen hundred travelers in "seven or eight coaches." Scott cautioned that migrating blacks should not leave in a panic and sell their homes "at a great sacrifice." The editor tried to reassure his readers that "if they must leave let them take their time in disposing of what they have and they will get more for it. There is no necessity for undue haste, the reign of terror is now over." But thousands of African American residents of New Orleans believed that the terror had just begun and did not want to risk their lives by staying any longer.[33]

Well after the violent summer ended, sporadic violence continued. In October, a Wild West show parade attracted crowds of angry whites who targeted blacks along the parade route. Scott reported, " 'There's a Nigger!' was the watchword" for an attack on black residents. Spectators also attacked black students at Southern University, pelting "the young people . . . with brickbats and other missiles, and cut[ting] one little fellow quite seriously." Random violence was not reserved for special occasions. After an African American resident, Sylvester Jordan, refused to step off the plank sidewalk into the muck and mud along the street to allow a white man to pass, he was beaten mercilessly by the man and a crowd of white onlookers. His attacker, a white man without a uniform who claimed to be a supernumerary police officer, argued that he was doing his job by enforcing racial order. After the assault, a semiconscious Jordan was arrested, and he died in jail after being denied medical attention. According to the *Advocate*, "He was simply placed in a cell and died like a dog." Scott was shaken by the violence. Rumors spread that the festivities of Mardi Gras might be turned into a mass lynching. The editor warned that unless the city took adequate precautions against violence, African Americans "should . . . not visit the city . . . when they usually flock . . . in such large numbers."[34]

Charles's work as a subscription agent for the *Voice of Missions*, which the *New Orleans Times-Democrat* described as a "religious paper" that "asserted the equal rights of the Negro," must have called attention to the content of all black periodicals, including the *Southwestern Christian Advocate*. In this dangerous climate, Scott addressed the Charles incident and the subsequent riot. In the issue following the first week of violence, Scott commended the city's elite whites, particularly the business class, for their efforts to stem the tide of violence. Scott's praise for "the better element of . . . white citizens" who were "forced . . . to rise up and put [the mob] down" was seconded by antilynching crusader Ida B. Wells-Barnett. She also praised "the courageous action taken by the best citizens of New Orleans who rallied to the support of civic authorities, that prevented a massacre of colored people too awful to contemplate." Indeed, Mayor Paul Capdevielle, who deployed a special police force of five hundred citizens to quiet the murderous gangs, and Governor William W. Heard, who called on the state militia to aid the mayor's efforts to restore order, helped to quell mob rule.[35]

Scott pointedly commented that the city's intervention protected not only black residents but also the city's fiscal interests. The editor argued that northern corporate investors such as the streetcar owners hesitated to finance projects in a lawless environment, so the city had much to lose if the riot had escalated. Scott aptly observed, "When the business men of New Orleans found that the work of the mob in assaulting and killing innocent Negroes had not only paralyzed their business but had [also] affected the standing of the city and state in the stock market . . . , they soon put a stop to such deeds of violence and blood." Efforts to promote New Orleans as modern and safe for investment may have been compromised by the chaos of a race riot. Scott concluded by lamenting, "It is a pity [the business leaders] cannot see their way clear to insist on the same right through the year."[36]

However, the mob violence may not have been completely antithetical to making New Orleans attractive to outside investment. The chaos of race riots may have frightened outside investors, but the terror of lynching and race riots targeted African Americans. The mobs threatened both the working and middle classes. Violence may have made black workers more pliable, less likely to contest low wages or poor working conditions. A volatile racial climate could have served as a way to keep black labor cheap while cementing elite rule. The mob also discouraged African American education and uplift by targeting black schools like the Lafon School and Southern University. The New Orleans race riot strengthened white supremacy by destabilizing black advancement and dissent.[37]

Scott denounced Charles's rampage as well as the wild violence of the mob. Using class-coded terms, the editor called on "the better class of the race" to ally with "the best white citizens." He believed that only elite whites could "recognize [the African American's] worth as a laborer and a well behaved citizen." Scott maintained that respectable blacks and whites shared the same interests in fairness, safety, and justice. He cautioned that middle-class blacks should not be too sympathetic toward the downtrodden among them: "The better class should seek to save the others if possible" but also "be broad enough and just enough to condemn . . . the bad element." Scott believed that African Americans such as Charles would "perish in their folly." Physical safety and financial progress would be the fruit of a discerning black middle class willing to break ties with those who were not striving for respectability. Scott held that the most important lesson learned in the riot of 1900 was that African Americans' "only hope [was] to keep close to the best white citizens of [the] city." Only leading whites would "stand by . . . in the time of need." Scott hoped that ties between the "better class" of African Americans and elite whites would help to preserve black citizenship.[38] But Scott's attempts to maintain such tenuous alliances with leading whites would prove hard to maintain in the long-term battle against the legal segregation of the city's streetcars. As the political tide turned even more forcefully against black citizenship, white leaders favored political expediency over interracial coalition building. The race riot played a role in accelerating the process of disfranchisement and the silencing of African American dissent.

African Americans contesting streetcar segregation won a brief victory. In the wake of the race riot, the 1900 bill sponsored in the state legislature calling for the segregation of streetcars failed, as did a proposed local ordinance. Vigorous opposition from African Americans coupled with the concern of sympathetic, business-minded whites stopped the attempt to divide the cars. The race riot had already damaged the city's image as a safe and stable location for new businesses; protest that started after the passage of the segregation law would only serve to make the city look more unstable. White businessmen believed that if blacks were restricted to special cars, black "laborers would be delayed in getting to their work." They also feared the financial price of black protest, citing a concern over "reducing the revenues of the companies."[39]

The city's African Americans won a temporary victory over the segregation of the streetcars despite the climate of chaos and violence. So when the state legislature renewed efforts to pass legislation segregating cars in the summer of 1902, African Americans believed that they could defeat the bill once again. But attacks on African Americans' voting rights had reshaped the state legislature into a body now elected almost exclusively by white voters. Few "friends of the race" could be counted in Louisiana's elective offices by 1902.

In June 1902, Scott reported that once again Harry Wilson, state representative from rural Tangipahoa Parish, was the sponsor of the legislation.

"The measure is brought forward now as two years ago by a member from one of the country parishes. He seems extremely solicitous that the races should be separated on the street cars of this city." Although he represented "a parish . . . that hasn't a street-car in it," Representative Wilson renewed his efforts to segregate streetcars. Wilson not only insisted that the cars be segregated but also refused an amendment that would have given the conductor the power to separate the passengers, modeled after a similar Virginia law. Wilson contested the compromise and insisted that New Orleans streetcars be compartmentalized by screens, or the streetcar company would have to begin running separate cars for blacks and whites.[40]

Given a legacy of successful opposition to Jim Crow cars, Scott wrote, "It is to be hoped it may share a like fate before the legislature." Scott believed that black opposition to the law, coupled with citywide white indifference to the racial conditions on the streetcars, would assure defeat of the proposed legislation. Despite the editor's hopes, and in keeping with a South-wide trend, New Orleans streetcar segregation became law in July 1902.[41]

AS EDITOR OF the monthly journal *Voice of the Negro*, J. Max Barber, a twenty-six-year-old black southerner, used his post to become a prominent spokesman on behalf of the streetcar boycotts. Barber wrote in 1904, "The rapidity which characterizes the spread of the Jim Crow idea is simply alarming." He warned his national audience, "With startling celerity the craze for separate street cars is spreading all over the South. Mere separation does not hurt the colored people half so much as the unjust discriminations imposed."[42]

The *Voice*'s offices were in Atlanta, where political cronyism and competition among rival streetcar companies led to the passage of a city ordinance segregating the cars. As W. E. B. Du Bois commented, the result was that "the black population of Atlanta [was forced to] walk, or ride in the rear."[43] Even though Atlanta's 1900 streetcar boycotts had been short-lived, Barber remained an advocate of protest, frequently publicizing the southern movement to contest segregation. In 1905, Barber's leadership in the boycott movement, his growing frustration with the destruction of black citizenship, and Booker T. Washington's acquiescence led Barber to become a founding member of Du Bois's Niagara Movement, an organization that worked on behalf of civil rights. The articulate young editor was the strongest national spokesman for the boycott movement.

Barber described what he called "the obnoxious laws" as "class-laws" designed to "give special privileges to the whites and to withdraw certain rights from the blacks." On Atlanta's streetcars, "The whites are allowed to sit in any part of the car without fear of molestation, while the colored are consigned to the seats in the rear." The segregated spaces of the cars made no allowance for black women: "If perchance a colored lady should stray toward the front seat, not knowing the vicious law, she is brutally ordered to the rear with some humiliating epithet by the gentlemanly (?) conductor. For this insult there is no redress whatever." Inequitable treatment on segregated streetcars insulted black customers, unfairly targeting all black patrons with possible policing by white conductors.[44]

Although the mere notion of seating blacks in the rear of streetcars insulted black humanity, some cities further humiliated black riders with various means of designating the physical difference between black and white seating. Barber described what he called "the most wicked of all 'Jim Crow' car laws." In the small town of Anderson, South Carolina, black passengers on the city's newly christened electric streetcars were forced to sit in seats that were turned around so that "the colored man must not only ride in the rear of the car but must ride backward." The rear-facing seats prevented black men from looking at white women on the cars. Anderson residents resisted the backward seating, initiating a silent boycott of their own when they "quietly refused to be thus humiliated" and "either walk[ed] or [rode] in their own buggies."[45]

In New Orleans, the 1902 act made conditions on streetcars equally humiliating. More than ten years after the passage of the law, Washington asked for a letter outlining "the actual facts bearing upon the method of separating our race in the street cars of New Orleans." Washington was making a late attempt to find "a way to have street railway conditions improved" and asked the Reverend Robert Elijah Jones, who had become editor of the *Southwestern Christian Advocate* in 1904, to write a letter Washington could "show to certain bankers who furnish the money." Such an approach aligned with Washington's view that economics, not politics, would drive change.[46]

Jones responded with a poignant and detailed account of conditions on New Orleans's segregated streetcars in which he described them as "the most abominable arrangement in the whole country" and "unlike anything else, even in the State of Louisiana." In contrast to most segregated cars, which simply had painted dividing lines or had black passengers fill in seats starting from the back of the car, New Orleans divided passengers with a "large and cumbersome" screen "a height of 12 or 14 inches" from the "top of the back of the seat, and invariably . . . inclined toward the face of the

Colored patrons." In fact, the screen was so close that a woman sitting in the segregated seat had to "hold her neck backwards or her hat [would] constantly [bump] against the screen." The "idea of sitting behind screens, as if they were wild or obnoxious animals . . . contribut[ed] to [African Americans' mortification."[47]

The law permitted only streetcar conductors to move the screens.[48] However, conductors regularly allowed white passengers to move "the screen backward at will." Forced to stand behind the screens when there was "room enough for the Colored passengers to sit if the screens were moved forward," black passengers were left with little room to maneuver. White conductors had no regard for black passengers' needs and did not adjust the screens for their comfort. On one occasion, according to the Reverend B. M. Hubbard, pastor of the First Street Methodist Episcopal Church, six black passengers stood in the aisle behind the screen in a car that had no white passengers.[49]

The last seats of the streetcar, those officially designated for black passengers, ran "lengthwise of the car" and were "shorter by several inches than the regular seat in the car." Thus, "two stout passengers [could not] occupy such a seat" on one side. But the law mandated only these four rear seats for black patrons. White riders resented the notion that even these few seats should be "saved" for black passengers, so when the cars became crowded, white passengers sometimes packed the aisle, blocking access to the screened-off seats. White men standing in the aisle near the black section often would "rest their feet upon these [rear] seats," refusing to allow African American passengers to sit. Jones fumed that "crowding upon the Colored passengers" cut down on "even the small space allowed." The *Advocate* frequently printed accounts of streetcar riders who were injured when crowded conditions distracted drivers or pushed patrons into the paths of oncoming streetcars. For example, John Green, "a member of Union Chapel . . . was run over" after being knocked out of a Magazine Street car, leaving him "badly bruised up." He "would have been killed only that he was a very large and portly man." The elderly Reverend B. M. Palmer, pastor of a local Presbyterian church, "was knocked down by an electric car . . . and seriously injured" while trying to board a crowded car.[50]

New Orleans had an unusual number of incidents of crowding, injury, and accidental ejection of passengers who rode on outdoor platforms or were pushed out of moving cars when the cars filled to capacity. Crowded conditions reached their peak during the hours when working people traveled to and from their places of employment. Streetcar segregation dramatically decreased the amount of space legally available to black riders. Although initially uncomfortable with being told where to sit, white passengers eventually used segregation to their benefit, crowding out the packed cars during rush hours. Rev. Jones hinted at this important factor when he commented, "The street cars in New Orleans . . . operated as if the Colored patronage was not wanted, or that the Colored people must take the accommodation offered without regard to convenience and comfort."[51]

The high number of white passengers had a determinative impact on the viability of the streetcar boycotts. African American passengers would have difficulty staging a boycott of New Orleans streetcars under these conditions. If boycotted cars remained packed with white passengers, the company might have been able to absorb the financial losses of absent black passengers. Anecdotal evidence even suggests that the streetcar company reduced the frequency of cars run on routes that were popular with black passengers in anticipation of the lost business.

Jones reported that a white man refused to remove his foot from the empty colored seat even when his wife directly asked him to do so. Jim Crow streetcars reaffirmed gendered inequities; both custom and laws allowed for the convenience and comfort of white women passengers. Much like earlier statutes segregating trains, black women nurses and caregivers were allowed to sit in the white section of the streetcar when caring for white children or elderly white patients. And by custom, white women received courteous and respectful treatment from both passengers and conductors, with conductors helping white women alight the steps of the streetcars and white men standing to allow white ladies to take their seats. These customs even took on the force of law: white women successfully sued streetcar companies when conductors spoke to them in a discourteous or slanderous manner. African American women's experiences on streetcars differed dramatically. But black women not only were denied the everyday considerations accorded to "ladies" but often bore the brunt of coarse interactions with rude white men, who refused to respect the few "rights" black riders retained.[52]

The *Southwestern Christian Advocate*, the city's only African American newspaper, spoke out only hesitatingly on behalf of a boycott. One group, led by some of the Methodist ministers associated with the *Advocate*, including A. E. P. Albert, the pastor of Wesley Chapel and a former editor of the paper; G. W. Henderson, a professor; and Scott, sought to exploit the streetcar company's reticence and wait for the outcome of a test case initiated by the company. After private meetings with company representatives, they hoped that building a coalition with sympathetic whites within the city's business class would be the best way to undercut streetcar segregation.[53]

In support of his inside strategy, Scott downplayed the viability of a boycott. Perhaps he hoped to bolster the possibility of a test case. Perhaps he did not want to offend the less progressive white delegates of the Methodist Episcopal Church who funded the *Advocate*; after all, political protest had led to Albert's dismissal as editor of the weekly in the 1890s. Perhaps Scott feared the consequences of open dissent in the wake of the riot. While informing his readers that the bill separating black and white riders with a wire screen had become law, the editor questioned the viability of a boycott. He contrasted 1900 with the current problem, insisting, "Two years ago, had [the law] passed we are sure there would have been a boycott by Negroes, for feeling at that time ran high." But Scott questioned whether a boycott would be an effective protest: "At this time many may refrain from riding, but it is impossible in a city of this size to inaugurate successfully a general boycott." Perhaps he truly believed that blacks who lived in distant areas would be unable to negotiate travel in the spread-out city. But he also hinted that the streetcar company asked him to discourage protest because it planned to take the issue to court: "We are not authorized at present to say what action will be taken in the courts." Private negotiations with streetcar officials seem to have tempered his public statements.[54]

African Americans did continue to turn to the courts to fight streetcar segregation in the 1900s—cases were mounted in Virginia, Alabama, and Florida—but in the wake of the *Plessy* decision, most courts did not challenge the separate but equal doctrine. Based on the precedent of the *Plessy* case, state courts often refused to even consider the question of the legality of segregation. Three separate attempts to challenge the constitutionality of segregation measures failed after 1896.[55] The Supreme Court of Alabama even refused to award punitive damages to a Sunday school teacher who was assaulted by a conductor and physically dragged out of her seat on a Birmingham streetcar for violating a local custom—not a law—separating the races. The court ruled that streetcar employees had a right to attack because there was a "natural, legal, and customary difference between the white and black races."[56] Although the New Orleans leaders who supported the test case hoped that the court might provide a remedy, boycotts increasingly became the only viable means of attacking Jim Crow laws.

Inactivity by these leading men led a group of black clubwomen to action. In July 1902, just a month after the law's enactment, the leaders of the Esther Chapter No. 1 of the Order of the Eastern Star, an African

American women's lodge affiliated with New Orleans's Prince Hall Masons, called for a meeting of the leaders of the city's black organizations to contest streetcar segregation. Ella Robinson, P. Thompson, O. B. Benton, Kate Price, and S. A. Gates wanted to unite New Orleans's black civic and fraternal organizations "for the purpose of determining upon some concerted course of action which will in some way free us from being separated from other civilized races in street cars by means of wire screens."[57]

New Orleans boasted a particularly rich organizational life. Countless churches, clubs, and fraternal and benevolent societies serving blacks of different classes and backgrounds bolstered their communities by aiding those in need and feeding African Americans' needs for spiritual and secular fellowship. The organizations that had helped to shape black civic and social life in New Orleans would also give structure to protest against the New Orleans Railways Company, a crucial factor in organizing as many people as possible, since about four-fifths of the city's African Americans belonged to at least one such organization.[58]

Spearheading the boycott fell in line with their work as clubwomen in key ways. All were members of multiple societies charged with addressing the concerns of the race. The particular difficulties black women faced on streetcars propelled them to become leading voices in the boycott movement. Eastern Star member S. A. Gates served as president of the Afro-American Club, which labored to improve health conditions by running a nursing class for black women and offering free nursing care, medical supplies, and clothing to those who could not afford proper treatment. Gates, the wife of a prominent Baptist minister, also played a major role in hosting the fourth annual national convention of the Southern Federation of Colored Women's Clubs, a sister organization to the National Association of Colored Women, in New Orleans in December 1902. At the meeting she spoke to participants about "the responsibility of mothers" to their sons and daughters to "make it as pleasant as possible for them in childhood" and to serve as positive examples through their actions and affiliations. Gates's effort to spearhead a movement against segregated streetcars melded with her mission to improve living conditions for the poor and to provide a good example for her children. Her work in civil society provided a training ground for the political realm. Women leaders tapped into their experiences working within the community to seek dignity for its members on the streetcars.[59]

The group's call for black New Orleans to organize was successful: more than two hundred members of at least sixty fraternal, union, and social organizations responded to the Eastern Star's request. To these leaders, the best way to regain equitable inclusion was to make a devastating economic impact on the streetcar company. Since the courts had given little long-term relief from segregation laws, group leaders decided that the most effective approach would be a boycott and formed a permanent protest organization. These community leaders returned to their unions, churches, and benevolent societies and encouraged members to walk, ride bikes, or use other forms of conveyance. Meeting attendees also declared their intention to start an independent line of "cabs and tallyhos" to aid the boycott.[60]

But the prominent leadership of the Eastern Star was short-lived. Only men were elected to head the boycott, relegating women to an auxiliary protest organization. Within many black organizations at the turn of the century, debates raged about whether women should adopt leadership roles. Many black women sought black men's protection from the public degradations of segregation. Some women leaders called on black men to fight segregation as part of the effort to protect black women in the public sphere. Nationally prominent clubwoman and educator Nannie Helen Burroughs, a leader in the Baptist Convention movement, wrote in 1904, "Our women need the protection and genuine respect of our men; if not unto them, unto whom shall we go?" Burroughs asserted that "whenever the men of any race defiantly stand for the protection of their women, the women will be strengthened morally and be saved from the hands of the most vile."[61]

Perhaps the Eastern Star chapter in New Orleans gave way to the leadership of local men to allow them to lead the fight to protect black women in particular and black people in general. But while black women called on black men to lead the fight, they also sought to protect themselves and their race as active participants in protests. The "politics of protection" did not necessarily stifle black women's participation in the fight for equitable streetcars; the outspoken leadership of black women jump-started the movement against segregated streetcars when others were unwilling to do so.[62]

As in most other cities where streetcar boycotts took place, African American organizations and institutions oversaw protest of Jim Crow streetcars in New Orleans. The boycott had the support not only of the city's Masons and Eastern Star chapters but also of members of the Odd Fellows, the multidenominational New Orleans Ministerial Alliance, and the Longshoremen's Protective Union and Benevolent Association.[63] Unlike in other boycott cities, however, New Orleans protesters found an ally in the white press. Some sympathetic writers from the more moderate local newspaper, the *Daily Picayune*, disapproved of the law, asserting that the separation was unnecessary. Most white southern dailies, including the more stridently segregationist *New Orleans Times Democrat*, maintained a policy of ignoring boycotts, mocking participants, or downplaying the effectiveness of the protests. The *Daily Picayune* accurately publicized the protests, published pictures of the offending screens, and highlighted the difficulties the new law presented to both white and black passengers. So with some hope for change, African American community leaders allied with sympathetic whites organized to contest streetcar segregation.

Although the editor of the *Advocate* failed to report on the meetings of the boycott organization throughout the summer and into the fall of 1902, Scott noted conditions during the first week the law was in force: "Screens required by law have been placed in very few of the cars," and "ropes are being used instead." The portion of the car designated for whites was crowded, with men and women "standing, morning and evening, in their end of the car, while there were vacant seats in the end for Negroes." Numerous blacks participated, and the streetcars had only "a very limited number of colored passengers"; the only black passengers "who seemed to be riding . . . had long distances to go." The boycott seemed to be succeeding without the participation of the dissenting ministers or the vigorous support of the *Advocate*.[64]

New Orleans blacks not only had used the streetcars for practical purposes but also had ridden the cars on special excursions to parks, balls, picnics, conventions, and holiday celebrations. So the boycott of the streetcars had to extend to the events sponsored by black clubs, lodges, labor organizations, and benevolent societies. Organizations supporting the boycott demonstrated a united front by canceling events that would require riding the cars. The *Picayune* reported, "The Jim Crow Law is playing hob with colored entertainments and public functions of the race" and "knocking the Railways Company out of considerable revenue." The white daily warned that "there will be no colored parks or picnics next summer under the Jim Crow Law" because "colored balls and entertainments are being discontinued because of the inability of the members of the organizations to go in bodies or get to their places in a reasonable length of time." Black organizations could easily have made special arrangements with the streetcar company to accommodate their members by running all-black cars hired to bring attendees to events, arrangements that were common throughout the South.[65]

For example, in an account describing the events at the Negro Young People's Christian and Educational Congress in Atlanta in the summer of

1902, the *Advocate* hinted that although "large numbers of persons who contemplated the trip to Atlanta dreaded to come in contact with the separate street car regulations of that city," the "street cars were largely given up to colored passengers, an effort being made seemingly to do nothing to mar the pleasure of the city's guests." When large events occurred in African American communities across the South, companies sought to avoid alienating black patrons or missing out on opportunities to reap the financial boost of increased patronage. However, as a show of will, African American organizations in New Orleans chose to cancel large-scale events rather than make special arrangements, sending a statement of their determination to the streetcar company and to the city.[66]

In November 1902, the Longshoremen's Protective Union canceled its annual memorial service, for which "at least 3,000 colored people [traveled] to and from the Seventh District." Union president William H. Penn simply explained, "There was nothing else to do. . . . We could not get transportation service in the cars. Under the law, when four colored people get in a car is full. At that rate . . . it would have taken a day and night to have gotten our folks up to Carrollton, and another day and night to have gotten them back. It is an ironclad rule of the Association that every member is fined $1 who does not attend the memorial services and who is not there on time. Holding the observance would have resulted in most all our members being fined."[67] Rather than make alternate arrangements, Penn, an important leader in the labor movement and the black community in general, canceled the event. Penn, who had served as the president of his union since 1895, was affiliated with twenty-nine clubs and fraternal societies, and a member of the First Street Methodist Episcopal Church. His willingness to forgo the event demonstrated to the entire city the power of collective action against segregated streetcars. Penn's break with the leaders of his denomination also suggests that the ministers' desires did not necessarily hinder their congregants from openly participating in the boycott.

The *Advocate* did not report the Longshoremen Union's cancellation.[68] Although Scott might have thought the story was impolitic, Penn's leadership in the boycott was particularly meaningful. Longshoremen were accustomed to negotiating with employers and had united with white workers to wage successful strikes. Penn's effective protest portrayed union members and their families as valued, revenue-generating customers as well. Black waterfront workers' valuable organizational and protest skills made them leading voices in the streetcar boycott.[69]

Although Scott did not encourage the boycott, he did not want his silence to be interpreted as support of the law. Writing a corrective to an article published by A. R. Holcombe in a national periodical, *The Outlook*, Scott disputed the claim that he and his cohort of dissenting ministers favored the separate streetcar law. Instead, the editor insisted that he had not spoken out vigorously because he had been asked to keep quiet until the test case was decided. Holcombe was "entirely misinformed," and the ministers' group had taken "the lead two years before in opposing the enactment of the law." These same leaders would have spoken out again had they not been "advised to keep quiet for fear of prejudicing the case." Scott dismissed the notion that he approved of segregating the streetcars: "Who there was among us who can be pointed out as favoring the law we are unable to say."[70]

By supporting New Orleans Railways' test case, the editor believed that he was indeed advancing the interests of the race. But his silence short-changed the effect of the boycott. Although the participation of the working class was the most important factor in the boycott movement, the press helped to fuel the protests. Newspapers quickly disseminated new information, calls for mass meetings, and changes in tactics. Protest was particularly difficult without the support of the city's primary African American news source.

However, local disagreements over tactics did not dull Scott's support for African Americans protesting streetcar segregation in other cities. The *Advocate* commented on boycotts throughout the South, praising other efforts to resist new laws. Scott reported on the success of the 1902 boycott of segregated cars in Montgomery, Alabama, where "colored people began walking after the enactment of the law and stuck to it." The protest in that city "made the company's business so unprofitable that [the law's] enforcement has been abandoned" after "one line of cars mostly patronized by them had to be closed entirely." The editor praised the unity of Montgomery's African American community: "We are gratified to know that our people united at something long enough to win a victory for the race."[71]

Scott also pointed out the irony of whites being arrested for violating streetcar segregation laws. When the daughter of Robert E. Lee was arrested in Alexandria, Virginia, for violating a local streetcar ordinance, the editor gleefully reported that although it was "not likely that Miss Lee will be prosecuted it does seem strange that the daughter of Gen. Lee should be among the first to be humiliated under this silly and senseless law." But, Scott reasoned, her treatment under the unjust law was indeed fair: "Since our white friends mixed the medicine, they'd as well take some of it."[72]

In November, Pearson, now serving as president of the New Orleans Railways Company, and a number of corporate officers were arrested for failing to erect the screens required by the state law. Pearson's attorneys argued that the law placed too heavy a burden on conductors, who were legally authorized to determine passengers' race and seat them accordingly. The challenge met with some initial success; Judge Auguste Alcoin of New Orleans's Second City Criminal Court found the state law unconstitutional, news that Scott printed in the *Advocate*. The state then appealed to the Louisiana Supreme Court.[73]

Scott's dissenters and streetcar officials may have made an odd coalition, but it had a logic of its own. Many streetcar companies in other parts of the urban South resented the extra cost and effort required to designate segregated areas on the cars. Indeed, some companies attempted to delay implementing segregationist policies as long as possible.[74] Most streetcar ventures were relatively new; the challenges of maintaining safe, reliable and well-maintained electric streetcars using brand-new and often unfamiliar technology tried companies around the country. Many companies teetered on the brink of bankruptcy and could not afford long-term decreases in their revenue in the absence of a public demand for segregated cars.

Some white passengers who had been accustomed to riding near or next to black passengers viewed streetcar segregation not as a necessity but as a problem of fewer seats on already crowded cars. On New Orleans's packed lines, "the only vacant seats were those set apart for negroes and on which the conductor would allow no [white passenger] to sit." A white woman wrote to the *Picayune* "to protest most forcibly against the new law requiring the Street Railways Company to reserve the last two seats on each side of the car for negroes." She had encountered difficulty on the St. Charles line while traveling with her young daughter and her "colored nurse." The woman asked, "What legal redress I would have, in case the conductor insisted on my nurse and baby sitting in the section reserved for colored people?" Although white newspapermen in most southern cities supported segregation, *Picayune* writers complained about the inconvenience, calling the law "obnoxious" and "unpopular." They declared that the designation of seats exclusively for blacks added to "the white man's burden, although the measure was passed to please him."[75]

Without public outcry by white passengers demanding racial division, northern corporate investors like those Pearson represented were not wedded to the idea of segregation, especially if it caused extra expense. An alliance with African American Methodist dissenters was practical for the streetcar company. Pearson could dull the effectiveness and cost of the boycott by asking the editor to downplay the daily events of the protest while appearing to be a quiet advocate on behalf of black passengers. In addition, the newly consolidated company could ill afford another battle after the labor disputes and fifteen-day strike waged by streetcar employees in October 1902. In this unstable context, the streetcar company did not want to become a party to long-term racial battles.

It is unclear whether the streetcar company officials truly wanted to upend the new law; the test case put forth by the company was poorly conceived and ultimately doomed to fail. Besides the formidable challenge of contesting the precedent of the recent *Plessy* decision, the test case was designed improperly. If the company had wanted to question the conductors' discretion, it would have dealt directly with their conduct rather than the condition of the cars. Perhaps the Pearson case was simply a stopgap designed to divide the city's black leaders poised for boycott: a unified and effective boycott would have cut into the profits of the newly consolidated company in its first year.

The uneven enforcement of segregation laws throughout the South led some blacks to believe that they could reach a fair settlement on the segregation issue. Streetcar segregation was not equally enforced from community to community. Black protesters hoped that inconsistencies in policy might hint at the possibility of positive change. Washington wrote in 1906, "In some of the Southern cities it is perfectly proper for members of the two races to sit side by side in the same street car; a few miles away it is considered practicing social equality for them to ride in the same manner."[76] The uneven application of streetcar segregation law throughout the South and the ambiguous nature of white public opinion in New Orleans gave Scott and the silent protesters hope. White passengers' reluctance, coupled with an effective test case put forward by streetcar officials, surely would put a quick end to the costly and unpopular policy.

As they awaited the verdict of the suit in the higher court, Scott and the dissenting group remained convinced that the case would effectively challenge the law. The *Advocate* increased its coverage of unfair conditions on the streetcars, assuring his readers that such inequities would not stand. Arguing that the majority of the city's African American community had "a disposition to await the action of the court," Scott insisted that the case would succeed because the policy inconvenienced white as well as black passengers: "Negroes are compelled to stand while more than half the seats of the car are unoccupied, and whites are often forced to stand while the few seats set apart for Negroes are vacant."[77]

In March 1903, however, Louisiana State Supreme Court issued its decision against the New Orleans Railways in *State v. Pearson*. Scott was crushed by the defeat. "With one stroke of the pen," he wrote, the judges "have dispelled the hope of thousands of persons." Citing the precedent of *Plessy* case, the state court upheld streetcar segregation. However, *Plessy* was just a cover: the gated streetcars offered separate but not equal conditions. Scott warned, "Under the circumstances it is impossible that the colored citizens of New Orleans will be satisfied with the manner in which the law is enforced."[78]

Following the decision, Scott's attack on the segregation law became more vigorous and vocal. The *Advocate* began to publish weekly reports detailing the uncomfortable situation on the streetcars: said one, "Few have been riding since the screens were placed in the cars, very little space has been allotted to Negro passengers." Although most blacks tried to avoid the cars, those "who did ride have been for the most part compelled to stand." The members of the dissenting group questioned the strength of their alliance with business interests. Although Pearson had appeared sympathetic to the complaints of aggrieved black passengers, the local men in charge of the daily operations of the company showed no concern for black passengers' well-being. On one streetcar, "the compartment for Negroes was so greatly crowded that many were compelled to stand on the platform. At a sharp curve the car jumped the track and four were more or less injured." Scott believed that New Orleans Railways behaved as if it wanted to get rid of its black passengers: "The company either does not desire the patronage of colored people or it thinks they will put up with anything." Unsure that black passengers had any friends within the company's ranks, the editor wrote, "Something will be done if our people have any self respect whatever. The Negro need not sit idly by and expect his rights to be respected." Scott began to believe that management was attempting to make the segregated cars as uncomfortable as possible to drive away black patrons.[79]

Finally, Scott began openly to encourage blacks to boycott, outlining the alternate forms of transportation available: "While many of our people are still walking, vast numbers of them have purchased buggies, surries, and other vehicles. Others still have joined what they are pleased to call the 'stay at homes.' Bicycles too are more popular since this law went into effect, than for two or three years." The editor touted the boycott's effectiveness, assuring his readers that the streetcar company "has been losing money." Citing not only reduced patronage but also a "large reduction in the number of cars run," he asserted "that from fifteen to twenty-five more cars would be absolutely necessary if the Negro patronage was up to the usual mark."[80]

Months after the Longshoremen's Union canceled its annual event, Scott supported the idea of canceling black events and rejecting the "temporary arrangements" the streetcar company was willing to make for those occasions. The *Advocate* publicized the call by the New Orleans Ministerial Alliance for the city's black organizations to cancel large events that would require members to patronize the streetcars. Scott hoped that the Odd Fellows would cancel their annual picnic in solidarity with the boycott and challenged company officials: "Our people are not as greatly in need of some regard for their comfort on picnic occasions as on everyday occasions, so as to enable them to get to and from their work, etc." But over time, the resolve to boycott the streetcars eroded. New Orleans was a large and sprawling city. If blacks, particularly members of the working class, wanted full opportunities for new homes, and employment, they would have to travel the city by streetcar. Within the next decade, black passengers traveling on the cars, cramped behind the prohibitive screens, was the norm.[81]

The dissenting group's hesitation had slowed the movement. Although the ministers did nothing to directly undercut the protests and eventually gave vigorous support to boycott efforts, that support came too late. Alliances with sympathetic white officials would not be effective in the battle against segregated streetcars. Confusion and disagreements within a community divided by tactics weakened those engaged in an already difficult fight. The New Orleans they loved had been shattered by legal repression and violence and reshaped in the image of Jim Crow. The movement for racial separation would continue to grow in cities such as Richmond, Virginia, where the postwar black community had found success.

Richmond's black women domestic workers carried baskets in their hands or on their heads. Streetcar travel made such chores easier. The boycott made them less efficient workers, yet they were some of the most active members of the streetcar boycott.

LEFT "Woman with basket on her head," ca. 1900 (1504, Cook Collection, Valentine Richmond History Center, Richmond, Va.). RIGHT "Street vendor," ca. 1900 (1490, Cook Collection, Valentine Richmond History Center, Richmond, Va.).

"Richmond Passenger and Power Co. Trolley," ca. 1900 (V. 55.126.2, Valentine Richmond History Center, Richmond, Va.). The 1904 streetcar segregation law authorized conductors to carry weapons to control any passengers that might protest. Here a conductor poses while pointing his pistol at two men holding bricks. The armed conductors would be a deterrent against the protests of striking workers and black passengers.

"Group in front of Virginia street car" (Valentine Richmond History Center, Richmond, Va.). Richmond's streetcars were symbols of the city's modernity and urbanity.

"1300 block E. Cary Street," ca. 1900 (1028, Cook Collection, Valentine Richmond History Center, Richmond, Va.). Most of Richmond's hackmen and teamsters were black men. These drivers proved to be instrumental during the streetcar boycott.

5 WHO'S TO BLAME?

Maggie Lena Walker, John Mitchell Jr., and the Great Class Debate

In 1899, Sutton E. Griggs, an African American native of Texas and a graduate of the Theological Seminary of Virginia Union University in Richmond, published a novel, *Imperium in Imperio*, that told the story of two lifelong friends, Belton Piedmont and Bernard Belgrave, and their membership in a black secret society, Imperio. Imperio was a mythical nation within a nation, an alternative government clandestinely organized by blacks shut out of America in the age of segregation. While the two well-educated race leaders strove for middle-class respectability, they disagreed about the best means to improve African American life in the face of segregation, disfranchisement, and racial violence. Belgrave, frustrated with the American South, dismissed all hope that America would treat black southerners equally, while Piedmont, the hero, argued that the South could be redeemed from racial polarization if black Americans worked hard to prove their worth and demonstrate their capabilities. If, after improving themselves, they were still rejected on the basis of race, they could start an independent black settlement and break away from the rest of the nation.

Imperium in Imperio pointed to the existence of a real divide within the black middle class. Like their fictional counterparts, African American leaders of the streetcar boycott in Richmond, Virginia, disagreed about the causes of racial strife and the best means to contest it. This generation of black leaders faced a formidable crisis. Leadership was a bleak task in a time when the choices were limited. How could they lead when there were few paths to follow? How could they best confront the problem of a dividing world?

WHEN SOME FOUR MILLION of slaves were freed at the end of the Civil War, many white sympathizers and critics agreed that the best way for them to improve themselves and become good citizens would be through education, thrift, and moral uplift. Thousands of northern white missionaries came south, helping to establish primary and secondary schools to transform former slaves into literate, moral citizens. Colleges, charged with the mission of creating a black leadership class, were founded throughout the region. At both institutions that emphasized industrial training and colleges that taught a classical approach, black students learned that respectable, civilized, moral behavior was essential to the growth of the race. Many African Americans agreed, seeking to educate and redefine themselves and their children according to the Victorian standards of the day.

By the turn of the twentieth century, the urban South was home to a new generation of blacks raised with the belief that their success would lead to greater opportunities for the race. Black Richmond embodied this transformation. In 1910, Richmond was a moderately sized city with 46,733 black residents, just over 36 percent of the city's total population. The city's African American leadership class was influential in part because Richmond was home to the largest population of African Americans in the Upper South.[1] The city's black middle class boasted a growing community of bankers, entrepreneurs, and journalists. In the former capital of the Confederacy, an increasingly prosperous and educated black community blossomed, prepared to play a major role in leading African Americans across the nation. At the 1900 meeting of the National Negro Business League, an organization founded by Booker T. Washington, Giles B. Jackson, one of the city's leading black lawyers, remarked that Richmond's blacks led the country in their development in real estate, banking, and insurance and that the state's black businesses had a capital investment of more than $14 million. The members of the league's local chapter included "eleven colored attorneys, eighty-three colored barbershops, three colored banks, sixteen beneficial insurance companies, sixteen blacksmiths and wheelwrights, one book seller, four butcher firms, one cabinet maker, two general caterers." The speaker argued that unsuccessful blacks had failed to advance only because of "the lack of individual effort"; poor blacks were "sitting by the pool of industry waiting for some one to put [them] in."[2]

Although Jackson was a particularly conservative force in Richmond's

African American community, he highlighted an ongoing tension between the small but prosperous community of race leaders and the working poor. Indeed, black Richmond was also home to communities of freed slaves and migrants from the surrounding rural counties who, despite the growth of black institutions, found neither ease nor prosperity. The working poor were in the majority in Richmond; most black men were day laborers who could not depend on a steady income, most black women served as laundresses, and together they cobbled together households on less than what was necessary to support their families. Even though the working poor may not have spoken or behaved as the middle class wanted, the leading class hoped to guide the poor toward greater success and full inclusion in American life. Perhaps if they could save more, purchase homes, raise mannerly children, and attend the right churches, they too would rise. Those African American residents of Richmond who had found a measure of success hoped that by building an institutional base of schools, civic orders, banks, and churches, they could serve their community and elevate their race. The city was home to several black congregations, among them the prominent First African Baptist Church; growing primary and secondary schools; and a black college, Virginia Union, as well as branches of national civic, religious, and fraternal organizations, including the Grand Fountain Order of True Reformers, the Knights of Pythias, the Lilies of the Valley, and the Independent Order of Saint Luke. The legacy of a strong free black community and the initiative of "new issue Negroes"—the first generation of African Americans to come of age after slavery—made Richmond a model for black urbanites throughout the nation. They hoped that their success would lead to greater advancement and opportunity for all black Americans.[3]

Instead, members of this educated class found opportunities shrinking and the doors of citizenship closing throughout the American South. Hostile state legislatures began restricting black voting rights, systematically underfunding or eliminating black schools, and providing few or no public services for urban black communities. In addition to the threat of repressive laws, black citizens were terrorized by the extralegal threat of lynching and race riots. During the 1880s and 1890s, more than one hundred African Americans were killed by lawless mobs each year, creating a climate of fear among southern blacks. Lynch mobs, often threatened by the success of black businesspeople, angered by the language of black journalists, or intimidated by black landowners, frequently targeted prosperous or successful black men and women.[4]

The wave of segregation laws was the final insult to black freedom and a major impediment to black success. Laws designed to separate white patrons from blacks assumed that racial equity contaminated the social fabric of the South. But African Americans who were educated in the mores of proper behavior believed that their dignity ought to be assured. After all, they had achieved more in a few decades than many white southerners had accomplished in generations. Many members of Richmond's black middle class were particularly angered by most white southerners' unwillingness to recognize that a segment of the black population was neither unclean nor uncouth. Educated and industrious blacks believed that their economic improvement would help to preserve their civic equality. In their view, those who demonstrated exemplary conduct ought to be spared the embarrassment of second-class treatment. Segments of the black middle class, along with southern white progressives such as George Washington Cable and Virginia racial reformer Lewis H. Blair, argued that segregation along class lines would remove the offensive members of both races from first-class seats.[5] But such proposals were ignored; ideas about cross-racial class alliances threatened the logic of white supremacy and could not be tolerated.

Angered by white southerners' general refusal to recognize that the rising black middle class was of a "different sort" than the poorer, uneducated "elements" of the race, the black middle class displayed a divided front in the battle against segregation. Seesawing between African American unity rooted in uplift and an outlook of division and blame, Richmond's middle-class leaders struggled for public recognition of their achievements and for the respect of public inclusion. For this generation of African Americans seeking the promise of freedom, the question became how black southerners should proceed. Was the onslaught of segregation laws caused by a cultural failure on the part of blacks who had not progressed? Was such moral progress helpful in making the case for black citizenship, or had the success of some black southerners caused white segregationists to begin erecting new barriers of separation and violent repression?

When Virginia Passenger and Power decided to segregate Richmond's streetcars in the spring of 1904, leaders and the lowly joined together to protest. The boycott depended on a unified black community. How could this diverse community unite on shared terms to form a successful defense of black citizenship?

RICHMOND BLACKS DID not contest the passage of the segregation statute of 1904 in any court of law. Blacks did not stage sit-ins like those that had taken place in Richmond during Reconstruction. Protesters did not engage in physical fights with streetcar conductors to keep seats in the "white" section. Instead, blacks across the city lodged a silent protest and began walking to work, to market, to places of worship, and to places of leisure.

On 14 April, "a conference of colored citizens" comprised of "a large number of the leading colored men and ladies" convened in Jackson Ward, the historical epicenter of Richmond's black political dissent, to address the new policy and decide the appropriate method of protest. Jackson Ward was originally a gerrymandered district created by the state's Conservative Party in 1871 to contain the black vote and weaken the Republican Party's power. Despite the efforts of Conservative-Democrats, Jackson Ward came to symbolize black political independence and self-sufficiency.[6]

At this small gathering at A. D. Price's Hall, the large hall at 212 East Leigh Street owned by a funeral director, community leaders decided to call a mass meeting to elect representatives and adopt a protest against the law. The group elected John Mitchell Jr., a former politician and editor of the *Richmond Planet*, as chair of the boycott organization and resolved that "colored people should do all in their power to promote peace and avoid any clash or disorder on the street-cars. It was decided that the best way to do this would be to WALK and STAY OFF the Virginia Passenger and Power Company's cars." Mitchell warned his readers, "This is no time to threaten or to attempt to retaliate." Characterizing the protest as "conservative," these "leading" men and women sought to set the tenor of the boycotts and to discourage black Richmonders from adopting other forms of protest. These leaders included some of black Richmond's most prosperous and prestigious businesspeople, including Mitchell's high school classmate, Maggie Lena Walker. Walker was the president of the Independent Order of St. Luke, a benevolent society dominated by black women of all walks of life. Walker, an extremely active and vocal advocate for the city's black women, also served as the editor of the *St. Luke Herald*. At a mass meeting a few days later, Patsie K. Anderson, a St. Luke member and manager of the Women's Union, stood up to reiterate Mitchell's program. In "terse, explicit language," she advised listeners "to do no talking, but walk, walk, walk. She carried the house by storm and sat down amidst great applause."[7]

Boycott leaders organized mass meetings to articulate the movement's goals. Black clerks, bankers, doctors, lawyers, and businesspeople were elected to serve with Mitchell on the Committee on Resolutions, mapping out protesters' objections. The committee was headed by R. E. Jones, a physician and president of the Richmond chapter of the National Negro Business League. Other members included H. F. Jonathan, vice president of the Mechanics' Savings Bank; R. T. Hill, a cashier for the True Reformers Savings Bank; H. L. Harris, a physician; and E. A. Washington, a member of the board of directors of the Mechanics' Savings Bank.[8] Richmond's three leading black newspapers, the *Planet*, the *St. Luke Herald*, and the *Reformer*, supported the boycott. Part of a new generation of the black middle class, boycott leaders walked a fine line between personal prosperity and the desire to lead all members of their community.[9]

Although many boycott leaders sought to police the behavior of black protesters by asserting standards of proper, genteel behavior, the decision to boycott, rather than to sue or adopt active resistance on the streetcars themselves, was not in itself a middle-class tactic. Close examination of Virginia's segregation statutes reveals that the boycott-centered protests and the absence of suits testing the validity of the new statutes were not caused by political indifference or a climate of accommodation. Rather, the comprehensive new laws themselves shaped the nature of the protests. Although historians stress that turn-of-the-century blacks were moving away from political protest, the segregationists who crafted the statutes presupposed black dissent. A comparison of streetcar segregation laws with older statutes that segregated trains makes it clear that the new generation of laws dividing blacks and whites undercut black southerners' ability to sue for equal accommodations and gave broad discretionary powers to conductors to quell spontaneous resistance on the cars. Indeed, the best indication of the tenor of the times might be drawn from the texts of Virginia's segregation statutes themselves: white lawmakers did not anticipate accommodation on the part of black citizens but drew on a knowledge of the history and contemporary nature of black resistance to shape the legal language of segregation.[10]

The text of the statute reflects that the Virginia law systematically limited the options for lawful protest. The absence of successful legal challenges to Virginia's segregation laws at the turn of the twentieth century reflected not a lack of political interest on the part of black southerners but rather calculated attempts on the part of segregationist lawmakers to limit effective legal challenges. In light of the text of the Virginia segregation law of 1904, the boycott becomes much more than a conservative plea for dignity. It was a valiant attempt to remove the wall of segregation one brick at a time.

The new Virginia law did not guarantee black men or women seats or require that a certain number of the seats be designated for black riders. Instead, it stated that conductors could "set apart [seats] in each car or coach a portion thereof, or certain seats therein, to be occupied by white passengers, and a portion thereof, or certain seats therein, to be occupied by colored passengers." Mitchell pointed out to his readers that "conductors can whenever they see fit cause a colored person, male or female, to get up and make room for any other person." The Virginia statute gave the conductor the right to determine how much space would be given to black and white passengers. Conductors could decide that few or no seats could be given to black passengers. Also at the conductor's discretion was individual seating; conductors could "require any passenger to change his or her seat when and as often as he may deem necessary or proper." Even as the *Richmond News Leader* insisted that law benefited black riders because "the negroes have rather the best of the new arrangement in being nearer the doors," in reality black passengers were not even afforded the luxury of being able to know that the seats they chose would be honored throughout their passage.[11]

Mitchell pointed out that a conductor "could keep [a black passenger] moving in a trip from the West End to the Post Office to such an extent that when he arrived at his destination, he would be as tired as though he had walked the entire distance." The *Planet* editor also pointed out that the law did not acknowledge of the proper gender etiquette of the day. Conductors "can whenever they see fit cause a colored person, male or female, to get up and make room for any other person." If black women sought to assert their status as ladies, to signify their equality with other southern women, they would not be treated as ladies on segregated streetcars. Black women could be made to stand on platforms or in the aisles while white men remained seated.[12] Streetcars would not be marked by clear boundaries dividing black and white sections, and the law offered no established rights to which black riders could appeal. There would be no set rules on Richmond's streetcars; black riders had no guarantee of their safety and protection from humiliation or harassment. If black riders chose to comply and find seats at the backs of cars, they could still be asked to stand, even if there was ample space for both black and white riders.

The fundamental illogic of segregation was also part of the 1904 segregation statute. The law complied with the custom of allowing black nurses caring for white children to sit in the section designated for white passengers. The *Planet* reported that one conductor mistakenly told a black nurse that neither she nor the white child she was watching could sit among white passengers. The motorman then explained to the conductor that "he was in error and that colored people could be permitted to sit with the white people for whom they are nursing." The *Planet* article points out that at least in that case, segregation might have saved the black nurse some work: "The nurse would have been relieved of the care and trouble during that trip at least."[13] No protesters were more effective at highlighting the discrepancies of segregation than black women.

In a break with earlier segregation laws in Virginia that did not deputize railroad officials, the statute made it a crime for riders to violate its provisions or the orders of white conductors. If African American passengers resisted segregation or refused to obey "the instructions and directions of the conductor," conductors and motormen could arrest riders. Streetcar employees were designated "special policeman," with "all the powers of conservators of the peace" and the authority to enforce the law. Not only were conductors empowered to enforce the law at their own discretion, but the segregation law also gave them the right to carry weapons while working on the streetcars and traveling to and from work. A documentary photographer took a posed image of a conductor standing at the front of a Richmond Passenger and Power Company streetcar with his pistol drawn at two men, each holding a brick. Each man seems to represent a threat to the authority of the conductor—presumably a striker or protester.[14] The comprehensive law even exempted conductors and the companies from any legal liability for any harm they might cause to others while enforcing the segregation statute.

Streetcar segregation did not end with the attempt to segregate riders; the 1900 Census listed only 12 black workers among the city's 196 street railway employees. The *Planet* reported that none of the African American employees were drivers. Although black workers had been hired to complete the hard labor of laying streetcar tracks, they were never entrusted with running the streetcars. The conductor's discretion, therefore, was always going to be the judgment of a white man over his black and white passengers. Boycott leaders had little reason to believe the president of the streetcar company when he insisted that "whenever we discover a rough conductor on our lines, we get rid of him at once." Black passengers had little trust in the behavior of the conductors or in company promises. Walker's *St. Luke Herald* warned that "the very dangerous power placed in the hands of hot headed and domineering young white men" would "certainly provoke trouble." Mitchell pointed out to a mass meeting of black protesters that "under the provisions of the law . . . white boys and ill-mannered men . . . in charge of the street-cars were empowered to carry revolvers and if they shot down colored men, they could not be punished for so doing." Mitchell believed that "white hoodlums" were often the source of racial violence; he thought the streetcars would be particularly dangerous, given the class of the conductors.[15]

Sit-ins like those staged in the Reconstruction era would be met not only with the threat of being ejected at gunpoint but also court costs and high fines, which most black Richmonders could not afford. A close reading of the segregation law reveals why black attempts to sue Virginia Passenger and Power Company for damages and the cost of the fare would have been virtually impossible. The state favored the conductor with virtually un-limited discretion in achieving the ambiguous "comfort" of passengers or issuing whatever directions he might deem "proper" or "necessary." Care-fully drawing on the parameters of *Plessy v. Ferguson*, the Virginia law re-quired de jure equality of segregated facilities, yet this equality was vir-tually impossible to enforce when conductors were not just citizens but empowered agents of the law. The law not only humiliated black riders but also threatened them.

In an era when black southerners daily faced indiscriminate violence, armed white conductors represented a threat to all black riders, resistant or otherwise. Lynch law governed race relations not only in the Deep South but also in "civilized" Virginia. The pages of the *Planet* regularly reported both local and national lynchings and in 1900 maintained a running tally of lynchings, "The Reign of Lawlessness," that crowned the political features page of the weekly paper. Lynch law threatened the lives of black women as well as men. As historian Elsa Barkley Brown has demonstrated in her account of an 1895 campaign in Richmond to protect three black women from extralegal violence, the threat of armed white conductors was dra-matic in the context of a national ethos that accepted the reckless and unwarranted murders of black men, women, and children. Mitchell's decla-ration that "the only safe plan was to stay off the cars and avoid trouble" represented not just political conservatism but practical advice. Boycott leadership hoped that a poised and proper protest would not only demon-strate the admirable character of a beleaguered community but protect the participants from violence.[16]

LEADERSHIP IN ONE FORM or another was required to make a boycott function. Leaders helped articulate a plan, goals, and tactical behavior for boycott participants. Encouragement, stories of progress, and news of ev-eryday victories helped sustain boycotts. And leaders had to speak to a broad audience, men and women, young and old, prosperous and poor.

Boycott leadership varied from city to city, but in Richmond, the growing black business class, led by Walker and Mitchell, provided an able voice for the protest. The questions that confronted black protest leadership in the streetcar boycott movement throughout the South can be traced through the outlook of these two local leaders. Aside from their gender, Walker and Mitchell lived parallel lives. Both were from humble slave origins, both had the opportunity to attend the city's only black high school during Reconstruction, and both emerged as leaders of their community. Walker made the Independent Order of Saint Luke Richmond's leading benevolent society, while Mitchell served on the city council. Mitchell was also active in fraternal life; he was the president of Richmond's African American chapter of the Knights of Pythias, an order founded by Abraham Lincoln in the wake of the Civil War. Both Walker and Mitchell started banks targeted at black customers, and both served as editors of well-respected and widely read weekly newspapers. And like the majority of blacks in Richmond, they lived in Jackson Ward. Walker and Mitchell were certainly peers, and given that they jockeyed for bank customers and fought for readers, they were probably friendly competitors. Hints of their tension can be found; neither mentioned the other frequently in print.

Walker's and Mitchell's articles and speeches provide key insight into Richmond's black middle class, but their newspapers did not just reflect their communities. Black newspapers of this era also were important guides for contemporary readers. As black Americans grew increasingly literate in each decade following the Emancipation, newspapers became key sources of information and political, social, and cultural direction. Thousands of black Americans nationwide read black papers, with friends, families, and communities sharing copies. And given that the newspapers depended on subscriptions for survival, editors were accountable to their readers. They could not be race leaders without readers' consent. Editors' opinions, therefore, not simply represented the insights of individuals but also were shaped by the will of the community. Walker's and Mitchell's writings provide a glimpse into the questions they and others of their class confronted during this turbulent era.

In 1904, Walker, the daughter of a white abolitionist and a slave mother, was by far Richmond's most influential woman of color. Her association with the Independent Order of Saint Luke fueled her career as an educator, philanthropist, banker, and businesswoman. Yet Walker had humble origins, working as a girl to help her mother pick up and deliver laundry across Richmond. Walker's mother, like thousands of black women of her era and the generations that followed, had worked as a laundress, an occupation that provided black women with little pay but ample autonomy and mobility. And although Walker and her family had shed the poverty of her youth by the 1900s, she remained concerned with the plight of women workers and the state of African American citizenship. Her work to uplift her community and defend African American dignity drew Walker into a boycott movement that defended the dignity of lady bankers and lady laundresses alike.

Although her lifestyle reflected her family's growing financial success, her work for the Independent Order of Saint Luke showed a sympathetic view of the African Americans many viewed as immoral. Walker was quick to remind her audiences, "I was not born with a silver spoon in my mouth, but with a laundry basket . . . on my head." Notwithstanding her personal achievements, her entrepreneurial visions for the Saint Luke Penny Savings Bank and later the St. Luke Emporium were always grounded in a concern for the health of the race and opportunities for black women workers. Brown has aptly pointed out that Walker's success was drawn "from the strength of the Saint Luke collective as a whole and from the special strengths and talents of the inner core of the Saint Luke women in particular." Unlike many other benevolent societies and clubs, the order drew its membership from all segments of society, including both women and men from all classes and walks of life. Walker joined the order at age fourteen, and her membership in the organization helped to shape her aspirations and her vision of a black society facing segregation.[17]

Women were the heart of Walker's cause. As a child working among the laundry women, Walker came to appreciate the dignity of hard work and the fellowship of sisterhood. To remind audiences of the importance of black working women, she always identified herself as a worker; "I have worked from a child . . . worked before I was married, worked after I married, and am working now harder than I ever worked in my life." Walker sought to use her status to protect and promote the cause of working-class black women. Walker called "the love I bear women, our Negro women" her "great all absorbing interest, the thing which has driven sleep from my eyes and fatigue from my body." Black working women were not only "hemmed in" "by the fears and prejudices of the whites" but also "ridiculed and sneered at by the intelligent blacks." She believed that African Americans could truly be free only when the dignity of working women was protected from both the barbs of segregation and the judgment of the black middle class. For Walker, the roots of black women's citizenship were grounded in love and respect. Walker preached to her audience, "Whatever

I have done in this life has been because I love women. Love to be surrounded by them. Love to hear them all talk at once. Love to listen to their trials and troubles." Her devotion to black women and her determination to provide them with economic and social options formed the heart of her efforts with St. Luke. This quest to protect the dignity of everyday women drew her into the fight against segregation.[18]

Writing as the managing editor of the *Saint Luke Herald*, founded in 1902, and crafting speeches for a variety of engagements, Walker outlined her vision for the future and described the reasons why the tide of segregation had risen against all black southerners, even those with the greatest success. Walker used her voice as an editor and spokesperson to clearly articulate a defense of black life and full citizenship. Walker's *Herald* spoke out against the horror and violence of lynching; she believed it imperative that "the Negro . . . cry aloud in anguish when he sees black men, women and children murdered and burned to death, tortured in the most inhuman ways."[19] Walker also fought against the imposition of Jim Crow laws throughout the nation, warning northern black readers that the concerns of the South were universal. "We have been telling our friends all along, that as long as the 'jim crow' business lasts in the South, and as long as disfranchisement exists in the South, it will continue to spread."[20] Lynching, violence, disfranchisement, and segregation constituted an attack on the health of black individuals, communities, and enterprises across the country. According to Walker, "We are being oppressed by the passage of laws which not only have for their object the degradation of Negro manhood and Negro womanhood, but also the destruction of all kinds of Negro enterprises[.] Every legislature in the South legislates against the Negro, and the effect of this same legislation is felt throughout the length and breadth of this country."[21]

Walker questioned the assumption that poor whites were at the root of black problems. In an article interrogating the *Washington Post*'s coverage of a Georgia lynching, she challenged the contention that elite whites played no role in the perpetuation of lynch law. She insisted that "criminal and worthless whites . . . do not mould sentiment, do not make public opinion, they are simply the curs who watching, take the silence of their superiors as permission to commit crime, and who follow gladly where they lead." Placing blame squarely at the feet of the white elite, Walker asserted that "the criminal and worthless white is not responsible for the bloody crimes of the South." She was not convinced that the impetus for racial violence and segregation originated from poor whites threatened by black success. The source of the problem was "genteel, white gentlemen." She saw little potential in appealing to white southerners as allies or friends in the fight against injustice. Only economic independence would steel black people against the assaults on their citizenship.[22]

However, Walker's belief in economic independence did not stop her from agitating against Jim Crow. Walker despised what she called the "song of segregation" sung by "the white press" and "the white pulpit." The spread of segregation to every aspect of daily life was like lawmakers telling black people "go to another country, get out, go away; if you want to remain here you must be my menial . . . my servant." She believed that segregationists were dismissing all black southerners to a separate sphere, their laws implicitly crying, "If you want to be what I am—a MAN—separate. Go where I can't see you."[23]

Walker found the spread of segregation laws into Richmond particularly offensive. She called for her audience to "examine what is going on here, right under our noses in Richmond City in the Capitol Square. The 'jim crow' car, once confined alone to our steam cars and long distance travel, is now upon every steam and electric line in the state." Segregation represented a profound inequity: "The Negro in traveling pays first class price, for second and third class accommodation." Walker believed strongly that segregation was a frontal attack on black citizenship. In the face of "the loss of citizenship," she demanded, "SOMEBODY MUST SPEAK. SOMEBODY *MUST* CRY ALOUD. The afflictions and the persecutions of our people MUST be told. WE MUST GET TOGETHER AND REASON TOGETHER. SOMEBODY MUST CRY OUT."[24]

To Walker, the women of Richmond were just as capable as the men of sounding the alarm concerning racial violence, the advance of segregation laws, and the degradation of black citizenship. As a leader of various women's clubs and organizations, Walker outlined a model of black womanhood that offered recognition of the lives of working-class African Americans. Asserting that African American working women were "noble, and true and clean," Walker countered the popular notion that black women were immoral because their employment caused them to cross the terrain of the city alone. Walker reminded her audiences that black women's labor was essential to the health of black families, arguing the black woman went "out into the world—not for name, not for glory and honor—but for bread, and for her babies." Improving the image of poor black women driven to lifestyles many would deem immoral and improper, Walker insisted "that ninety-five percent of our women who go astray, do so from absolute need, selling their souls to clothe their bodies!" She spoke directly to black male leaders who offered no assistance to black women: "Instead of scoffing at the efforts of your women, instead of criticizing them, every Negro man, every Negro Newspaper, every Negro preacher should be extending the hand which helps and giving forth the words which encourage—for the path of the colored women is dark and thorny."[25]

Walker sought to explain the socioeconomic context for the difficulties of the poor and dispossessed. Although she also differentiated classes within African American communities and scolded those who practiced immoral behavior, she sought to revive and uplift black women through the development of black institutions and enterprises. Black immorality arose out of the awful circumstances of racial oppression and the lack of viable choices. She identified the absence of opportunity and the repressive politics of race, not black behavior, as the cause of the shortcomings within black communities. Although Walker became Richmond's most elite black woman, she always remained hesitant to judge the least among them, instead seeking to value the role that all black women played for the health of their families and communities. The plight of the dispossessed was her fight, and she encouraged black women: "The fact that we are at the very bottom of the ladder should not dishearten us."[26]

Asserting that the race required both black men and women to succeed, Walker believed that one remedy for the attack on black citizenship might be the advancement of black women. Like many of her contemporaries, including Mary Church Terrell, Anna Julia Cooper, and Nannie Helen Burroughs, Walker believed that black women had to "do the work which the race must do"—that is, work at the forefront of the fight for black citizenship. Each of these spokeswomen had a distinct approach to women's contributions as race leaders. Clubwoman Terrell believed that the race could best be served through black women's role as early childhood educators, while Walker promoted black business as African American women's path to success. Walker's belief that the black woman could best be served by "striking out boldly, for herself, doing credit to her state, her sex and her race" transmitted to her approach not only to business but also to the fight against segregation.[27]

Mitchell's approach to the problem of segregation was mapped out in his weekly newspaper. The *Planet*, which was read both locally and nationally by more than six thousand subscribers, was founded in 1883 "to foster enterprise and encourage literary culture." The paper grew when Mitchell took over the editorship in December 1884, making Mitchell prominent if not wealthy. Despite Mitchell's humble birth to a literate slave mother in the midst of the Civil War, he sought out education and opportunity and used his talents to become a local politician, writer, and businessman. He used his newspaper to articulate his stalwart opposition to lynching. At an 1889 meeting of the National Colored Press Association, Mitchell read the names of more than two hundred victims of racial violence, inspiring a young Ida B. Wells to remember his "personal bravery and courage."[28] Mitchell's fight against lynching came close to home during the 1895 battle to prevent the lynching of two black women, Pokey Barnes and Mary Abernathy, and a black man, Solomon Marable, from rural Lunenburg County, Virginia. While the accused were held in Richmond's jail, he championed their cause, using keen reporting to cast serious doubt on their presupposed guilt and eventually helping to gain their freedom. The effort brought Mitchell national renown.[29]

Mitchell subsequently used his newspaper to continue to contest racial violence, to sound the alarm about black disfranchisement, and to promote black education and uplift. By the turn of the century, the *Planet* had become well known as a vibrant voice of race advocacy.[30] In addition to local events, the paper featured accounts of national news, stories reprinted from other black and white newspapers, snappy editorial notes, an ongoing account of racial violence throughout the South and the nation, and ads run by Richmond's business owners and fraternal lodges and orders. The *Planet* was at its best reporting the events of the city and the ins and outs of the Southwide battle to retain black citizenship.

The circulation of each issue of the *Planet* extended beyond the list of subscribers and even beyond the literate; copies of the paper were often shared in public spaces such as barbershops, and crucial articles were often read aloud.[31] But for the most part, like most black newspapers, the *Planet* operated in the separate sphere of black community, and few whites read it. Hoping for a medium that could highlight issues of race to "thinking white people," prominent African American author Charles W. Chesnutt lamented that "few white people . . . read the present newspapers published by colored people."[32] But having an audience comprised mainly of other blacks gave Mitchell and other editors the ability to be frank about issues of race. But to survive, black newspapers had to temper their tone; editors operated under the spotlight of white supremacy. Nothing could have prevented white southerners from reading the African American periodical in their city. In fact, black journalists were frequently targeted for speaking frankly about race and racial violence. Both Alex Manley, editor of North Carolina's *Wilmington Daily Record*, and Wells, of Memphis's *Free Speech and Headlight*, were popular journalists driven into exile by the threat from white mobs. To avoid having his newspaper offices destroyed and his life threatened, Mitchell had to moderate his outspokenness. But Mitchell was noted not for his moderation but rather for his willingness to provide vocal leadership from the bully pulpit of the *Planet*. His leadership on behalf of the streetcar boycott was just part of his larger campaign to defend black citizenship.

An examination of the *Planet* also reveals that part of Mitchell's racial advocacy was an effort to outline the best course for African Americans to take culturally and socially to advance the race. Yet Mitchell's writing on this subject gets mired in the difficulties of defining the cause of black southerners' political dilemma. He personally had felt the barbs of repression when he and three other black councilmen were pushed out of elective office by Democratic Party fraud and threats during the 1896 election.[33] Mitchell battled with the idea of whether the problems confronting black citizenship were emerging as a response to the pathologies he believed were present in black communities or simply resulted from outside attempts to punish all blacks regardless of class. Such vacillation was emblematic of the frustration of the members of Mitchell's class. Faced with a mounting tide of segregation law, fraud, and disfranchisement, middle-class African Americans asked themselves, should African Americans continue pushing for "progress" while perhaps being punished for the very progress they espoused?

At times, Mitchell clearly stated that black behavior was not the source of African American difficulties but rather that black success had instead posed a fundamental challenge to racial hierarchy in the American South: "It is evident that these discriminating laws are aimed at the intelligent, property owning colored people, because the servant class are welcome from one end of the 'Jim Crow' train to the other. Should the colored servant save his meager earnings, take off the apron of servility and embark in business for himself, he immediately becomes the object of suspicion and is subject to all of the onerous discriminations of caste."[34] Mitchell also aptly pointed out the illogic of segregation law, questioning why the rules changed at every venue: "'Get behind, Mr. Negro' says the Virginia Passenger and Power Company. On the railroad trains, they say, 'Get in front.'"[35] Mitchell highlighted the nature of a nonsensical and unnecessary system that degraded African Americans of every background. But because he had been raised to believe that education, thrift, ingenuity, and moral behavior would enable black Americans to thrive as citizens and find friends among sympathetic whites, he was sometimes harsh in his criticism of blacks who had not or chose not to adopt proper moral and cultural standards.

In a commentary on a *Richmond Times-Dispatch* article calling on cultured and educated blacks to remove uncouth elements from the black community, Mitchell argued that "in the matter of public conveyances which are operated by virtue of a public franchise, there should be no such thing as the establishment of private comforts to the discomfort of any large portion of the public." In a strategic move, Mitchell also agreed with white journalists' efforts to highlight class differences within the African American community. In contrast to Walker's insistence on the importance of the working poor, Mitchell concurred with the idea that "there is always room at the top. . . . In Richmond there are Negro lawyers, Negro doctors, Negro bankers, Negro merchants, Negro teachers, Negro real estate owners, all of whom are making a place for themselves at the top. This simple statement should be enough to stimulate every ambitious Negro to greater exertion."[36]

Mitchell believed that the "Genteel Negro" deserved special treatment and should separate from the common African Americans; blacks who desired success could improve their society by "flocking to themselves, and . . . establishing their rules of culture and morals . . . and serve notice that the low-lived and unclean [Negroes] shall not enter." But Mitchell took this logic a step further, insisting that if segregation should exist, it needed to be instituted along biracial class lines and remove "white jail-birds, penitentiary convicts, dive keepers, white women of questionable character" from respectable society. Poor whites who lacked morality and achievement were just as problematic as poor blacks. In fact, Mitchell often blamed non-aristocratic whites for the advent and enforcement of segregation law. When Mitchell agreed with white authors, he often commented that they were probably "an ex–slave owner or the son of one of the Southern autocrats," highlighting his belief that upper-class whites had no inherent aversion to blacks. Mitchell's mother had been owned by James Lyons, an aristocratic Confederate, and he and his mother continued working for the Lyons family after the close of the Civil War. Mitchell often credited his ties with this elite white family as part of the basis for his postbellum class status as a successful and cultured man. Indeed, Mitchell's concerns with the class status of both blacks and whites seemed to stem from his background in the Lyons household. In contrast with Walker, who blamed elite whites for repressive law, Mitchell always believed that wealthy whites, who had lived closely with black slaves prior to Emancipation, were more comfortable then poor whites with the idea of black citizens in the public sphere.[37]

Mitchell shaped his response to the race problem around his observance of the violations of the color line by white men in relationships with black women. Touching on these sexual politics, Mitchell insisted on "true separation," a divide where "white men . . . living in clandestine relationship with Negro women, degrading white society and assisting God Almighty in obliterating the color-line," receive punishment. He suggested that "a bill be passed making it a felony for white men to associate with colored women and vice versa."[38] Mitchell was always a critic of the faulty logic of southern segregation.

Just as he believed that poor whites were at the forefront in demanding race segregation, Mitchell also believed that poor blacks were a big source of the "race problem." Mitchell's two-handed approach to the fight against segregation is evident in the short editorial notes featured in the *Planet*. These brief quotes in the first column had a political bent and often were comments directly related to the articles on the rest of the page. The quotes were not news, but rather enjoinders directed to black citizens about their political, moral, and social behavior or political criticism aimed at segregationist lawmakers and their policies. The juxtaposition of blame directed at the black community and anger directed at segregationists is a microcosm of Mitchell's divided approach. Disturbed and confused by the passage of new Jim Crow laws—what Mitchell called "the storm of condemnation"— the *Planet* editor wavered between internal judgment of black behavior and external condemnation of the plans of segregationist lawmakers.[39]

In the column, the editor directed his readers to "not be insulting to white people or to colored ones. Let us cultivate true gentility. We will win friends by this." Indeed, Mitchell had benefited from his relationships with whites. His bids for the Richmond City Council beginning in 1890 were backed by white politicians in Virginia's Readjuster Party. Thus, Mitchell's insistence that black Richmonders had white allies was not simply wishful thinking but a testimonial based on his past political alliances with white politicians.

To avoid alienating influential whites who might have spoken on behalf of black citizens, Mitchell warned blacks to "be as polite as possible to white people."[40] He encouraged blacks to teach their children proper manners, believing that courtesy, not public resistance, was the best method of political change. However, Mitchell distinguished between politeness and cowering before white authority; he warned, "Politeness and good behavior do not mean cringing and servility. Don't forget that."[41] Mitchell clearly believed that kind, proper, and dignified behavior could help turn white public opinion about African Americans.

But despite his fear that behavior might precipitate repression, the editor gave constant reminders of African American status under federal law: "We are American citizens and insist upon having all of our rights under the law."[42] Mitchell did not believe that blacks should be so self-sufficient that they would stop asking the federal government to protect their rights in the South. Given his personal political disappointments, however, his expectations of help were low: "We do not tell our people not to look to Washington for relief."[43] Mitchell often argued for universal rights under the law with no prejudice toward any particular class or color: "The Declaration of Independence is a platform of principles, upon which we all should stand regardless of race, politics or religion."[44]

Mitchell presented a picture of black southerners at war for their rights and their reputation: "The guns of persecution are being steadily directed against us and the shrapnel of falsehood and the shells of misrepresentation burst steadily about over our heads." He encouraged his readers to fight this war by maintaining their right to vote, and he reminded readers, "Have you registered? Do so next Tuesday. The polls will be open from sunrise to sunset."[45] But Mitchell was concerned that immoral behavior and black failure to succeed jeopardized African American citizenship. While reiterating that "the law guarantees certain rights and the Negro-haters defy the law," he also suggested that "good behavior will help us wonderfully," encouraging African Americans to put down "the lawless elements in [their] midst." The editor warned that "some white people are great enemies" but added that "some of us are even greater enemies to ourselves." Indeed, at the insistence of election officials who asserted that illiterate African Americans were incapable of interpreting increasingly complex ballots and slowed the lines at black precincts, Mitchell reluctantly went along with plans to profile voters, screening out the badly dressed and those who appeared uneducated.[46]

However, Mitchell was quick to condemn white segregationists who directly threatened the quality of black life and the character of black citizenship. Constant sarcastic reminders of segregationists' mortality filled the columns: "The Negro-haters are here. But thank God the grave-yards are filling up and others more friendly to us are taking their places."[47] He asked readers to "pray to God to provide a separate hell" for John E. Epps, the sponsor of the law requiring train segregation, and his supporters, continuing, "So few of these Negro-haters will reach heaven that it is useless to bother the good Lord about that place."[48] On another occasion he quipped, "Colored folks, these Negro-haters will be dead after a little while, the grave-yard is receiving them right along. This is encouraging."[49]

In contrast to his harsh denunciations of segregationists, Mitchell reminded readers that other whites were willing to defend the rights of worthy blacks: "It is gratifying to come across white friends who sympathize with us in our troubles and wish us God-speed in our endeavors to better our condition."[50] He hoped aloud that the numbers of white anti-segregationists were large; "there are thousands of white people who think well of and know us."[51] Occasionally, Mitchell's proclamation of white advocates of black rights took on a sad tone; the editor seemed to be trying to reassure himself that there were still whites who sought a racial middle ground: "Colored men, do not despair, our white friends are not all dead; neither have they gone on a long journey." He encouraged his readers, "Do not get weary. Do not imagine that all white people are against us. We have thousands of friends who plead our cause whenever the opportunity presents itself."[52]

Mitchell constantly warned his readers to be thrifty and to engage in business because "a penniless race of people cannot command respect."[53] Arguing that blacks could somehow use their behavior to sway whites into respecting black citizenship, Mitchell suggested that his readers should "merit the confidence of the white people by good conduct," perhaps by keeping "tidy" and saving "at least a portion of [their] earnings."[54] Perhaps Mitchell's status as a self-made son of slaves led him to believe that all African Americans could achieve greater success if they made the effort. Mitchell fervently advocated black self-help and often encouraged readers to work harder, save more money, and start businesses of their own. He believed "one thrifty colored citizen is worth a thousand indolent ones."[55]

Mitchell's editorial notes expressed a great deal of anger toward blacks who lacked the will for self-improvement: "Colored men, we must afford no encouragement to the low disrespectful elements among us." Sounding almost like a segregationist, Mitchell went so far as to say, "They should be sent to the rear and kept there. They retard our progress and hinder our onward march to material prosperity."[56] "The disreputable insulting, lazy, 'no count' element amongst us must be made to understand that they retard our progress as a race and would be more service to us under ground than they are above it. Let them improve themselves and help us."[57] Couched in a language of "us" versus "them," Mitchell cited "the turbulent, low-bred classes" as one of African Americans' "greatest drawbacks." Borrowing the language of colonialism, Mitchell asserted, "We must do missionary work to the extent of showing them that they injure not only us but themselves as well." In contrast to Walker's identification with the working poor,

Mitchell had little patience for African Americans who failed to meet his standards of behavior.

But Mitchell's editorial proclamations also included encouragement for blacks who had achieved some measure of success. He told readers, "We have succeeded to a remarkable extent and even the Negro-haters can see it."[58] Overall, Mitchell believed that blacks should not be discouraged from their efforts at uplift: "It is no use to stop and complain. Keep on working while expressing your disapproval of conditions which obtain." He urged his fellow black southerners, "Let us not be disheartened, but press onward doing the best we can, and meriting the good will and esteem of our white friends."[59] Sometimes discouraged but always hopeful, Mitchell believed that if the leading class of African Americans was "manly and courageous, politic and God-fearing," they would "win in the end."

Walker and Mitchell shared the belief that segregation fundamentally threatened black citizenship. The two risked their status in the community to serve as willing and vocal leaders in the streetcar boycotts. But leadership included governing the terms of protest, offering advice not only on tactics but also on protesters' demeanor and behavior. Throughout this era, African American leaders often sought to guide a diverse community toward standards of cultural, social, and political behavior in hopes of proving black citizens' worthiness to the nation. Richmond's burgeoning black middle class had mixed feelings about the black poor, simultaneously protecting and chiding them as the objects of social uplift and the targets of charges of "loafing" and "ill-mannered" behavior. While progressive reformers such as Walker worked diligently to provide a safety net for the black poor, especially women, some within the black middle class seemed to resent the inappropriate behavior of some of the black working class. Mitchell constantly spoke from both sides of the spectrum, one day stating that "unacceptable" behavior, lawlessness, laziness, and ignorance were the root cause of repression aimed at African Americans and on the next day castigating white segregationists for their blanket attacks on black citizenship. Mitchell clung to the hope that changes in black behavior would lead to changes in state policy. The black middle class despaired at the notion that even the best among them would be rejected by white society as unacceptable and uncivilized. It may have been too difficult to consider that second-class citizenship for African American southerners was inevitable no matter what they did.[60]

Despite the effort to uplift the African American community, the tide of segregation rose even higher, leaving the middle class to question whether

African Americans could ever prove themselves worthy in the eyes of segregationists. African Americans' struggles to create distinct cultural, social, and political strategies illuminate the ways in which they defined themselves and others during a difficult period. However, both Richmond's working poor and its rising elite found a place in the protest against Jim Crow streetcars.

6 NEGROES EVERYWHERE ARE WALKING

Work, Women, and the Richmond Streetcar Boycott

Texas and Virginia have been added to the list of "Jim Crow" street carism.
Well boys, swallow the pill manfully. Don't begin crying, but walk. Negroes
everywhere are walking.—"Walking Everywhere," *Fort Smith Arkansas
Appreciator*, reprinted in *Richmond Planet*, 30 April 1904

At the turn of the twentieth century, most black residents of Richmond,
Virginia, were working class. African American men helped to maintain
their households by working as day laborers, loading on the city's docks,
hauling goods to and from its marketplaces, working in the tobacco factories, or serving white patrons in hotels and businesses. Although some
working black women found limited opportunities in the city's factories,
most, both young and old, were employed as housekeepers or nurses in
white homes or more independently as laundresses for a variety of customers throughout the city. Each morning thousands of working class
black Richmonders set out for their places of employment. People of all
walks of life traveled to work on the city's streetcar system.

Richmond was home to the first electric streetcar system in the United
States, with forty cars operating under the authority of the Richmond
Union Passenger Railroad in 1888. Short-track electric streetcar experi-
ments had taken place in Montgomery, Alabama, and South Bend, Indiana,
but Richmond was the home of the first fully functioning commuter system.[1] By the turn of the century, the street rail system had been expanded,
with tracks crisscrossing Richmond.[2] Streetcars symbolized the power and

prestige of corporate investment in the growing southern city. The cars served all sectors of society, providing access to all city wards, including the majority black Jackson Ward, with routes running past the city's shopping districts and marketplaces as well as past black churches and places of business. The streetcars made Richmond's historic seven hills easier to travel and allowed the city to expand geographically. Black residents of older neighborhoods could commute to work in distant areas of the city, and the black middle class could seek newly built housing outside of the city center.[3] Blacks of all classes enjoyed the benefits of the system, but the streetcar particularly allowed working-class passengers to conserve energy before hours of arduous labor, provided a rest after a hard day's work, and expanded opportunities to find work in neighborhoods across the city. For black women carrying the burdens of their labor and households, a seat on the streetcar brought a needed rest from toting groceries in their hands and laundry on top of their heads. Black men who worked as hackmen, peddlers, and teamsters on Franklin Street in Jefferson Ward could, for a small price, find a quick journey home. The cars provided a great deal of convenience at minimal cost.

Black laborers laid the streetcar tracks just prior to the turn of the century. These same black men who worked to pull up the city's cobblestones in order to lay the new tracks could pay their fare and chose any seat on any of the city's streetcars because of the victory of Reconstruction-era blacks over Jim Crow policies.[4] So although formal and informal racial segregation governed where black Richmonders could reside and find lodging, entertainment, and employment, the stain of segregation did not mark the city's streetcars.

For working-class African Americans, rides on the city's streetcars were one of the few spaces in which they sat on relatively equal footing with white Richmonders and elite blacks. Although the heavy hand of southern racial etiquette shaped nearly every public interaction, riders of all classes and races paid the same fare and could sit anywhere on the streetcar or stand in the aisle. This is not to suggest that streetcars were spaces in which racial hierarchies were undone; there is no record of streetcar drivers pausing to help black women with burdens to board or white men standing up so black women could take their seats. However, history suggests that these relatively equitable rides were meaningful to working-class black Richmonders. Their status on the streetcars was indeed so important that they were willing to sacrifice convenience in the fight to maintain the dignity worthy of all first-class citizens.

IN 1900, RICHMOND was the fifth-largest southern city, with a total population of 85,050 and a black population of 32,230 (38 percent), the fourth-largest black community in the urban South. Blacks were not the majority of Richmonders, but they exercised a degree of political and economic autonomy. Black Richmonders grew politically stronger as the majority in Jackson Ward; although it had been originally conceived as a way to contain and stilt black influence, the Ward became the heart of Richmond's black community and the epicenter of black political organizing in the city. Nearly half of the city's black residents lived in Jackson Ward; in fact the rates of residence may have been underestimated at 15,592.[5]

Black residents from all over the city took pride in Jackson Ward, with its record of electing black city councilmen and its fledgling banks, newspapers, and small businesses. After the close of Reconstruction, Richmond's black electorate was particularly vulnerable, but the residents of Jackson Ward continued to vote despite fraud and informal efforts to disfranchise them. Black voters faced a direct attack after former Conservative-Democratic Party members united around the platform of stopping "Negro Domination." In 1902, they sponsored the passage of a new state constitution that dramatically cut the size of the electorate, both black and white. In the wake of this political manipulation, only 21,000 of the 147,000 black men of voting age in the state remained registered. Jackson Ward was dissolved as a voting district as a consequence of gerrymandering by Richmond's Council Committee on Ordinances in the summer of 1903. The passage of a poll tax designed to target poor and working-class black voters delivered a final blow, and by 1905, the number of African American voters in Virginia had been reduced by half.[6]

Despite this explicit attack on black political engagement, the community of Jackson Ward was still socially and politically meaningful to black residents, and most African Americans continued to refer to the community as Jackson Ward long after no such place could be found on a map.[7] Jackson Ward remained a center of black organization and identity, and its institutions continued to provide black voters with a way to resist efforts to strip them of the franchise and tried their best to remain engaged citizens.

Virginia Passenger and Power's spring 1904 decision to segregate the streetcars that cut through the streets of the largest black community added insult to injury. Despite the growth of a literate and successful black community, African Americans were rejected as voters in favor of white supremacy. The effort to humiliate paying customers simply because they were African American went too far. Many black Richmonders were self-reliant and proud despite the devastating political defeats of the past decade. The majority of Richmond's black community spoke back, boycotting the company that sought to render them second class in their own neighborhood.

SINCE THE ERA OF Reconstruction, black Richmonders from all segments of the African American community had fought Jim Crow restrictions on the city streetcars. Richmond's horse-drawn streetcars, owned by the Richmond Railway Company, initially refused to carry black riders in 1865. The company eventually relented somewhat and allowed black riders on the hazardous running boards. By custom, black nurses tending to white children were allowed to sit inside segregated cars. But Black Richmonders soon tired of second-class conditions, and in 1867, led by black militiamen, they staged sit-ins on public streetcars. Like their counterparts in New Orleans, Charleston, Mobile, Savannah, Nashville, and Baltimore, black streetcar riders in Richmond staged dramatic spontaneous protests.[8] Emboldened by the presence of the local Lincoln Mounted Guard, Richmond's black streetcar passengers sought to force the Richmond Railway Company to recognize their right to equal accommodations. African Americans, usually militia members, would pay their fare and then quickly sit down in seats designated for white riders. When the conductors stopped the streetcars to remove the black passengers and have them arrested, blacks riding on the running boards and passing on the streets rushed to protect the black riders, shouting that they had the right to ride in integrated cars. Through these impromptu sit-ins and mass meetings, blacks demanded that their federally protected rights be enforced. The fight against segregated facilities continued for three years and resulted in the desegregation of Richmond's public streetcars.[9]

Although the federal court in Richmond ruled in favor of the legality of transportation segregation in 1876, clamor on the part of white citizens in favor of segregated trains and streetcars did not begin in earnest until the 1890s. Segregationists, who worried how restrictive laws might be perceived outside of the South, were emboldened by the U.S. Supreme Court's 1899 decision in *Louisville, New Orleans, and Texas R.R. v. Mississippi*. The federal court's implicit endorsement of segregation reawakened efforts at segregation throughout the South. In 1891, the white segregationist Democrats of Richmond's Powhatan Club began to push for segregation on the streetcars while fighting to oust black teachers from black schools in an attempt to undercut not only black rights but also Richmond's African American professional class. Train service was segregated first. Sensational news reports fueled renewed calls for race separation. In the winter of 1899, the story of a "dirty, intoxicated negro" sitting next to a white woman caused outrage. Then Virginia governor J. Hoge Tyler's fanciful account of riding in a sleeping car with "a Negro opposite him, above him, and in front of him," was the final straw. The governor supported a bill, sponsored by segregationist legislator John E. Epps, requiring Jim Crow on Virginia trains and steamboats. The bill passed unanimously, becoming state law on 25 January 1900.[10]

Virginia did not break new legal ground. The brief law fined companies and employees if they failed to enforce a policy of separate but equal and contained exceptions for black nurses and white officials in charge of black prisoners. The law did not give police powers to conductors, nor did it give them complete discretion over where to seat passengers.[11] The law carefully asserted that the separate accommodations had to be equal accommodations. Virginia blacks' protests against train segregation would be difficult in the wake of Homer Plessy's failed case, which called for equal but racially separate facilities on Louisiana's trains. Legislators had taken great care to adhere to the federal precedent, making sure that the text of the Virginia statute stipulated that accommodations be equal as well as separate.

The offensive law drew widespread attention from black Virginians. John Mitchell Jr. reported in the *Richmond Planet* that the law would force insulted blacks to respond and would "humiliate" blacks and "awaken a spirit of antagonism which increases as the objectionable features of the requirement are enforced." Blacks would not accept the "dangerous doctrine" without a fight.[12] In July 1900, the *Planet* announced that to avoid humiliation, blacks would refuse to ride the trains. Although cars for black riders were running, "few colored people could be seen occupying a whole car." Mitchell believed that Richmond's blacks would maintain their pride with the attitude, "If you do not desire my company, I can assure you that I have no wish for yours."[13]

However, difficulties of mounting effective collective protests on trains coupled with black Richmond's precarious political future derailed efforts to protest the 1900 law. Seeking to regain the political losses in Richmond caused by fraud in 1896, the black voters of Jackson Ward sponsored black city council candidates in the fall of 1900. Intimidation and fraud again derailed their campaign. Thwarted by an illegal local election and statewide efforts at black disfranchisement, black leaders were forced to put their energies behind fighting the "unconstitutional 'constitutional' convention" organized to eliminate the black vote. Unable to fight both battles at once, they had to "yield an unwilling acquiescence to the law" and accept the segregation of railroads. Richmond blacks swallowed the bitter pill of segregated trains but did not take the insult to heart as the essence of their condition. Mitchell wrote, "It is unfortunate, but a people who withstood 250 years of galling slavery, four years of bitter war and thirty years of so-called liberty will not die or get out of breath because a few Negro-haters choose to force the railroad companies to haul them as quarantined patients suffering with the smallpox."[14]

Future attempts to segregate black Richmonders were met with more than words. In 1900, a proposal to segregate streetcars put forward by the all-white Richmond City Council was thwarted by the protests of the Constitutional Rights Association, a group of black Richmonders led by lawyer Giles Jackson, one of the unsuccessful candidates for the council.[15] Born in 1852, Jackson was a decade older than Mitchell, with whom he was often extremely competitive, and was a longtime member of the Republican Party as well as a leader in the Grand Fountain of the United Order of True Reformers and a national spokesperson for Booker T. Washington's National Negro Business League. Jackson's Constitutional Rights Association sought to bring suits to test the constitutionality of Virginia's separate car law as well as the grandfather clause, which allowed most white men to avoid the laws that blocked black voter registration. Although a lack of financial resources stymied the association's efforts to lodge federal suits, it did, in Washingtonian style, negotiate a private compromise in which the Richmond City Council agreed to "an indefinite postponement of the . . . ordinance."[16]

For more than twenty-five years, through sit-ins, mass meetings, petitions, and political appeals, black Richmonders had successfully fought off legal attempts to segregate the city's streetcars. In the early spring of 1904, when state lawmakers enacted a law segregating the streetcars, black Richmond therefore hoped to prevent its implementation. But this new law was part of the segregationist tide that swept the South. Richmond was at a dismal juncture in American racial politics. African Americans' newly championed rights were threatened by repression and diminished by compromise. Mob violence threatened blacks throughout the state, with sixty-two African Americans lynched in Virginia between 1880 and 1909.[17] In addition to disfranchisement, threats to black education and the federal endorsement of racial segregation also wore away at black rights. But it was also an era when many blacks felt compelled to choose between conservative opportunities for economic advancement and a principled defense of their political rights. The residents of the city of Richmond faced the same bleak choices. However, by launching a boycott—what Mitchell often called an attack on the streetcar company's "pocket nerve"—Richmonders combined their growing economic strength with their campaign for full citizenship.

By 1904, the Virginia Code had been amended to segregate street railways in addition to trains and steamboats. The exhaustive nature of the text of the law made effective black dissent virtually impossible. The flexible new statute did not legally require segregation but instead "authorized and empowered" streetcar companies to change corporate policies and begin separating black and white passengers at their own discretion. Mitchell was angered that the Virginia Passenger and Power Company chose to enforce a voluntary law and decried the separation of the races when no conflicts had occurred on the city's streetcars. In a fight that symbolized their citizenship as a whole, black Richmonders of all walks of life decided to value their dignity and citizenship rights over comfort.[18]

ON 9 APRIL 1904, news of the boycott first appeared in the pages of the *Planet*. The story did not carry a large or flamboyant headline, but Mitchell was outraged. The editor believed that there was no reason for the streetcar company to begin enforcing a voluntary segregation law when no obvious racial tension had existed. Mitchell explained that he did "not know a place where there is less friction on the street-cars than in this city."[19] Mitchell would have accepted loud, rude, or unruly black behavior as a valid reason for white segregationists to divide the races. But he was uncomfortable with the idea that race alone could have precipitated the passage of this repressive law.

In response to Virginia Passenger and Power's new policy, Mitchell warned African Americans to "stay off the street cars" and encouraged them to use their "big feet" to put economic pressure on the company. Other prominent business and fraternal leaders called for protest, among them W. L. Taylor, president of the savings bank founded by the Grand United Order of True Reformers; R. T. Hill, the president of the Nickel Savings Bank; and Maggie Lena Walker, president of the St. Luke Penny Savings Bank. Mitchell believed that a boycott was the best way for blacks to express their grievances and cause "agony produced on the white man's nerve center, which is his pocket." But he warned protesters not to ride and complain: "We hope that our people will comply with the rule of law, if they ride on the streetcars. To get on there and 'jaw' at the conductors will afford some satisfaction, but it will not pay in the long run or the short one either." Mitchell believed that the segregation statute was designed to make black riders angry and thus appear lawless: "The evident intention of the Negro-haters is to foster bad-feeling between the races and to force the colored people to commit some overt act which will be used as argument to prove that their desire and purpose is to over-ride the law."[20] Thousands of black Richmonders heeded Mitchell's call, many of them wearing buttons "bearing the inscription, 'I will walk.'"[21]

Concerned not only with participation but behavior, boycott leaders encouraged lawful actions on the part of participants, in part because of fears that a race riot would be precipitated by angry black riders confronting conductors and white passengers or angry whites trying to oust resistant blacks from streetcars. Calls to stay off the streetcars were often coupled with advice about gentility and decorum. Boycott leaders discouraged backtalk and street arguments and urged boycotters to resist silently. Improper behavior, leaders believed, would derail their protest.

Instructing black Richmond to "show to this corporation that independence and liberty are sweet and the day of the time-server is past," Mitchell argued that despite the recent blows to black citizenship, the boycott would reaffirm their status as a liberated people. Because the protest was invested with these important symbolic dimensions, the editor was deeply concerned with participants' conduct. To Mitchell, African Americans' behavior would be a direct reflection of their image in the public eye: "Conduct yourselves, colored people, as becomes a well-bred, but long-suffering people." Adherence to this code of conduct would be just as important to the success of the boycott as the full participation of black streetcar patrons. Mitchell needed all segments of black society, not just the middle class, so that the protests would have a meaningful effect. As all of black Richmond participated, Mitchell would continue to remind readers about appropriate conduct and reaffirmed the importance of dignified, nonconfrontational comportment.[22]

Indeed, all segments of the city's large black population joined the protest. Walking up and down Richmond's steep grades, working-class women toted their employers' laundry and groceries, which they previously had been able to rest in the aisles of the streetcars. Middle-class black women in refined clothes on their way to teach or work as clerks also gathered their skirts and took on Richmond's hills. Black men who depended on the streetcar to travel to work caught rides, and it became "a common thing to see wagons on their way down town carrying three to six laboring men free of charge." The boycott was so effective that it left the once-bustling Clay

Street line, which usually carried "a packed crowd of colored people" to work from Jackson Ward, appearing as if "the colored population had left the city."[23] Mitchell refused to ride the segregated conveyances that passed directly in front of the *Richmond Planet* office on Broad Street, walking even when he was carrying luggage. Although African Americans had grown accustomed to the convenience of using the streetcar system for short-distance travel, they refused to be herded to the back like second-class citizens.

The protest of black Richmonders garnered praise from black advocates across the country. In *Voice of the Negro*, J. Max Barber reported to thousands of readers that "in Richmond the Negroes are walking. It looks rather strange to see great crowds of colored people walking all the way to Church Hill or Manchester from the Western part of Richmond on Sunday mornings when the sun seems to shine particularly hot; but the colored people would rather do that than compromise their self respect."[24] Letters from places as far off as Chicago; Mt. Vernon, New York; and rural Texas arrived in support of the city's "walking Negroes." Blacks across the South were inspired to take action; as one black newspaper editor suggested to his readers, "Don't begin crying, but walk. Negroes everywhere are walking."[25]

The boycott's initial success suggests that black Richmond's communication networks effectively disseminated news about the segregation law. The participation in the boycott was supported by the *Planet* and six other local black newspapers. However, the boycott network went beyond the press to include the local grapevine of churches, clubs, and fraternal orders. These organizations helped to supplement the press, leaving the streetcars empty.[26]

Blacks remembered or shared a collective memory about the protests blacks held in response to their exclusion from the Richmond Railway Company in 1867. The direct confrontations black Richmonders had staged almost forty years earlier were not the conservative expressions of displeasure turn-of-the-century black leaders would have supported. Working-class black Richmonders may have had a different inclination than their leaders, seeking to adopt tactics that had succeeded in the past. The rigorous effort to police protester behavior hints at the tension that may have existed between those who promoted politely abstaining from riding on segregated streetcars and those who would have boarded streetcars with the intention of breaking the rules.

Throughout the protest, middle-class black leaders' desire to maintain an "outspoken, but conservative" protest was reaffirmed. Stressing that if "some thoughtless colored man" became "involved in an altercation," "it would be the same as touching a match to a powder magazine," Mitchell reminded the attendees at a mass meeting that he believed "the evident intention of the regulation was to goad the colored people into resistance, and to cause them to commit some overt act which would be construed into a disposition on their part to over-ride the law." Mitchell reaffirmed his belief that the conductors were white men of the lowest class, asserting that the streetcar company "secured anyone it could at the low rate of wages it was paying." In Mitchell's eyes conductors were poor whites, who he believed were the source of the kind of race hatred fueling Jim Crow segregation.[27]

Black leaders around the country offered similar advice about behavior. The national leader of the black Knights of Pythias, Robert R. Jackson, wrote in support of the Richmond boycott. He commended the "the manly stand upon the part of the citizens of the city" and encouraged the boycotters to "walk until Judgment Day." Jackson also suggested that black Richmonders "establish bus and car lines" and pledged that his group would purchase one hundred dollars worth of stock in any independent transportation line black Richmonders might seek to establish. Unlike the attempts to organize black-owned streetcar companies in Jacksonville in 1901, New Orleans in 1902, and Nashville in 1905, black Richmonders put most of their energies behind the boycott and relied on hack drivers to transport boycotters. Also, like the boycott leadership, Jackson encouraged black Richmonders to behave according to strict standards and to avoid acting with "brutality, murder, coercion and conflagration"; rather, they should behave "like the good citizens we have been for forty years."[28]

Beyond concerns about African Americans' comportment, Mitchell and the boycott leaders may have feared a race riot. Full-scale confrontations between white and black Richmonders were not common, with the worst such conflicts having taken place during the Reconstruction era.[29] A race riot fueled by angry black passengers and armed white conductors on Richmond's streetcars could have easily been sparked. The fears of Richmond's boycott leaders were not unfounded; black passengers were targeted on New Orleans streetcars during the riot of 1900, and confrontations between black passengers and white streetcar conductors also took place in the months prior to and during the Atlanta race riot. Richmond's boycott leaders feared the violence, criminal prosecution, and economic destabilization that would have come in the wake of a riot in their city and sought to avert violence at all cost.[30]

As much as they tried to police behavior, the boycott leaders were willing to risk their status for the protest. Not all of black Richmond's "leading class" supported the boycott. A group of community leaders—notably, Giles Jackson; the Reverend W. P. Burrell, from the Committee of the Baptist Sunday School Union of Richmond and the general secretary of the United Order of True Reformers; and representatives of the Committee of the Baptist Ministers Conference, which represented "the pastors of three fourths of the Negro churches of Richmond"—met privately with Virginia Passenger and Power Company. Burrell had written to Virginia Passenger and Power to request that law not be "used to discriminate" against black passengers by treating them rudely or refusing to provide them space. However, Burrell's letter was conciliatory and did not directly challenge the segregation of the cars; he insisted that black Richmonders would "make no kick on the law if properly administered." During the private meeting, company officials assured these leaders that segregation would be "used kindly, discretely, and with as little unnecessary inconvenience" as possible. Virginia Passenger and Power president Fritz Sitterding and general manager S. W. Huff promised the African American delegation that segregation would be enforced with "perfect fairness and courteous consideration" and urged these secular and spiritual leaders to provide their "kindly assistance in the way of explanation and good advice." Although the leaders insisted that they did not approve of the segregation law, their silence and inaction was just as good as an endorsement.[31]

The race-baiting *Richmond News Leader* seemed to enjoy the rift, characterizing the ministers as conservative, the boycott leaders as promoting "social equality," and black Richmonders as too lazy and stupid to protest. Despite evidence to the contrary, the *News Leader* asserted that the ministers' do-nothing approach was the most popular and that the boycott was a failure. Reporting in format reminiscent of a "darky story," the *News Leader* claimed that when one unnamed black pedestrian discovered, after a "cold," "hard" walk, that other blacks were riding in the streetcars, he exclaimed, "Look hy'ah . . . is I de only fool nigger is gwine tuh monopolize dis street cyar line?" In "Aunt Jemimy's Point of View," the *News Leader* suggested that black residents should simply accept the change: "A pin-prick 'll grow intuh a sho-nuff mis'ry ef you keep on a-complainin' uv hit." Richmond's segregationists hoped that the rift would weaken the boycott, bringing the protest to a quick end.[32]

The pact of nonresistance between the streetcar company and the dissenting group led to divisions among the city's black churches and organizations. Jackson, who in 1900 had led the efforts to prevent the city council from segregating the cars, split with members of his own organization, such as Dr. R. E. Jones, president of the Richmond chapter of the National Negro Business League, to side with the boycott opposition. Dissatisfied with conditions on segregated cars, Burrell too subsequently broke with the dissenting group and joined the boycott organization, using his organization's weekly *Richmond Reformer* to publicize boycott efforts. W. T. Johnson, Mitchell, and Maggie Lena Walker's minister at First Baptist Church remained silent about the protest; indeed, the First Baptist Church records make no mention of either financial or moral support for the boycott. Walker kept a copy of the private agreement between the leaders and company officials in her papers. Walker did not keep active journals or political correspondence during the duration of the boycott, no other document recounting the protest was preserved in her papers, so the presence of this document hints at her disappointment in her pastor. Despite what historians since August Meier and Elliot Rudwick have characterized as the conservative tone of the protest, Walker, Mitchell, and the other leaders of the boycott led a controversial movement that did not enjoy universal support among Richmond's most prominent African American leaders.

Even in the face of the silent condemnation of some church and business leaders, many of the people of Richmond believed in the boycott. On the occasion of their monthly meetings in May and June 1904, the more than three thousand members of the colored Baptist Sunday School Union took to the streets, marching to the First African Baptist Church in May and to the Ebenezer Baptist Church in June. They carried no banners or placards on either occasion, but their support for the boycott was clear and consistent. After the marchers made their way to each of the monthly gatherings, the ministers who spoke made no mention of the protest. The members of the Union, young and old, who represented the most elite and the most humble African American Baptist churches in the city, marched to show their support for the boycott, making a public break with the ministers at the head of their organization. Although their demonstrations were not as grand as the parades held annually to celebrate Emancipation Day, the Sunday School Union's monthly protest march was also an expression of freedom, an endorsement of a movement that already had the support of people from all walks of life, and a signal that when official leadership failed, the people could lead themselves. When each of the meetings ended, all three thousand walked home.[33]

Mitchell's *Planet* provided ongoing updates on the status of the boycott, seeking to encourage boycott participants, pressure officials at the streetcar company, and win over black Richmonders who still used the streetcars. In one article, Mitchell mentioned the general manager of Virginia Passenger and Power by name, arguing "that General Manager S. F. Huff is the only person who stands between a restoration of the former conditions and the present unsatisfactory condition." The same article carefully pointed out that boycott participants should not ostracize any African Americans who failed to adhere to the boycott; however, Mitchell was quick to dismiss any blacks who did experience arrest or poor treatment while riding on the streetcar as persons who should have known better. Mitchell had little sympathy for black riders who violated the boycott and subjected themselves to the barbs of legal segregation. Mitchell used the newspaper to laud the progress of the boycott. He declared that "the 'Jim Crow' streetcar system here has proven anything but a success and the cars are studiously avoided by the colored people." The editor also reminded participants of the importance of their struggle. If passengers calmly avoided the cars, their patience and control would be rewarded: "The colored people have certainly conducted themselves in a manner befitting a long-suffering, humble, but patriotic people."[34]

The only resistance demonstrated on cars themselves came from white passengers who were unwilling to move in accordance with the conductor's orders. The *Richmond Times-Dispatch* reported that a white passenger and conductor got into a fistfight when the conductor asked the passenger to "move forward." The confrontation started in the city and continued out into the county, near Thirty-second and Q Streets. Some white Richmonders resented the effort to separate black and white passengers on nearly empty cars, while others objected to the inconvenience. Mitchell enjoyed chronicling the confrontations between white passengers and conductors, pointing out that segregation laws were uncomfortable for whites and blacks alike.[35]

The boycott of Richmond's streetcars weathered the summer of 1904. Mitchell reported that "colored laborers are walking and the drays, produce and delivery wagons haul quite a number down town free of charge." Richmond's roughly nine hundred black hackmen became the city's most important workingmen during the boycott, offering alternative transportation for those displaced by the boycott. Without the aid of an organized taxi service or the help of a black streetcar line, black workers traveled to and from work with the help of black wagon drivers. The time and effort black drivers committed to aiding workers with rides to their jobs was clearly a sacrifice. In the day-to-day staging of an effective boycott, the risks hack drivers braved were essential to the boycott's initial success. The aid and leadership of working-class men who gave rides and shared information meant as much to the ongoing boycott as official resolutions. The unique mobility afforded the black transportation workers allowed them to make adherence to the boycott less arduous for the participants.[36]

Life for Richmond's working-class African Americans was precarious, and the boycott could not have made the situation any easier. Employers may have targeted and punished workers who arrived at their jobs late or exhausted.

Many of the city's white leaders did not welcome the black working poor. Local tobacco entrepreneur L. B. Vaughan wrote to the *Richmond Planet* to inform black readers of his belief that "the country Negro is making more rapid progress in the acquisition of property than the city Negro" and that in rural settings, the black would have the opportunity to "work his own farm, of which no fair-minded man must complain." Vaughan closed his letter with the suggestion, "Don't worry about the franchise, avoid politics, make yourselves worthy of the high privilege to vote. . . . [L]ook well to this and all will be well."[37] Like Vaughan, many southern white leaders believed that the natural place for southern blacks to labor and become worthy of full citizenship was a rural agricultural setting.

Even though working-class African Americans provided the labor essential to the Richmond's economic health, the city's white leaders did not make life easy for the black working poor. Some of Richmond's workers lived in miserable conditions. The poorest urban blacks often resided in parts of the city that received the brunt of pollution from riverfront factories, lacked clean water or proper sewage, and received little public funding for improvements. But through participation in labor organizations and community organizations such as Walker's Independent Order of Saint Luke, poor black Richmonders improved their working and living conditions. The members of Richmond's African American working class battled hard to reshape their communities by contributing to the growth of their schools and churches.[38] Their participation in the streetcar boycotts should be understood as an extension of efforts to affirm their place and to demonstrate their right to dignity, comfort, and respect.

Working-class black women were some of the most visible and willing participants in the boycott. The *Planet* regularly cited working women's sacrifices in support of the boycott. On one occasion, "A colored woman walked from Fulton up to 24th and Leigh streets and then went back again"—more than twenty city blocks up and down a steep grade. In another instance, Mitchell sarcastically reported, "One colored female weighing approximately two hundred pounds has been walking from up-town to Church-Hill although she has been unfit for service when she reached her place of employment."[39] By highlighting working women, Mitchell demonstrated the ways that they led with their feet and provided examples for a local and national audience.

Like the wagon drivers, female boycotters faced resistance from white employers. A cook charged with delivering dinner to her boss wanted to walk rather than ride. Her employer, however, insisted that she would have to ride the streetcar, telling her, "Your time belongs to me. You bring [dinner] on the car." The cook delivered the meal quickly by riding the streetcar and then disembarked when she thought she was out of sight.[40] Cooks like this woman would have been responsible for household tasks such as delivering meals and traveling to the market to purchase food.[41] Even when employers may have objected to their employees' participation in the boycott, black laborers found creative ways to adapt their practical responsibilities to their political goals. Resistance to Jim Crow law was a common sentiment among the black working class; after Maryland state representative William G. Kerbin sponsored Jim Crow legislation, his cook and laundress lodged a two-woman boycott, refusing to continue working for him.[42] Even when participation involved personal risk and complex negotiations, working black women demonstrated that members of all social classes felt that the fight against segregation was essential not only to their dignity but also to the preservation of their citizenship.

The occupations in which most working-class black women engaged required both carrying burdens and moving frequently in the city. Of the 8,213 black women and girls over age ten who worked in Richmond in 1900, 6,319 (77 percent) worked as laundresses or household servants. Black women overwhelmingly dominated the field of domestic work. The census of 1900 listed only 25 white laundresses and 187 white female servants and waitresses.[43] The labor of black women domestic workers and laundresses was in high demand.

Work as a laundress required the difficult task of moving bundles of heavy clothes of customers from their homes to the homes of the laundry women. As historian of working-class black women Tera Hunter has pointed out, "The sight of 'tall, straight Negro girls marching through the street carrying enormous bundles of soiled clothes upon their heads' was common every week." Although they made very little money for their hard work, laundresses enjoyed the autonomy of working in groups in their own communities, away from the supervision of white customers.[44] Affordable streetcar travel made the work of Richmond's laundresses less difficult and perhaps allowed them to generate more income as they could handle more customers from a broader area. The streetcar enabled laundresses to increase the volume of customers they handled, take in laundry from broader areas such as white suburbs, and pick up and deliver more quickly and efficiently. Boycotting the streetcars must have been a serious sacrifice.

Even if Richmond was a walking city, women had burdens to carry such as laundry, food for sale, and perishable groceries that had to be purchased frequently. Richmond historians Elsa Barkley Brown and Gregg Kimball have argued that "except for the relatively small number of men engaged in trades like huckstering, the black Richmonders who may have had the widest gaze on the city were women, those thousands who worked as laundresses or domestic servants, and who, by virtue of their employment, had to traverse and were seen as 'belonging in' the widest range of spaces." Brown and Kimball thus question the concept that household labor occurred in the private sphere and that the streets belonged to a male public.[45] In this framework, black working-class women made the greatest sacrifices to participate in the boycotts, and without their active participation, no boycott could succeed.

Large numbers of working-class black women participated in the boycott. Even as historians have characterized the fight for equal treatment on streetcars as a middle-class desire for ladylike treatment, the history of working women in Richmond reminds us that working-class women also sought the dignity, respect, and equity of first-class treatment.[46] Even the vast majority of middle-class black women who could not afford to hire servants had to tote groceries and carry the bolts of fabric and other goods necessary to maintain their households. Mass support for the boycott had to originate with women of all backgrounds.

The black women also stood at the rhetorical epicenter of the fight against the segregation of streetcars. White Richmonders insisted that blacks were too savage, untutored, and dirty to sit among white passengers and that to protect white passengers, especially vulnerable white women, strictly enforced codes of segregation were necessary to prevent the mixture of the races. This argument implied that black men, who supposedly had a propensity for raping white women, had to be physically cordoned off from white women. These arguments that the "social equality" of black men would endanger white women were akin to the claims of white southern lynch mobs and angered both black men and black women.

Debating the terms of segregation also entailed arguing for black men's right to protect black women. A supporter of the boycott applauded the "manliness of the black men of Virginia, in the stand that they have taken."[47] Flipping the rhetoric of the day on its head, black men increasingly argued that segregation and its accompanying climate of everyday violence threatened their ability to protect black women. Aptly pointing to the history of white men's sexual violation of black women and the contemporary threat of lynching, black men and women argued for the need to protect black women as vigorously as white men sought to protect white women. Walker agreed with the belief that black men should defend the honor of black women but also argued that black women had a role in the fight for their own honor, encouraging all to stand against "the degradation of Negro manhood and Negro womanhood."[48] The political dynamics of gender did not alienate black women's participatory leadership; rather, it helped to make them some of the most important participants in the daily battle against the streetcars.

Women also dramatized the politics of skin color within the African American community. Describing white conductors' difficulty in distinguishing white people from light-skinned people of color, the *Planet* reported that "several white colored folks have been forced to ride with the white folks, the conductors having ordered them to ride there." Tapping into the myth of the tragic mulatto, Mitchell recounted a case of color confusion: a Virginia Passenger and Power streetcar stopped for "to all appearances what was a white woman, neatly attired in a black skirt, white shirt-waist and black hat carrying a white sun parasol with black ribbons and a black shopping bag." The streetcar conductor quickly offered his assistance to help the woman board and directed her to a front seat, to which the woman replied, "No, thank you sir, I am colored." The conductor dropped her arm and quickly moved away.[49] This woman and others light enough to pass may have enjoyed secretly sitting with white riders, silently challenging the flawed reasoning of segregation. As had been the case in New Orleans, some light-skinned blacks who could pass did not mind the benefits of white-skinned privilege, gaining individual inclusion under segregated circumstances. But the majority of African Americans of all colors were loyal to the boycott.

The absence of black passengers helped to push the already financially insecure Virginia Passenger and Power Company into receivership in the fall of 1904. When the company defaulted, Mitchell believed that victory was sure, declaring, "The colored people have maintained their self-respect and have stayed off the street-cars even when it seemed that human nature could stand no more." According to Mitchell, "As soon as the objectionable signs are removed by the receivers and the conductors are instructed not to interfere with the comfort of the passengers, there will be a return of the old time patronage."[50] Black media across the South lauded the victory. Atlanta journalist J. Max Barber wrote that the bankruptcy was inevitable, commenting, "it is no surprise to us" and congratulating black Richmonders on their ability "to teach such a lesson and administer such a rebuke to violent race prejudice."[51]

Indeed, the streetcar company was suffering because of dramatic changes in its corporate structure. A contingent of stockholders had split the stock and brought in two new major outside investors from New York City, Frank Jay Gould and Helen Miller Gould, the son and daughter of the infamous Jay Gould, robber baron railroad financier. Jay Gould had made his fortune in part by bankrupting competitors and his own companies. The Goulds dominated their new company, adding a small board of directors that met regularly in New York City, and alienated longtime, small stockholders whose investments were now virtually worthless. Their family legacy, in addition to their outsider status and dramatic changes in the rules of how the company was governed, created chaos as the company sought to expand. Under the direction of Frank Gould, the company purchased smaller competitors, including the Richmond Traction Company, which was in the midst of a labor dispute with its workers and had prohibitive debts. Virginia Passenger and Power inherited these labor disputes: "This controversy was, therefore acquired with the property."[52]

Strikes in 1903 severely hurt the company, vulnerable from its major expansion that year. Even with an 11.48 percent increase in passengers in 1903, increases in salary for protesting workers and the revenues lost during the strike resulted in a $23,311.77 deficit in the company's street railway division by 1904. The losses caused by the boycott hammered an already hobbled company. But the enforcement of the voluntary segregation law may have been precipitated by the Goulds' investment. The segregation policy and behind-the-scenes efforts to stop black protest may have been an effort to prove that although the streetcar company was northern owned, it remained beholden to the interests of southern whites. The dominance of the Goulds was short-lived; competing stockholders' and lenders' interests forced the company into receivership under the direction of Virginia Passenger and Power officeholder and stockholder William Northrop. With Northrop at the helm, Virginia Passenger and Power served the interests of both local investors and segregationists.[53]

The belief that Richmond blacks had won this victory over the streetcar company might have taken the fire out of the boycott. The financial ruin of the company had been protesters' long-term goal, so protesters surely believed that the end of the Jim Crow policy was in sight. Citing the twin blows delivered by the 1903 strike and the boycott, which had "over eighty per cent of the colored people . . . walking and sweating," Mitchell was certain that the laws would change.[54]

Mitchell underestimated streetcar investors' determination to continue the policy despite the cost. Believing that the receivers would be pressured to change segregation policies on the streetcars, Mitchell declared an early victory. But the court-appointed receiver, Northrop, received considerable financial backing that enabled the company to withstand further losses.[55] Mitchell continued to insist that that the boycott had succeeded because it forced Virginia Passenger and Power into the hands of receivers. He reported that "the receipts fell off to such an extent that the street-car company was unable to pay interest on its bonds."[56] But the newly charged company withstood the pressure of the boycott and refused to desegregate the streetcars.[57]

Black efforts to avoid Richmond's streetcars continued in earnest for the next two years. The *Richmond Reformer* reported in January 1905 that despite cold weather, the boycott held: "It is now nine months since the Jim Crow street car rules went into effect and the there are thousands of the best class of citizens who are walking yet." The True Reformers' newspaper also pointed out that blacks, especially the better class, had to be careful not to be hypocritical in the fight against segregation. African Americans of all classes must not only reject segregated streetcars but also eschew the "poorest accommodations" and entrance through "side alleys and side doors" offered to black patrons at the local theater. No amount of cultural exposure could outdo the harm of accepting the buzzard's roosts in the backs of Richmond's theaters.[58]

Although all black Richmonders had difficulty avoiding the use of the streetcars as the city expanded, many continued to try. As 1906 began, Mitchell sought to maintain a positive outlook on the future of black Americans, commenting, "No, we do not think the out-look is dark for the Negro. We think the out-look and the in-look is better than it has ever been."[59] Mitchell continued to encourage his readers to save their "self-respect" and their money by avoiding the streetcars: "Every time you want to ride on a street-car, put five cents in a bank and at the close of the year, count the fund and see how happy you will be." The boycott could cure all manner of illnesses as well: "Walking cures insomnia, sleeplessness, indigestion, stiffness in the limbs, constipation, dizziness and sometimes reduces swelling in the joints."[60]

The *Planet* was full of encouraging words: "Except in case of sickness or disability, street-car travel is a luxury anyway, when it comes to a city the size of Richmond. . . . When a colored person rides on a car here, it is strictly business and no pleasure. More colored people in Richmond own their horses, buggies, wagons and bicycles than ever before. It has been so long since we had our feet on a streetcar in Richmond that we have well-nigh forgotten the feeling of electric traveling. God has been kind and good to us and we find that we can make as good time footing it as we can going over a given route on a street-car with its numberless stoppages for passengers."[61]

Revivals of their efforts came with news of other communities beginning boycotts or starting efforts to start their own lines. When the mayor and city council of Newport News, Virginia, passed ordinances segregating the streetcars, local blacks reorganized their effort to stay off the cars. Mitchell continued to believe that the Newport News battle could be won: "With the level ground in that neighborhood and the numberless carriages, private and public owned by colored people, it seems to us that somebody's pocket will feel the effect of the crusade." Mitchell used the news of this boycott to spur his community to maintain its efforts.[62]

The *Planet* also highlighted the protests in Nashville, Tennessee, where a law segregating streetcars was passed in 1906. The local paper, the *National Baptist Union*, reported that white teenage boys jeered black passengers as they boarded, using racial epithets and crying, "Jim Crow, Jim Crow, take a back seat." Although some of Nashville's African Americans continued to ride the streetcars, efforts to organize were spurred by the arrest of Mrs. W. B. Phillips, "a very respectable colored lady," for refusing to give her seat to a white woman. Following the gender etiquette of the day, Phillips insisted that "Southern courtesy would demand that respectable Southern white men would at all times give their seats to Southern white ladies." She insisted that a seated white man rather than a seated black woman should be willing to give up his seat for the white woman. But the conductor and a plainclothes officer arrested Phillips for her insistence that she too deserved the respect due a lady. Following Phillips's, arrest, Nashville's African American community organized a boycott and began efforts to start an independent transportation company. Mitchell encouraged Richmond's blacks to take note when Nashville's black-owned Union Transportation Company purchased a small fleet of automobiles to carry boycott participants to and from work while the company sought to purchase electric streetcars that could climb the city's steep grades. Mitchell wished aloud that the company could grow and put "electric motor cars in every Southern city where the infamous Jim Crow street-car law is in practice." It was a principled effort: one of Union's African American investors promised that Union Transportation would be integrated: "We are not going to exclude whites from our automobiles."[63]

That same year, southern efforts to stop Jim Crow streetcars experienced brief success in the courts. Florida's segregation statute, known as the Avery Law, made an exception for black servants, as did segregation laws in Georgia, Virginia, and Louisiana. The Florida Supreme Court found that the exception for black nurses caring for white children violated the Equal Protection Clause of the Fourteenth Amendment and declared the Avery Law unconstitutional just one month after it was enacted, ruling in a suit secretly funded by the streetcar company. Victorious black Floridians who had staged boycotts in Jacksonville and Pensacola returned to the cars, conspicuously riding in the front seats. Although the suit was publicized in black newspapers throughout the nation, it was secretly funded by the streetcar company officials in Florida in the attempt to halt the costly boycott. Even if streetcar company officials simply had their costs in mind, the success of the case buoyed efforts to stop streetcar segregation and inspired boycotts in new cities. However, the victory proved short-lived: the Avery Law was rewritten without the nurses' exception and found to be constitutional by the state supreme court.[64]

The brief court victory seemed to lead to a further hardening of Jim Crow laws throughout the South. A flurry of attempts to pass new laws followed in the wake of the Florida decision. As part of the backlash, J. Thomas "Cotton Tom" Heflin, a congressman representing Alabama's Fifth District, which included Tuskegee, proposed a law segregating the streetcars of Washington, D.C. Heflin's proposal did not make it to a vote. In his reporting, Mitchell pointed out the sad irony of a proponent of states' rights forcing legislation on a city that was not his own. Mitchell bitingly suggested that Heflin purchase a carriage and stay off the streetcars himself.

Heflin continued to ride the streetcars in the District, carrying an unlicensed weapon after purportedly receiving threats from people opposed to segregation. In 1908, while on his way to the Metropolitan Methodist Episcopal Church to speak about temperance, Heflin ordered a black man, Lewis Lundy, off a streetcar for drinking in the presence of white women. When Lundy argued and fought back, Heflin threw him to the ground as the other passengers ran away. When Lundy tried to run, Heflin fired two shots from the window of the car: the first hit a white bystander, and the second struck Lundy in the head. Even though both Lundy and the bystander were severely injured, Heflin faced no consequences in criminal court and remained proud of his actions: "Under the circumstances, there was nothing else for me to do. I am glad to say I have not yet reached the point where I will see a negro . . . take a drink in the presence of a lady without saying something." He was indicted but never convicted and continued to hold his seat in the U.S. House for another twenty-four years, bragging that the shooting was the highlight of his career. Even as Heflin's violent determination to segregate the cars passenger by passenger was condemned by the *Richmond News Leader*, his legislative intent had come to dominate the political landscape in Virginia.[65]

In the wake of the Florida case, the legislature of Virginia passed a new bill, without an exception for nurses, mandating that streetcars throughout the state be segregated. The 1904 law had given individual lines and cities the power to segregate if they chose; the new law made segregation the rule. Even though members of the legislature suggested that Richmond blacks would favor the law, Mitchell insisted that "Richmond Negroes fought the 'Jim Crow' law in every way conceivable and there are many there still fighting it." Almost two years after the boycott began, Mitchell pointed out, "There are colored people here who do not ride on the streetcars and hope never to have to do so. They accept all of these discriminations under protest."[66]

In fact, the renewed legal efforts to harden the segregation of the cars gave new energy to blacks' refusal to ride segregated conveyances. As Mitchell hoped in the pages of the *Planet*, "Racial discrimination is a great spur to racial activity."[67] After a lull of almost a year, Mitchell's weekly suddenly buzzed with stories reporting on renewed protest. Black Richmonders purchased "new bicycles, young horses and new buggies and appear as the owner rather than the driver."[68] Mitchell reminded his readers that "street-car travel is a habit. It is a luxury and not a necessity." Mitchell held onto the notion that the boycott had succeeded despite the passage of the new state law. "The street-cars of this city are crippling both white and colored people. In this respect it draws no color line. Some colored folks

continue to get on there to be insulted and crippled. Others
their trips few and far between. The line has not yet been able to ͺ
hands of the receivers."⁶⁹

Mitchell believed that segregation precipitated increased viole.
tween white and black riders. Did the new state mandate give black rᵢ
right to the seats at the backs of streetcars? Could they ask white passenͺ
to move and make way, or should they be forced to stand on empty streetcars to avoid sitting in front of white passengers? The new law continued to
be applied in an uneven manner, giving increased privileges to white conductors and passengers and increasing the burden for black riders. One
black man was punched repeatedly in the face for asking a white man to
move to the front of the mostly empty car. The black man, traveling home
from work, wanted to sit in compliance with law and not be arrested, but
he violated unwritten racial norms by asking a white man to move. Mitchell
cited this assault as just the type of violence caused by Jim Crow streetcars
and questioned why the conductor, vested with police powers, allowed the
white passenger to sit in the rear and failed to arrest him for the attack.
Mitchell hinted that such an attack could have led to greater violence or
even lynching: "There are some colored folks around here that would have
made a 'grease spot' out of him. . . . But then this feeling will not do."
Continued boycotting of segregated cars was the best way for African
Americans to avoid violence, insult, and injury.

The *Planet* continued to point out glaring inconsistencies in the law.
Mitchell mocked the police powers given to conductors when he reported
that an overzealous conductor ordered a police officer to stop assaulting a
boy during an arrest and himself ended up under arrest.⁷⁰ Mitchell took joy
in reporting that even the *Richmond Times-Dispatch*—notorious for its hostility toward African Americans—admitted that the conductors abused
their authority, annoying passengers both black and white: "There have
been more white people ordered around and made to change their seats,
sometimes without any apparent reason." Even with just one or two black
passengers on the cars, conductors ordered whites to move. Protesters remained hopeful that their continued effort to avoid the cars, combined
with the irritation of white riders, might slow the progress of Jim Crow.⁷¹
Even a black postal employee, who had special rights to ride the streetcar
without being charged, was arrested by an overzealous conductor for failing to move when ordered. The charges were dismissed after a brief investigation found that the conductor had overstepped his legal bounds.⁷²

Mitchell used the state law as a rallying point, calling on black communities throughout Virginia to organize boycotts. He asserted, "These laws were passed on the theory that financial loss would not follow for the reason that colored people would soon get accustomed to the changed conditions and ride just as much as before. . . . A determined constituency will command respect."[73] Indeed, African Americans in both Portsmouth and Norfolk organized boycotts and started new wagon companies to accommodate the transportation needs of former streetcar passengers. A local paper reported that "the car companies feel the cut in their receipts." Such protests seemed to result in the Norfolk streetcar company ignoring the law and allowing black passengers to sit among whites if there were no seats available in the back. Norfolk's chief of police then met with officials of the Norfolk Railway and Light Company to instruct them about the new state law's requirements.[74]

But in the end, passage of the comprehensive new law requiring segregation must have been a blow to the movement. Boycott organizers had hoped to squeeze Virginia Passenger and Power, but the state law meant that the streetcar company no longer had the authority to change its policy. As time went on and the city and its surrounding communities grew larger, African American workers had an increasing need to reach ever more distant locations. To reach the growing streetcar suburbs in Henrico County, domestic workers had no choice but to ride the streetcars. Over time, lower rates of participation blunted the boycott's financial sting.

But in that fateful year, devastating defeats ultimately dashed African Americans' hopes for political rights and opportunities. Throughout 1906, Mitchell continued to counsel blacks not to be their own "worst enemies" and encouraged "bad Negroes" not to set out to prove the "charges [of white supremacists] to be true" through bad behavior. Even in the face of increasing violence and decreasing black rights, Mitchell continued to believe that the "great mass" of African Americans would strive "to improve their condition educationally, religiously, morally, industrially, and financially." He encouraged blacks to "be more polite and obliging to the better class of white people," arguing that such efforts might "win [whites'] friendship and merit their approval."[75]

In 1906, the Atlanta race riot and the Brownsville incident dimmed Mitchell's hopes for an intervention by the "better class." Atlanta had been lashed by violence after false rumors of black men raping white women whipped local white men into a frenzy of murderous anger. That violence was followed by another riot in which black soldiers stationed in Texas fought back against local whites angered by the presence of black men in uniform. Despite evidence of self-defense, President Theodore Roosevelt, a Republican who had enjoyed broad African American support, dismissed the black soldiers without a fair trial. Angered and ashamed, Mitchell had expected more from the president he had endorsed, the elite whites in charge of Atlanta, and the white leaders in his own city. He again found his wish for interracial coalition of the "best" blacks and whites defeated by violence and betrayal. Mitchell could only hope that "this trial by fire" would not discourage blacks from their path. Calling on the history of slavery, he continued to wish that America would live up to its promises. "Our future prosperity and permanent glory rests in this land where we have borne the heat and burden of the day and suffered from the chilling blasts beneath the rays of a heatless sun."[76] Even as segregationists hardened new laws, boycotters would continue to walk, suffering in the heat of summer and in the cold of winter in Richmond and throughout the South.

7 BATTLING JIM CROW'S BUZZARDS

Betrayal and the Savannah Streetcar Boycott

If any "buzzard" cares to ride let them do so. Those of us with the least spark of race pride will continue to glory in our walk.—SOLOMON JOHNSON, *Savannah Tribune*, 22 September 1906

In Savannah, Georgia, a small port city with a rich colonial heritage, Emancipation Day was celebrated annually on the first of the year. For decades, African Americans marked the day freedom came to the former slaves. The band from Georgia State Industrial College drummed a beat as black fraternal orders, church organizations, unions, and labor organizations took to the streets to march in remembrance of how they became a liberated people.[1] But as freedom became increasingly threatened by Jim Crow laws, racial violence, and disfranchisement, the parade took on a different tone.

On Emancipation Day 1906, the parade was said to stretch twelve city blocks. In previous decades, the parade had been led by the First Battalion Infantry of the Colored Georgia State Troops. The Colored Infantry had been a source of pride within the black community, a mark of citizenship and African American manhood. However, the Colored Infantry was viewed as a threat to white authority, they were systematically underfunded by state lawmakers and forced to purchase uniforms and build an armory with funds they had raised on their own. The infantry was denied the right to serve during the Spanish-American War even though the men had volunteered for the fight. The final attack on Savannah's black servicemen came when the state disbanded all African American regiments in 1904.[2]

Without the infantrymen, the parade took on a different tone. The parade column marched a bit more solemnly, fighting off any signs of disrespect from white passersby. First, the marchers refused to let an obstinate white man cut through the parade, and he was beaten up by the crowds watching the festivities. Later, parade watchers threw a streetcar conductor out of his vehicle when he tried to drive through the marching masses. The crowd even attacked a white journalist who attempted to photograph the fights.[3]

Turn-of-the-century Savannah, a small city of 65,064 where an African American population of 33,246 held a slim (51 percent) majority over whites, was distinctive not only for its rich architecture and quaint squares but also for its unusual racial legacy.[4] It was a city where race relations had been governed by a unique system of compromise. The historic city's oldest African American institution, the First African Baptist Church, was born out of this compromise between free and enslaved blacks and leading whites. This pattern of negotiation continued after the close of Reconstruction. But as the force of de jure segregation grew, the pattern of compromise wore thin. By 1906, Emancipation Day had become a symbol of a growing rift in the fabric of compromise. African Americans would no longer accept any intrusions on their citizenship without a fight. They, too, held a claim on Savannah.

SOLOMON JOHNSON MOVED to Savannah as a child in the 1880s from Laurel Hill, South Carolina. Having learned the printing profession working for the *Savannah Echo*, Johnson became a protégé of John H. Deveaux, editor of the *Savannah Tribune*, and took the helm of the *Tribune* when Deveaux accepted a political appointment as the head of the Savannah customhouse. Much in the style of the day, Johnson was an outspoken editor of the newspaper Deveaux had established. Under Johnson, the *Tribune* retained its political character; weekly articles followed the state Republican Party, elections, and local, state, and national events.[5] But under Johnson's leadership, the *Tribune* also grew into a reflection of the character of Savannah's African American community. The header announced that the paper was the official organ of the Georgia Prince Hall Masons, a secret society in which Johnson was a leading figure, and local news was dominated by events in local black churches, reflecting the fact that most secret societies had close ties to black churches. The paper provided "Ministerial Dots" with reports from the First and Second African Baptist, First Bryan Baptist, and St. James African Methodist Episcopal Churches. The *Tribune*'s weekly reports reflected the extent to which church life was the center of black Savannah's community.

But the *Tribune*'s most important function was its defense of the quality of African American life in the South. Johnson sounded constant alarms against the erosion of African American citizenship. He monitored white efforts to disfranchise black Georgians, reported on the rise of lynch law and racial violence, and contested every effort to expand segregation laws. The editor did not condone any form of racial segregation and believed that every small ordinance restricting black access to public facilities was a step down the slippery slope toward the destruction of African American citizenship.

Throughout his tenure as *Tribune* editor, Johnson voiced his opposition to Jim Crow accommodations of all kinds. For decades he railed against the white-owned Savannah Theatre, which provided only segregated accommodations. Characterizing some residents' willingness to climb "the long flight of stairs up to the peanut gallery of the Savannah Theatre" as "disgusting," Johnson was ashamed that many of black Savannah's civic leaders also traversed the narrow staircase to the theater's segregated balcony. Johnson was particularly pained that black schoolteachers provided a poor example to young people by being counted among those willing to accept second-class accommodations. The editor dismissed any acceptance of Jim Crow as a "lack of race pride" when people had the option of simply avoiding the theater. "Stay away just one season," he wrote, "and we will assure you better accommodation will be given."[6]

Johnson always protested vehemently when local officials made any attempt to segregate Savannah's streetcars. In the fall of 1899, when the streetcar company segregated the Thunderbolt and Isle of Hope streetcars, which traveled from Savannah to the outlying suburbs (including the black Georgia State Industrial College), Johnson demanded a boycott. The small suburbs of Thunderbolt and Warsaw passed municipal laws requiring passengers to be divided by race. Johnson reported that the streetcar suburbs segregated in response to complaints of "rude Negroes" and "bad conduct on the cars."[7]

Johnson drew on community history and reminded his readers of earlier victories. When the streetcar company had attempted to segregate in 1872, black residents staged boycotts. The company reformed its policy in response to the boycott, and integrated cars had operated for the next three decades. Johnson recalled this historic legacy, asserting that "what was accomplished twenty-seven years ago in a lawful manner can be accomplished now if it is necessary. The same pride of race and love of principle and law that our people had then, have not only been retained, but increased."[8]

While encouraging the community to resist, Johnson warned the streetcar company that its losses would be significant if black residents ceased to ride the cars. Estimating that nearly half of the streetcar patrons were African American, Johnson insisted that patrons would not sit idly by; African Americans had "aided materially in building these lines. . . . Can the street railway company afford to lose this large patronage by consenting to mortify and degrade colored people?" Johnson countered charges that blacks were ill behaved by asserting that poor whites were just "as rude and distasteful on the cars" as any rowdy black passengers and that any disturbances should be individually addressed. Johnson was offended; segregationists had attacked all black riders because of the alleged actions of a few. He stated, "The colored people of Savannah will never consent to be herded as cattle on the street cars."[9]

Black congregations and their pastors provided the best network for organizing resistance to the offensive segregation law. Johnson called on Savannah's ministers to urge their congregations to stay off the segregated streetcars in response to the segregation of the Thunderbolt line. While the boycott continued, the interdenominational Ministers' Evangelical Union responded to Johnson's call and organized a committee to negotiate with the streetcar company. The union elected the Reverend J. J. Durham, pastor of Second African Baptist Church, chair of the streetcar committee. Durham was an esteemed community leader, not only pastoring his congregation but also serving as chaplain of the First Battalion Infantry of the Colored Georgia State Troops.[10] Durham was charged with negotiating with city officials from Warsaw and the streetcar company to reach a settlement of the boycott.[11]

Johnson used the *Tribune* as a platform to warn African American visitors to the city about conditions on the streetcars. Praising a group of excursionists who refused segregated seating, Johnson warned visitors to "keep off of the cars." But in the following weeks, the problem became Savannah residents who were willing to ride second-class on the Thunderbolt streetcars. A few black residents, under the watchful eye of a *Tribune* reporter, rode the segregated streetcars to a musical performance in a suburban streetcar park. Johnson was "proud of the fact that none of the respectable class . . . went out there. It was only the jim crow class who cares nothing about principle." The *Tribune* observer lauded a group of unsuspecting women who had not heard about the passage of the law; when they discovered that they would be seated in back, they walked home. Johnson scolded a group of men who were demeaned by the conductor and "didn't have sufficient manhood to resent it by getting off the car." Some black riders were embarrassed by the presence of the *Tribune* reporter and tried to board the streetcar without being seen. Johnson claimed, "They knew that they should not accept the accommodation, but on account of their jim crow nature they could not do otherwise." Johnson warned that any acceptance of segregation was simply a green light to segregationists seeking to discriminate on all of Savannah's streetcar lines.[12]

But while the pages of the *Tribune* demanded just treatment, the editor also cautioned black people about proper deportment in public places. If segregationists pointed to black behavior as a cause for the new laws, Johnson noted that some residents could improve their dress and behavior with the hope of deflecting outside criticism. He believed that perfect deportment would demonstrate that African Americans were worthy of inclusion. Johnson warned, "There is a class of people who are too careless with their . . . apparel in public" and cautioned that those who were "slouchy and dirty" should not "intrude in the most prominent places." Johnson also offered the critical comment that "the boisterous action of a class of our women on the streets, does not reflect creditably upon them." Not only boycotts and agitation but also good hygiene and civil behavior were important for the pride of the race.[13]

Eventually the boycott made an impact on streetcar revenues. Local officials and company representatives became eager to regain black patronage. Town officials and the streetcar management reached an agreement with boycott leaders. With the understanding that order was to be maintained and that any instances of "boisterous behavior" on the part of black patrons would be punished, Warsaw town officials revoked the offending law by the end of November, just a little more than two months after the measure had gone into effect. Black Savannah welcomed the new year with the dissolution of segregated cars. The *Tribune* congratulated Durham, thanking him for his "persistence as chairman of the committee that waited on the street railroad company and the authorities of the Town of Warsaw." The leaders of the Ministers' Evangelical Union, coupled with the resolve of the boycott participants, won out. The *Tribune* sang out, "No more jim crow cars in Savannah. It has been abolished."[14]

Although the 1899 boycott had been a resounding success, there was dissention within black Savannah. The editorial column of the *Tribune* was peppered with hints of the difficulties within Savannah's black leadership class. Johnson warned, "Underhanded and treacherous methods never win. Manliness tells." "Masquerading as race leaders and stabbing the race in the back at the same time, seem to be the delight of certain men." He cautioned, "As a race, we can well afford getting rid of some of the traitorous Negroes among us, who have pious mien, and pose as leaders." Tellingly, Johnson advised, "Whenever you find a Negro advocating the cause of a man of the opposite race who has in any manner acted inimical to the best interest of the Negro, he does it not from principle's sake, but because he is well paid for it." And, indeed, the third and final boycott of segregated streetcars would be plagued with men willing to undercut African American protest efforts for a price.[15]

EVEN ON SAVANNAH'S integrated streetcars, conditions were sometimes rough; black and white passengers lodged frequent complaints against aggressive conductors and motormen. Conductors were responsible for the safe travel of their passengers, observing those boarding and leaving, assisting people who needed help stepping on and off, and signaling the motormen when it was safe to continue. However, as in most southern cities, all the conductors employed by the Savannah Electric Company were white men. Of Savannah's 121 street railway employees listed in the 1900 census, only 6 were black, and they were probably unskilled laborers. The practice of hiring primarily white men as conductors extended throughout the nation; of 56,932 conductors working in the United States in 1910, only 44 were black.[16]

Some of the Savannah conductors had a nasty habit of signaling the motormen to proceed before passengers could board or disembark. Conductors caused passengers whom they disliked or who had offended them to be thrown to the ground with an unexpected jerk of the streetcar. Hostile conductors also ignored passengers' signals, causing riders to miss their intended stops. Although both black and white riders complained about the conductors, the clashes between black patrons and white conductors were the most frequent and violent.

George Baldwin, the Savannah Electric Company president, asked a company investigator to examine the claims of Andrew Monroe, an African American man Baldwin knew as an employee of the Merchants' National Bank of Savannah. Baldwin ordered the investigation because he believed Monroe to be "a perfectly respectable and reliable man." Monroe alleged that his wife and child had been assaulted while attempting to get off the East-West Broad Street line car. The family frequented the line on journeys to and from their West Broad Street home.[17] Matilda Monroe, while "holding her baby in her arms," was thrown down to the ground when the streetcar was intentionally "started before she could alight." The conductor did nothing to help the fallen woman and child, nor did he stop to see if they were injured. Baldwin was willing to acknowledge the complaints of "respectable colored persons" and asserted that "conductors must be taught that a passenger must be treated in the same way by the Company, no matter what his color may be." Recognizing that African American passengers would be unwilling to accept second-class conditions quietly, he warned, "We want no race question sprung on us here in Savannah; the consequences are altogether too serious."[18]

Johnson mentioned this incident, along with other attacks on black streetcar patrons, in the editorial notes of the *Savannah Tribune*, warning, "The attention of the manager of the Savannah Electric Company is called to the careless action of some conductors. . . . They pay but slight attention to colored patrons, especially females."[19] Johnson believed that black women with children or burdens needed respect and help getting on and off the cars, not hostile treatment. On average, black passengers made up almost a quarter of the streetcar company's passengers, and on some lines, black passengers were a majority of riders. The streetcar company could not afford to offend black passengers by ignoring the abuse and mistreatment doled out by prejudiced conductors or motormen. But black passengers found themselves in a tight spot: if they were not judged to be "respectable colored persons" or failed to submit quietly to abuse, the company cared little about how they were treated on the cars.

A local white attorney, H. E. Wilson, wrote privately to the streetcar company to complain about the mistreatment of a black couple that he witnessed on Savannah Electric's A & B line. The man and woman, whom Wilson did not know, were "most unjustly and discourteously treated" by a conductor. First, he refused to stop at the destination they had requested. Then, when the couple was allowed to exit several blocks from their original stop, he signaled the motorman to start before they could fully exit. Only halfway off the streetcar, the man was thrown down, while the woman passenger was forced to jump from the moving vehicle.[20]

The conductor at fault disputed Wilson's claim and instead cited the black woman's behavior as the source of the conflict. Although Wilson had not noted that the black passengers were unruly, the streetcar company manager reported that when the car finally stopped to let the black passengers disembark, "the woman instead of getting off stood on the platform chewing the rag with the conductor about not letting them off before." Because the woman dared to complain out loud about their mistreatment, the conductor "became impatient" and signaled the motorman to restart the car. Her complaints were sufficient explanation for the conductor's attack. The streetcar manager insisted that perhaps the conductor was "guilty of carelessness" but found that he "was justified in the way he handled his car on account of the excessive talk on the part of the negroes." Baldwin agreed with the manager's investigation and sided with the conductor. He explained to Wilson that although company policy required that employees "at all times be not only courteous to any of the public with whom they come in contact, but that they should be unusually so and equally so to all," "one or two things" about the couple's treatment were "apparently not quite definitely clear." Baldwin dismissed Wilson's complaint and asserted that the conductor was justified in his rough treatment of the offending black passengers. Black passengers who defended themselves were treated poorly, even when their complaints were justified.[21] On Savannah Electric streetcars, "uppity" black passengers had little protection from abuse and mistreatment, even when prominent whites argued on their behalf.

Although African American passengers had maintained integrated cars prior to the fall of 1906 and the streetcar company purported to give "the same attention" to the concerns of black riders, complaints by black passengers did not lead to improved conditions. In contrast, the Savannah Electric Company took very seriously the complaints of white passengers. When a white passenger wrote to complain about an incident when a conductor signaled the motorman to restart the car before he could get on, there was a prompt response. The incident was similar to those reported by black passengers: when he attempted to board, the man was forced to leap onto the moving vehicle. When asked why he had restarted the car before the man could get on, the conductor responded, "Well if you don't like it you can report me." The passenger did so, and the conductor was quickly fired from the company.[22] Although African American passengers had defended their right to ride unimpeded by segregation since the 1870s, a climate of hostility created by some abusive conductors and motormen remained.

IN THE FALL OF 1906, politicians on the Savannah City Council, fueled by their interest in breaking the Savannah Electric monopoly on the city's electrical power, began to push for a new policy segregating riders on the streetcars. Concerns about the danger of monopolies were part of nationwide Progressive attacks on unchecked corporate power. The political interests that organized against Savannah Electric knew that an ordinance would place the company in a bind. Any attempts to enforce the policy would anger black patrons and reignite their long history of resistance against streetcar segregation. Black anger might lead directly to a costly streetcar boycott. Any refusal to comply with the new policy would alienate white riders who supported segregation, and company officials would risk being labeled as race traitors and outsiders operating at the behest of northern corporate interests.[23] Black Savannah was unaware that local politicians were manipulating the civil rights of African Americans in backroom business schemes. The reasoning behind the legislation did not matter; black streetcar patrons would protest any erosion of their rights.

The *Tribune* alerted African American readers about the new attempts to segregate Savannah's streetcars, reminding local whites that there was no need to separate the races. Johnson wrote, "This ordinance is altogether uncalled for. At present the white and colored citizens ride together without friction. The purpose of the ordinance is to segregate and abuse the colored citizens of this city." Arguing that the city's progressive image could be at stake, he made the generous claim that "the white people of Savannah are looked upon as being the best in any Southern city." Johnson cautioned Savannah's city leaders: "There is no reason . . . to besmirch this reputation by the proposed jim crow ordinance." Asserting that segregationists did not have "the best interest of the entire people at heart," Johnson was confident that new attempts to segregate streetcars would be defeated. He reminded readers that "the last attempt was only fostered by one member of the city council and he went down in unanimous defeat." Despite his hopeful tone, the editor called for ministers and community leaders to meet at the historic First African Baptist Church to organize a strategy to contest the ordinance's passage.[24]

The city's black ministers and leading men met that week to form a permanent organization. The regular meeting of the Baptist Ministers' Union was postponed, and ministers of all denominations joined with business and political leaders to develop a plan. The meeting was contentious, with debates about how the group should proceed, who was best suited to lead, and whether to make the protest public. Although "the opinions of many were different," group members finally united in vocal opposition to the segregation of Savannah's streetcars and established a resolutions committee to draft statements of protest to the city council and another committee to recruit new participants and spread the word to Savannah's congregations not represented at the initial planning meeting. Unity was essential for success; as Johnson implored in the *Tribune*, "For once let us stand together as a people and let our enemies know that we are capable of resenting insults."[25]

Divided between ministers and members of the city's rising black middle class, the elected leadership of the boycott organization was a broad group of African American men. Given the community's long history of church-based leadership, the city's ministers were the first line of defense in contesting segregation. However, a new generation of skilled workingmen and professionals also led the protest. Black Savannah's sacred and secular leadership united in the fight against segregated streetcars.

The Reverend J. A. Lindsay of the St. Philip African Methodist Episcopal Church headed the newly formed organization. At St. Philip, Lindsay inherited a legacy of community leadership from the Reverend C. C. Cargile, who had also battled on behalf of the black community. Lindsay gave his time to the protest and helped to provide the space necessary for mass meetings by opening St. Philip as one of the boycott's regular meeting places.[26] The Reverend J. W. Carr, leader in the Baptist Ministers' Union, assumed the pastorate of First African Baptist after the passing of its nationally renowned pastor, Emmanuel K. Love. Carr served as a leader in the boycott organization and also opened his sanctuary for the boycott's first mass meeting.[27] Carr's commitment to protest may have been bolstered by his role as an officer in the February 1906 Georgia Equal Rights Convention, which was inspired by W. E. B. Du Bois's Niagara Movement. The convention called for a broad platform of change for the state's black citizens, including the abolition of Jim Crow cars. Carr represented Savannah and served as a vice president of the statewide organization.[28]

Four other ministers made up the core of the boycott leadership.[29] The Reverend Henry L. Haywood, the pastor of the Union Baptist Church, a leading member of the Baptist Ministers' Union, and the president of the Evangelical Emancipation Association, served as the boycott organization's secretary.[30] The Reverend J. H. May, pastor of the Second African Baptist Church, had a mandate from his congregation to serve in the boycott leadership, continuing Durham's legacy.[31] The Reverend J. A. Brockett of St. James African Methodist Episcopal Church, rounded out the list.[32]

Leading men from outside the ministry also played a crucial role in the boycott leadership. One of the most prominent lay leaders was Johnson, who not only served as editor of the *Savannah Tribune* but also worked in the Republican Party, served as a leader in Savannah's Prince Hall Masons, and had been a member of the First Battalion Infantry of the Colored

Georgia State Troops before they were disbanded.[33] Local attorney Abraham L. Tucker and physician J. Walter Williams were also appointed as leaders in the boycott organization.[34]

Some of the most prominent leaders of the 1906 boycott were skilled workingmen. One of a few African American boat pilots licensed in Savannah, William D. Armstrong, captain of the coast-trading steamer *D. Murchison*, served as a boycott leader. Armstrong also served as chair of the Republican Party's county committee and was a member of several of Savannah's most prominent clubs and secret societies, including the Odd Fellows, the Olympia Lodge of the Knights of Pythias, the Eureka Lodge No. 1, and the Prince Hall Masons. He was also a member of the St. Philip African Methodist Episcopal Church. Through Armstrong, the protest tapped into a variety of networks: the black maritime laborers, the state's Republican Party, fraternal societies, and churches.[35]

Two barbers, John W. Armstrong and Richard Barnes, were an essential part of the boycott leadership. Barnes owned an independent black barbershop on West Broad Street and served as an officer in the Olympia Lodge of the Knights of Pythias.[36] Armstrong worked as a barber for a white clientele in the shop run by C. B. Guyer, a white man. Armstrong was also a leading businessman, serving as general manager of the Metropolitan Mercantile and Realty Company and vice president of the Metropolitan Mutual Benefit Association. Armstrong made an unsuccessful bid for the state House of Representatives and ran for tax collector on the Republican ticket in 1906.[37] The presence of barbers among the leadership was meaningful. Black men in Savannah dominated the trade, with the 1900 Census showing that 139 of the city's 169 barbers were African American. Like ministers, barbers were economically autonomous, since their salaries came from their customers. Such independence fostered a spirit of resistance; a core group of African American barbers had long been active in the fight for fair accommodations in Savannah.[38]

Coupling negotiation with a plan for protest, the resolution committee asked the Savannah City Council to maintain the existing rules on the streetcars to preserve the "harmony and peace now existing between the white and the colored people." The committee reminded the city council that African American patronage was a substantial portion of streetcar traffic and that the voices of "the more than thirty thousand colored people of the city" should not be ignored. The resolutions committee also asked Savannah Electric to consider a path other than racial separation. The committee reminded the streetcar company that black patronage was essential to the company's profitability and that black riders would not ride on segregated cars. The committee argued that segregation would exacerbate existing racial tensions and put "innocent, hard-working, well-disposed colored passengers" in harm's way. The policy would "engender strife and confusion between the races" and increase "brutality on the part of some of the street car employees," who had a history of abusing black passengers.[39]

Johnson used the *Savannah Tribune* to express his hope that the Savannah City Council would not segregate the cars. In the days before the decision, Johnson continued to affirm the community's intent to contest the segregation ordinance. Before the vote, the *Tribune* called on the council to act "for the best interest of the entire people regardless of race." Reminding them again that "the two races have been getting along amicably," and reporting on the African American community's willingness to protest, the *Tribune* encouraged the council to defeat the offensive proposals.[40]

On 10 September, the Savannah City Council met to decide the fate of the streetcars. On the advice of the city attorney, the council withdrew both ordinances proposing racial separation and passed a resolution demanding that the Savannah police begin enforcing the state's dormant 1891 segregation law.[41] This strategy effectively shut black residents out of the decision-making process. No new ordinance was on the table, so the council refused to hear the presentation of the resolution committee representing the concerned black citizens. Reliance on the fifteen-year-old Georgia statute also stunted any opportunities to challenge the legality of a new ordinance in a court of law. The Georgia law, which had served as a model for segregation laws in other southern states, had already been defended and implemented in other cities, most notably Atlanta. With this move, the Savannah City Council left few options for protest.[42]

Indeed, Georgia law stated that "all conductors of dummy, electric, and street cars shall be required, and are hereby empowered, to assign all passengers to seats on the cars under their charge, so as to separate the white and colored races *as much as practicable*." The Savannah Electric Company had previously used the law's vague language to avoid segregating the cars and precipitating a black boycott. Streetcar company managers remained "skeptical as to the practicability of enforcing separation on the suburban lines without causing a great deal of friction and leading to increased trouble on city lines." The company's general manager, L. R. Nash, forwarded a copy of the Georgia law to Baldwin that summer with the phrase "as much as practicable" underlined. Although the streetcar company had effectively avoided explicit efforts to segregate black and white riders by claiming that the law was not practical and could not be enforced effectively, the Savannah City Council pressed the issue and used the current law to force the streetcar company to either comply or reject the law outright. The streetcar company, which immediately began segregating riders, knew that it would face a formidable protest from black Savannah.[43]

"Let us walk! Walk!" cried the *Tribune*, "do not trample on your pride by being 'jim crowed.' Walk!" By mid-September, vehement protests were under way. African American streetcar passengers doggedly refused to be complicit in efforts to usher them to the backs of streetcars. Even though the local white press insisted that "the most sensible and self-respecting" "colored people" were "not anxious to ride with the whites," black riders valued complete equality, including their right to sit where they chose. As Johnson vigorously replied, "The separation law was never designed to give the Negro a square deal" but was instead intended to "put a lasting mark of having been a slave on [the] colored man." Fighting this "mark" of slavery was important to all classes of people in black Savannah.[44]

Several mass meetings were held after the city council resolution was passed; community members had "aroused themselves from a semi-dormant state to one of almost complete activity." The *Tribune* reported, "The people feel that they have been forced to take a decided stand in this matter" and would meet the insulting condition of the cars "with manhood and self-respect." Savannah's African American men, women, and children participated in the well-organized boycott; by Savannah Electric Company estimates, black passengers, who had constituted almost 24 percent of all streetcar passengers, were less than 4 percent of the total number of passengers by the week of 16 September. Some streetcar lines that had enjoyed large numbers of black passengers saw their ridership drop to almost zero, including the West End, Battery Park and E & W lines. As the *Tribune* reported, with an allusion to white supremacist political organizations, African American "people refused to ride, and the cars have been since nearly completely 'lily white.'" All fourteen of the streetcar lines operating in Savannah and the surrounding suburbs were affected.[45]

The *Tribune* reported that organizing efforts were more "than temporary enthusiasm"; boycott leaders were planning for the long haul. Protest leaders met with the city's African American hackmen to organize efforts to provide alternate transport, especially for those who lived in outlying areas. Much as in other southern cities, African American men dominated the driving and hauling trades; according to the 1900 census, 518 of the city's 612 hackmen, draymen, and teamsters were black.[46] These black drivers' mobility and relative independence made them a crucial ally in the fight against segregated streetcars. The hack drivers agreed to support the boycott, and many reduced their prices so that working people could afford their fares. In an effort to become even less dependent on Savannah Electric, black residents of the city's western suburbs began efforts to organize an independent transportation company. Independent hack lines or streetcars provided alternatives for black passengers while enabling black residents an opportunity to reinvest in their community. African American residents also began to search out more permanent solutions for the problems of reliable transportation.[47]

By the end of September, the boycott was a sure success; Johnson gleefully reported, "'Lily White' street cars are among the popular sights these days, caused by the proud colored citizens who are determined not to be 'Jim Crowed.'" Indeed, on almost every line, according to the streetcar company's records, only a nominal number of African Americans still rode the cars. Endorsements by the city's black congregations, social clubs, and benevolent societies were essential to extending the boycott beyond the workweek. The streetcar company depended on weekend passengers to make the cars run profitably seven days a week. The weekend before the boycott began, for example, black passengers constituted 97 percent of all riders on the West End Line. When black organizations supported the boycott by changing or canceling events that would require people to ride the streetcars, they took away some of the company's most important passengers.[48]

Special trips out to the city's parks were also important to company profits. One of Savannah's middle-class black societies, the Adelphia Club, canceled a scheduled outing in Lincoln Park, the segregated park for black residents accessible only by streetcars owned by Savannah Electric.[49] Lincoln Park was one of the urban South's many segregated streetcar parks, designed to boost the number of African American passengers on weekends, holidays, and in the summertime. Black residents had used the park for both formal gatherings and informal outings. African American community leaders felt a symbolic ownership of the park, even attempting to have a say in the way it was administered. For example, a 1902 petition signed by seventy-seven black residents, including leaders of the 1899 and 1906 boycotts, was sent to the Savannah Electric, recommending that the company rent the park to Tom Golden, "a good friend to the colored people and a law abiding citizen," in an effort to ensure that Lincoln Park remained "a place of amusement where our race can go without any fear of having the law violated." The petitioners, led by Johnson and John W. Armstrong, suggested that abiding by their interests would help make the park prosperous: "We know that by making this place popular your Company will reap much larger returns than they have ever received." But the same groups that had used Lincoln Park prior to the boycott chose to avoid both the park and the segregated cars, since, as the officers of the Adelphia Club put it, they were "unable to offer number one accommodations in every particular, even public conveyances."[50] Both religious and secular organizations supported the boycott by ending the sponsorship of events that required their members to ride the streetcars.

Such endorsements were essential to the movement's overall success. Savannah's diverse community of churches, benevolent societies, and social organizations, many of which had been established in the antebellum era, served as a network of support and a center of social activities. The Masons' participation in the boycott was assured because Johnson served as the "right worthy grand secretary of Savannah." But the boycott needed the participation of all the city's black social organizations, not only national groups such as the Order of the Eastern Star, the Knights of Pythias, and the Odd Fellows but also innumerable local clubs and church organizations like the Friendly Brothers Aid and Social Club, the Sons and Daughters of Jacob, the Sons and Daughters of Moses, the Crescent Aid and Social Club, and the Browns Aid and Social Club. The participation of churches and social clubs was effective; no rise in black patrons was recorded on Saturdays or Sundays.[51]

The boycott did not enjoy universal support, however. Several members of the Savannah Men's Sunday Club, one group of leading black men, did not openly support it. Although the group had a tradition of protest and agitation on behalf of the race under the leadership Monroe Nathan Work, who would become a leading sociologist and statistician at Tuskegee, most members remained silent during the months of the protest. Work and several other group members were educators at the Georgia State Industrial College, and their journeys to campus were considerably eased by passage on the Thunderbolt line. Also, because the school was funded by the state, Work and other state employees may have feared reprisals from Georgia's segregationist government. Whatever the reasons for their decision not to participate, their silence hurt the unified front of the boycott. Black traffic on the Thunderbolt line remained much higher than on other lines during the first weeks of the protest.[52]

But on the whole, the community continued to protest. According to the streetcar company's statistics, 88 percent of black patrons avoided the cars during the first six weeks of the protest. To accommodate African American laborers traveling to work, the city's hackmen reduced their fares and increased their hours. All forms of transportation were used: the *Tribune* reported that "buckboards and street wagons have also been pressed into service by their owners." But Savannah was a small city, with most of its black population living in the outlying parts of town. W. E. B. Du Bois's 1905 study of urban residency patterns described black Savannah as a community where "the distribution of the population resembles a great O, with the whites in the center and the blacks in the circle around."[53] Blacks in most parts of the city could walk into the city center to their jobs and churches, and walking indeed became the favored form of transportation for most people. Johnson came up with creative ways to reallocate money not spent on carfare for community needs, proposing that "those who have been constant riders . . . donate the amount they would otherwise spend toward the purchase of a suitable site for a school building in the southern part of the city."[54]

Despite the "beneficial" effects of walking "to the physical and financial condition" of the boycott participants, a few black riders remained on the segregated cars. Johnson ridiculed blacks who continued to ride on Jim Crow streetcars, calling them "buzzards" and questioning their manhood and their good judgment. Buzzards were mythic creatures in African American folklore and were synonymous with Jim Crow. The Jim Crow rhyme, originally a game similar to Ring around the Rosie, was made famous to white audiences and linked to segregation by the black-faced minstrel character played by white performer Thomas "Daddy" Rice in the 1830s. Although most accounts of Rice's performance begin in the middle of the rhyme, traditionally it began,

> Where yo gwine buzzard, where yo gwine crow?
> Ise gwine down to de new ground to jump Jim Crow.
> Wheel around and turn around and do jes so;
> Evy time you turn around, you jump Jim Crow.

Johnson dismissed those who did not boycott as "buzzards" willing to "jump Jim Crow" on Savannah's segregated streetcars.[55]

PROTESTERS FACED VIOLENT intimidation during the first weeks of the boycott from the Savannah police force, which was doubled in size to deal with the boycott. Officers taunted and attacked African American walkers and created a climate of "intimidation to make them ride." Such efforts to frighten African Americans back onto the streetcars were not terribly effective because walking broke no laws. Pedestrians could not be charged with the city's punitive vagrancy laws if they were moving along on their way to work.[56] In this dangerous climate, African American protesters were cautioned not to provoke white authorities and warned to "learn to 'boycott their tongue'" as well.[57]

Questions of safety and behavior became central issues in the last days of September 1906, when race riots shook the upstate city of Atlanta. Race-baiting politicians and fabricated news stories about black men who raped white women inflamed Atlanta. The frenzy came to a head on 22 September, when black residents were stoned, beaten, shot, and tortured by angry mobs of armed white men, with some women and children joining in. The mobs roamed downtown streets, attacking black barbershops and restaurants. As in New Orleans in 1900, the terrain of the Atlanta streetcars was especially volatile—"the most fearful of all," in Johnson's words. Gangs of white toughs monitored the city's streetcars, and each car that passed "would be eagerly scanned for negroes." If the mob saw black riders, the cars were "immediately boarded and a rush made for the blacks." Black men and women were dragged from at least twelve streetcars before the company halted service.[58]

Atlanta's African Americans avoided leaving their homes. In response to rumors that black residential areas would be attacked, black neighborhoods armed in self-defense. African American snipers fired on streetcars that passed through black neighborhoods to prevent rioters from riding streetcars into residential areas. When a battle took place in Darktown, a poor section of the city, armed black residents were able to hold off white attackers. The following day, a mob of "police" turned on the middle-class community of Brownsville, where two of the city's respected black educational institutions, Clark College and Gammon Theological Seminary, were located. Confrontations resulted when police and white civilians attempted to disarm black residents defending their community. Black residents ambushed the incoming force, killing the group's leader. The next day, police went door to door in Brownsville, arresting hundreds, including professors and students from Clark and Gammon, and confiscating all weapons. African Americans' efforts at self-improvement through education and economic advancement did little to protect them from violence; in fact, their achievements may have made them more vulnerable.[59]

When the riot was finally quelled after four days of violence, black residents remained withdrawn from the city's downtown. Atlanta's street-cars were free of black riders. The *Savannah Tribune* reported, "On the trolley cars not a Negro was to be seen all day. They did not seem to think that the trolley cars were healthy places for them, and if they went out, they preferred to walk." Such stories must have shaken Savannah's protesters as they continued their boycott. The riot was a devastating blow to those resolved to defend black life in the South.[60]

Some Atlanta residents facing the torrent of racial violence and weary of the battle against Jim Crow began to argue not for segregation but for separation—that is, for building a world separate from whites that would provide some safety. In a striking article written in the wake of the riot, J. Max Barber, who had been a vocal advocate of streetcar boycott movements throughout the South, wavered in his resolve to battle segregation. Barber had been driven out of Atlanta by segregationist legislators as a consequence of his outspoken denunciations of both local and national politics and his accusations that white rather than black men were responsible for rapes in the South. Faced with a tribunal of local white leaders who intended to bring criminal charges, Barber moved his person and his press to Chicago. In an angry edition of the *Voice of the Negro*, the first published in Chicago, Barber used the streetcars as an example of the difficulties of racial politics in such a bleak time, vacillating between support for separate streetcars and demands for fair treatment on racially integrated cars.[61]

Barber asserted that it was not "a humiliation for black men to ride with black men," but humiliating rather "when, because we are black and for no other reason, we are denied our rights, robbed at the ballot-box, driven out of courts with lynch justice, refused common civic treatment that belongs to decent men and loyal Americans." Worn down by his former outspoken stance and by the trials of being driven out of the South, Barber argued, "If it will conduce to the peace of society and to the protection of our women from the insults of white men and to the comfort of all parties concerned, we say it deliberately, 'as for me and my house,' give me a separate car or a trailer."[62]

In his frustration, Barber insisted that spaces where African Americans, particularly black women, could avoid white threat and violence must be created, now arguing in favor of all-black cars despite his years of protest to the contrary: "A separate car will save our ladies from the insults of white men and give us men passengers decent seats and guarantee to us protection." In his bitterness, Barber wrote, "This is the dictum of self-respect. We are not clamoring to ride with white men; but we are clamoring to ride with decent men." But Barber set clear terms under which such compromise would be possible: "Frame the law in such a way that no white man shall be allowed upon the car set apart for the Negro race and the conductor shall be liable to a fine . . . for permitting a violation of the law." Finally, Barber, who recognized that segregated conditions always implied black inferiority and degraded the humanity of all African Americans, concluded his bitter thought experiment by completely rejecting any acceptance of separate cars. The streetcar boycotts' greatest advocate reaffirmed his desire to fight for integrated cars, insisting, "If nobility of character, decency of person, purity of life and genuine gentlemanship and womanly department count for anything," African American southerners were more than worthy of inclusion.[63]

News of the Atlanta riot also dampened the hopeful spirit of the Savannah protest. Fearful that white mobs might begin to target African American protesters in Savannah, boycotters found themselves in a precarious and volatile situation. An odd mixture of fear and blame characterized the *Tribune*'s tone following the violence in Atlanta. The newspaper initially reported that the "cause of the outbreak" was attacks by black marauders who had raped four white women. Although Johnson later noted that "it seems . . . strange that there should be so many reported alleged assaults near Atlanta," he was initially unaware that the stories of rape had been fabricated by the *Atlanta News* and that no white women had in fact been attacked by black men. Thus, the *Tribune* argued that the violence could have been prevented if the community had done more to control its "criminal" element. Johnson cautioned that "the good colored people and the good white people must join hands and put down lawlessness in every community. The criminals of each race must be apprehended and punished. When this is done, lawlessness will not be so rampant." Yet despite the hope that the riot was uncommon and specific to the problems in Atlanta and that good colored people could avoid similar fates, the fact that defenseless blacks of all walks of life were murdered, beaten, and hunted like animals on the streets of a modern city was jarring. Blacks in Savannah knew that the potential for violence was not unique to Atlanta and that their families and homes could also become targets of angry mobs of white men eager to put blacks "in their place." Black Savannah mourned the "helpless, harmless, innocent, murdered sisters and brethren" in Atlanta.[64]

Savannah's streetcar protesters continued to walk, but the community clearly was much more fearful in the wake of the Atlanta terror. Segregationist vigilantes threatened to attack those attending a meeting to organize and fund the United Transportation Company, an independent venture to create "immediate and ample transportation." Rumors spread throughout the community that the meeting at St. Philip "would be raided by white men," and some "advised the people not to attend." Despite the threats, hundreds of brave boycotters eventually arrived—so many that the meeting had to be moved to a larger auditorium.[65]

The Atlanta riot also spurred boycott leaders to be more vigorous in their attempts to police participants' behavior. Such demands suggest that boycott participants were becoming increasingly vocal in their opposition to racial violence and more interested in self-defense. Johnson called for "cool heads and rightful action and speech" and demanded that people "be discreet and particularly law abiding." Johnson clarified that his warning was not directed toward "the better element," who were "always conservative and law abiding." Instead, he directed his warnings about good behavior at those who were "not so careful." The editor cautioned, "The carrying of concealed weapons is a grave crime," implying that some protesters had begun carrying weapons. Although Johnson claimed that his calls for calm and control were a long-standing part of his journalism, the tenor of the protest changed in the weeks following the riot.[66]

On the whole, the riots did not quell the boycott's momentum. In fact, avoiding the cars may have been not only a resistant stance but also a wise course of action at a time when racial tensions were high. Local whites who wanted to emulate conditions in Atlanta might have targeted black streetcar riders. The boycott allowed black travelers to move in groups, riding wagons or walking from black neighborhoods to downtown places of business. Avoiding the cars, which had been the site of mayhem in Atlanta, might have kept black residents safer in the weeks following the violence. The boycott helped to invigorate a beleaguered community; by saving money and investing in black enterprises, the community imbibed a spirit of independence. If whites were hostile, black Savannah would seek to be as autonomous as possible; as Johnson counseled, "Self-help is the best and it should be in this case." In the end, the violence of the Atlanta riot strengthened African Americans' resolve not to accept the degradation of their citizenship.[67]

Many white lawmakers, including Georgia governor Joseph Terrell, blamed the black community for the Atlanta violence, making no distinctions between black middle class and the poor. To Terrell, both successful and poor blacks bore responsibility. The governor argued that "two classes of Negroes"—the "idle and vicious" poor and "the semi-educated with high-flown notions of social equality"—provoked violence in southern cities. In a bold move, the *Savannah Tribune* reprinted a fiery response to these charges written by T. Thomas Fortune, an African American journalist and co-founder of the Afro-American League. Fortune blamed conditions within black communities for fostering a self-destructive underclass. The existence of an "idle and vicious" class was fueled by the poverty and vice allowed to flourish in black communities with the consent of the police, "white dive keepers," and city officials. Fortune also described the governor's African Americans with "high-flown notions" as in actuality "self-respecting people who work hard and want to obey the laws, but who resent and will always resent, the jim-crow car laws." For Fortune, the battle against segregation was essential to the fight against violence. Although "Governor Terrell and his sort have come to believe and to class [public equality] as 'social rights,' . . . no right made the subject of contract is a social right, but always is a civil right." Equality was not a privilege but the right of all citizens. Fortune poignantly concluded, There will always be 'bad Negroes' in Georgia, and their numbers will continue to multiply, as long as jim-crow laws are made and enforced, because they violate the sanctity of contract and debase the manhood and womanhood of the people at whom they are aimed, by the inferiority of the service they make possible, by the insolence and the brutality of the enforcement of them, and by the stigma they place upon a body of citizens who have as much right to fair and equitable laws and human administration of them as the white citizens of Georgia."[68] The fight against the "stigma" of segregation was a fight in defense of black humanity and the quality of African American life. Savannah residents could protect themselves against brutal attacks and random violence of race riots only by refusing to accept any deterioration of their citizenship. The most debased black Americans would rise only when the country respected them as right-ful equals. The *Tribune* offered ongoing encouragement: "Our people must continue to stand together. Do not fall by the wayside. We are now achiev-ing that which is and will do an everlasting good." And as winter set in, the boycott did not wane. Johnson commented, "The weather . . . was an excellent test, and has shown that our people are deeply set in their deter-mination not to be 'jim crowed.'"[69]

ALTHOUGH AFRICAN AMERICAN communities throughout the South had demonstrated tremendous solidarity in contesting the segregation of public conveyances, divisions among leaders and the treachery of a few undercut their efforts. Although protest organizers in New Orleans and Richmond had faced intracommunity conflicts, African American men who operated clandestinely at the behest of the streetcar company sabotaged the fight in Savannah. The success of the boycott depended on both integrity and unity. Johnson published a plea for harmony when the boycott began, arguing, "This time more than any other calls for united action of all of our men. There should be no division whatever." Johnson believed that the fight against segregation would be best served by those willing to sacrifice their personal gain for the good of the community and the race. He hoped that the collective pressure of a united community could keep everyone in line. He warned, "The person who does the least thing to stir the people into a division should be frowned upon as an enemy to the best interest of the race. Let there be a unanimity of thought and action."[70]

The records of the Savannah Electric Company demonstrate, however, that two ministers and a host of petty informants undermined the boycott. Black Savannah's class divisions splintered the leadership, and the streetcar company exploited these divides to its benefit. By targeting an opportunistic minister of a working-class congregation, engaging the services of a questionable black "leader" to speak out against the protest, and offering jobs to working-class blacks, the utility company sought to diffuse the protest. The duplicity of a few key men gave the Savannah Electric Company the opportunity to stifle the boycott from the inside.

The boycott devastated the Savannah Electric Company's revenues. In November 1906, Baldwin, the company's president, commented that its earnings were "very seriously affected by the boycott." Baldwin believed that a cadre of Savannah businessmen had pushed for the enforcement of the 1891 state law segregating streetcars in an attempt to bankrupt Savannah Electric and take over streetcar service. City councilmen knew that the segregation of streetcars would be met by a formidable boycott by African American passengers, as had been the case in 1872 and 1899. In response, Baldwin resolved to "use every possible effort to eliminate this boycott otherwise, the strain upon the company's resources will be entirely too severe." Baldwin argued that the best strategy would be to spend "as much as $2000 in hiring a lot of workers among the negroes" to quell the protest. Baldwin hoped that the employment of a few black streetcar employees would be the best way "to change [protesters'] sentiment and put them back to riding again." Baldwin hesitated to hire the workers, believing that he would be committing "blackmail," but he was afraid; he ultimately decided that "conditions . . . are so serious that we must take this risk." Baldwin assumed that the men leading the protest could be paid off; he did not understand African Americans' willingness to stand on principle. Baldwin sought to "make the payment to these workers contingent upon the cessation of the boycott" and assumed that the boycott leaders could be paid off with a few jobs for black workers.[71]

Savannah Electric's parent company, Boston-based Stone and Webster, affirmed Baldwin's belief that the city's efforts to segregate the streetcars were aimed at bankrupting Savannah Electric. Company officials knew that black ridership was essential for success but remained unsympathetic to the conditions that African American customers faced and did not want to challenge the segregation law. Officials cautioned that "the signs required by the ordinance" should be hung and "any other details, which may be objectionable to the negroes [should be] taken care of in order to eliminate possibility of trouble" with the city. The corporate office never considered negotiating openly and fairly with boycott leaders; rather, Stone and Webster believed that the best approach to ending the boycott was Baldwin's plan. Given the tight situation, the corporate office agreed that the "expenditure of $2000 to quiet the negro boycott is entirely warranted." Management would have been reluctant to make such a deal had there not been an ongoing attack on the holdings of Savannah Electric; officers wrote, "We look upon the proposition of conciliating negroes as merely a choice of two evils, and it is a policy which we should hesitate a long while before adopting if it were not for the other troubles affecting the Company's interests at the present time."[72] Stone and Webster's willingness to uphold white supremacy demonstrates that northern companies contributed the capital necessary to make the segregated South.

In the fall of 1906, Savannah Electric's manager wrote, "As soon as the colored people organized themselves to handle the matter the riding fell to 10% of normal." Conductors noted that black ridership had "worked back to about 25%" of usual levels as the boycott entered its second month, and the company hoped for "probabilities of further increase . . . considering the colder and less favorable weather" in the winter. But despite the cooler weather of the late fall, African Americans continued to avoid riding the streetcars. The manager believed, "The longer conditions remain as they are the more firmly the walking habit will become fixed and the greater the permanent loss of riding." Unless the Savannah Electric Company took action, black passengers might never return to the streetcars. The company began to seek out agents within the protest community to do its bidding.[73]

Although he promised fiery sermons filled with "sparks, live coals and flames" and advertised that at his church, the "gospel of human rights is the gospel of Christ," the Reverend J. H. Brockett, pastor of St. James, was the first Savannah minister poised to try to undo the boycott. Brockett was a founding member of the African American streetcar boycott organization, but in the days prior to the boycott, he secretly proposed a deal to Savannah Electric's manager. He sought a charter for a streetcar line "for the exclusive use of colored people" that would appear to be an independent venture. Brockett would gain "some notoriety" from the venture, and the profits would be returned to the company. Savannah Electric declined, saying that it did not have enough cars to start a new line and maintain its original franchise. Brockett then suggested "the liberal use of money" to end the boycott, offering to serve as an "agent to get control of a sufficient number of influential citizens to counteract any efforts toward a boycott." Claiming that he had made a "list of ten negroes of influence," Brockett promised that the money required to bribe the local leaders would be less than losses caused by the boycott.[74]

Although Brockett was an insider in the streetcar boycott organization, the company manager remained suspicious of Brockett's true influence, investigating the minister and discovering that although he had "a large congregation" and "considerable influence among the less intelligent negro element," he did "not stand very high among the better class of colored ministers." Company officials doubted Brockett's effectiveness in influencing not only his own congregation but also other community leaders. Baldwin asked trusted local blacks about Brockett and learned that he was "universally known as a sharper, exploiting both races to the utmost of his ability." Yet Baldwin felt that actively engaging Brockett's services was the company's best opportunity to stunt the boycott.[75]

Johnson hinted in the *Tribune* that he was aware that one of the boycott's leaders was working against the cause. As early as September, he commented, "We are fearful of the foes within the ranks"; a "contentious man" was "one of the worst enemies of the race."[76] But the *Tribune* never targeted Brockett by name, and it is unclear whether Brockett's schemes were ever uncovered. His name remained in the news of the boycott, and he was listed as a speaker at prestigious events at black Savannah's churches. However, Brockett was never a part of the United Transportation Company venture, and articles about the boycott did not highlight his activities within the boycott leadership.

Savannah Electric's attack on the streetcar boycott also included a war of words in the *Savannah Press*. The Reverend E. Jonathan Nelson, the secretary and treasurer of the Colored Orphans' Home, began correspondence with Baldwin in December 1906. Nelson, who was not the pastor of any church, launched a letter-writing campaign against the boycott in a local white newspaper. Nelson characterized the boycott as "a money making scheme on the part of a few designing men." In his "Good Word to the Colored People," he accused the boycott leaders, particularly those affiliated with black-owned transportation ventures, of being deceptive to "reap the harvest in cash from the misguided simpletons" who participated in the boycott. Nelson believed that the boycott was unwarranted because the company had not pushed for the enforcement of the streetcar law. The minister asserted that seating at the fronts and backs of city streetcars was the same and that segregation "would work no hardship upon the race." In an effort to "convince the more ignorant and easily misled of the race" that the boycott was unnecessary, Nelson wrote a series of articles that sought to "teach submission to all law," and "order among men. Nelson argued that protest against the law was futile, because "God alone is the only effective panacea for all human woes." The pieces appeared under the initials "D. E. F." Nelson hid his identity for fear that he would be called a "white man's nigger . . . in the pay of the Street Car Company." He did not want his identity to distract from his mission to uncover the "utter foolishness" of the streetcar boycott.[77]

Nelson insisted that the boycott was not intended to advance racial equality but rather to advance the careers of a "the class of immoral scamps —self-poised leaders among the people, many of whom, because they are of a lighter hue from the masses, holds [sic] themselves 'as good as the white people.'" Referencing Savannah's long-standing intracommunity color line, Nelson argued that boycott leaders were estranged from the people and operated as, "designing human sharks," exploiting the allegiances of the poor and working class for their own benefit. He asserted that the boycott worked extreme hardships on those who had to walk to work and could not afford to hire hacks to carry them the great distances they had to travel. Nelson believed that the boycott was waged "at the expense of the poor and needy—the peaceful and law abiding of the race who would merit the good opinions of our white friends and benefactors."[78]

Johnson dismissed Nelson's attempts to speak out against the boycott, scoffing, "The jackleg preachers who are trying to induce our people to use the trolley cars, should be completely ostracized." He described all those working on the behalf of the interests of Savannah Electric as "disgusting" and "contemptible." Despite the condemnation, Nelson continued to publish articles calling for the end of the streetcar boycott.[79]

Nelson's articles and letters to Baldwin were filled with conversion tales, stories of the "ignorant" who immediately began riding the streetcar after he informed them that there was no harm in the segregated cars. He recalled one "painful incident" in his first published article: "I met a poor old woman plodding along wearily south on Whitaker Street, bearing a very heavy basket that seemed out of proportion to her bent form." Nelson reported that "she intended to walk, as she hadn't enough money for a hack." When Nelson suggested that she ride the streetcar, she replied, "Colored people are not allowed to ride on the street cars now." Nelson insisted that the elderly were participating in the boycott only out of confusion. As soon as he informed the "poor old woman" that it was safe to ride on the segregated streetcars, she quickly boarded a passing car.[80] Nelson asserted that his articles would change the minds and hearts of boycott participants; he frequently told Baldwin that "the people are now thinking for themselves."[81]

But Nelson's work on behalf of Savannah Electric came at a price. At first he framed his requests for payment as a donation to the orphans' home. At Christmastime, he hoped that "the Company may be encouraged to remember the 'orphans and poor old people' while Santa Claus is here." Nelson later claimed that other Savannah ministers had begun withholding funding from the home after discovering that he opposed the boycott. Nelson initially hesitated to ask directly for cash payment, but he clearly sought to be rewarded for his work. As a Savannah Electric memo stated, "He does not ask for a contribution, but *between lines*, he intimates that some results already having been obtained, one would not be entirely inconsistent on the company's part." Over time, Nelson's tone became desperate; in February, he thanked Baldwin for his note and let him know that the Colored Orphans' Home was "greatly pressed just now for means to further [its] work" and that "any financial aid that the Company may see fit to make us at this time—knowing that we are not in sympathy with this boycotting scheme but have done and are doing all in [our] power to break it up once and for all in Savannah."[82]

Nelson eventually fell out of favor with Baldwin and the streetcar company, perhaps because the minister could truly do little to help end the boycott. The company informally investigated Nelson, asking African American informants for background information on his character. One informant described Nelson as "what is known as a jack leg preacher. He is Secretary and Treasurer of a small colored orphans' home at the Corner of Waters Road and Wheaton Street, but he is not authorized to collect any money for same, nor is he authorized to sign any letters on behalf of the home." Nelson's status with the streetcar company was finally seriously damaged when he was arrested and charged with embezzling funds and violating state pension statutes. Nelson then directly requested help from Savannah Electric: "I ask you to help me out in the name of common humanity and my humble occupation—as I lack proper means for my defense." He hoped that Baldwin "might be in a position to aid me otherwise with your influence."[83] Outside of anonymously authoring the antiboycott articles, Nelson had little influence or political clout to back up his letter-writing campaign against the streetcar protests. But other investments made by Savannah Electric began to bear bitter fruit in the spring of 1907.

By that time, the boycott had reduced the company's earnings so much that according to its accountant, "Owing to the peculiar conditions now existing in Savannah, it is possible that the net earnings of the company . . . will not be sufficient to pay the dividends on the preferred stock" for the six months ending on 30 March 1907. The company's advisory committee met at the end of January to make its projections for 1907. The committee estimated company earnings "based on the assumption that the boycott will gradually diminish, causing a loss of earnings . . . of about 15%, and will finally become negligible about July or August, at which time, the customary increase of 7 or 8% may be looked for." Officials believed that the success and survival of the Savannah Electric streetcar franchise depended on ending the boycott in the spring or summer of 1907.[84]

Brockett's schemes to undercut the boycott came to fruition in May, when he helped to organize the First Annual Interstate Convention of Negro Composers and Musicians. The five-day gathering, organized by a committee Brockett headed, called on musicians from throughout the region to come to Savannah to participate in the workshops and contests. The company would run special cars for the use of attendees, and Baldwin hoped that the "Musical Convention of Colored People" would help raise revenues and break the spirit of local protesters, although he hesitated to trust Brockett. Baldwin warned the company's manager to "see that [Brockett] gets no money until he produces the riding": payment would be made only "after the convention if he does what he says he will do, instead of paying him beforehand."[85]

Brockett's plan may have caused irreparable damage to black Savannah's collective will. The boycott efforts had gotten a second wind in late March and early April. In response to rumors that Lincoln Park would reopen for the spring, Johnson renewed his vocal condemnation of segregated streetcars and the company-owned park. He declared that "under the existing jim crow law . . . every institution should boycott [Lincoln Park], and not a member of the race should enter its gate." Any patronage would "sanction the present enforcement of the jim crow law." Johnson stated that in no uncertain terms, "any individual or institution attempting to give a picnic at Lincoln Park, or do anything to cause our people to patronize the street car company under the present restriction should be frowned upon."

Some local organizations joined the effort or renewed their support for the boycott. The Chatham County Emancipation Association and the Savannah Men's Sunday Club sponsored a march from Chatham Hall to the Prince Hall Masonic Temple on a Sunday afternoon, followed by a mass meeting in support of the boycott. This very public display sought to renew boycott efforts and "urge . . . people not to patronize Lincoln Park." These actions did a great deal to revitalize the collective spirit of the protest participants. Savannah Electric noted a dramatic drop in African American patronage in the month of April, one equivalent to the losses at the beginning of the boycott more than seven months before. At first, Savannah protesters heeded Johnson's advice to "sacrifice your pleasures for your manhood and your womanhood. Keep on walking and tell everybody to keep away from Lincoln Park."[86]

Brockett's convention at the beginning of May was perfectly timed to counter the success of the prior month. Despite Johnson's attempts to announce to outside visitors "that the colored men, women and children of Savannah, with the least taint of race pride, do not use the trolley cars and . . . desire . . . visitors doing likewise," the conventioneers patronized the special convention cars.[87] Other African American groups in Savannah also began to make private arrangements with the streetcar company. Although the *Tribune* praised the congregation of St. Stephen's Episcopal Church for its "novel" approach in transporting people to and from church events, other groups now openly made arrangements with the streetcar company. The Baptist Ministers' Union, whose members had originally supported the boycott, voted unanimously to hire "special cars" from the streetcar company for the Georgia State Industrial College commencement. Instead of making alternate arrangements, the union chose to patronize Savannah Electric and encouraged students and commencement attendees to do the same.[88]

The Baptist ministers may not have viewed "special" all-black cars as a complete acceptance of segregated streetcars, or perhaps some of the ministers were among the "ten negroes of influence" who had been paid off by the company to make the arrangements. It is unclear whether the ministers affiliated with the state-funded institution were pressured by state officials to break the boycott, but the group could have sought to establish a plan that avoided the cars. Johnson condemned those leaders who were "pocketing their pride to accept jim crow fare."

Johnson finally learned of some of the offers of bribes by April 1907 and publicly rebuffed attempts to buy his influence: "In reply to an inquiry," he declared that he was "not a 'jim crow' editor" and would not abandon his "manhood and pride of race to ride on the jim crow street cars" no matter "how great the provocation may be."[89] There is no evidence that Johnson accepted the bribes. Other leaders were less determined than Johnson and their concessions helped to wear down the resolve of the protest community.

Although Johnson continued to condemn "a certain class of traitorous men in the garb of preachers" willing to "sell their manhood rights and endeavor to ruin those who are weak enough to follow them," Savannah Electric's attack on the streetcar boycott undercut the protest community's will. Black Savannah returned to riding the segregated cars, worn down by the long fight and weakened by the lack of resolve on the part of key leaders. The streetcar companies' willingness to invest in segregation stunted the effectiveness of protest. With nowhere else to turn, many Savannah riders returned to the cars, although a few never did.[90]

8 BEND WITH UNABATED PROTEST

On the Meaning of Failure

In 1912, race leader and author James Weldon Johnson penned the *Auto-biography of an Ex-Colored Man*, a novel that explored the consequences of second-class citizenship. Initially published anonymously, the story so carefully traced the details of turn-of-the-twentieth-century black life that many readers believed that it was a real-life account of a man of mixed racial ancestry who had decided to pass for white. Johnson's fictionalized account captured the tragedy of violence and discrimination for many black Americans. In his assessment of racial dynamics, the main character pointedly observes that "the progressive colored people" are just as shut out of the larger society as dispossessed blacks, a group that he calls "the desperate class." Whites accuse those striving for inclusion through education and attainment of "putting on airs," and demands for fair treatment breed "disgust" among white southerners. One character takes comfort in the fact that at least his battle for citizenship is just, commenting, "When I am discouraged and disheartened, I have this to fall back on: if there is a principle of right in the world . . . if there is a merciful but justice-loving God in heaven . . . we shall win; for we have right on our side." However, Johnson's protagonist is not hopeful. Believing that being right is not enough, he chooses to break with his past, change his name, and silently pass for white. He does so not out of "discouragement or fear" but instead out of "shame at being identified with a people that could with impunity be treated worse than animals." Whether African Americans retreated within their own separate communities, escaped to the North, or remained hopeful that change would eventually come, the failure of their fight to defend their citizenship exacted a cost.[1]

In the end, this generation of African Americans failed to stop Jim Crow's advance. Court challenges and letter-writing campaigns to improve conditions on trains never realized success because disfranchisement left African Americans voiceless in the courts and in southern legislatures. The popular movement to boycott segregated streetcars faltered in the face of lawmakers' unflinching support for separating the races. Segregation was promoted in every realm of public life—residences, parks, schools, and places of amusement. They could not stop Jim Crow. What did failure mean to this generation of resistant African Americans?

J. MAX BARBER, the Atlanta-based journalist who had been so vocal in his defense of the streetcar boycotts, paid a high price for his activism. Barber had courted Booker T. Washington's support for the *Voice of the Negro*, allowing Washington's secretary, Emmett Scott, to take up the position as associate editor when the journal was founded. As Barber's political consciousness grew, so did Washington's desire to silence him. Washington, who had hoped that Barber would follow a much more accommodationist path in the pages of *Voice*, was angered by Barber's radicalism and his membership in W. E. B. Du Bois's Niagara Movement.[2] Barber used the *Voice of the Negro* as a forum for supporting both the streetcar boycott movement and Niagara. Barber saw the two efforts as interconnected and was unaware of the degree to which Washington would try to stifle his dissent. In response to his outspoken agitation, Washington crushed Barber, stunting his career as a race leader and journalist.[3]

The attack came from a source close to home. Washington used his influence with a competing Atlanta newspaper editor, Benjamin J. Davis of the *Atlanta Independent*, to begin a campaign to dethrone Barber as an emerging race leader.[4] Davis encouraged his readers not to protest Jim Crow laws: "As a race we are always complaining about our political rights. Let us exercise the rights we have and their manly exercise will add to us many of the things we contend for on paper."[5] Moreover, he also openly attacked Barber. With Washington's encouragement, the *Independent* accused Barber of working for whites, asserting that the *Voice* was just a front for its white co-owners. The *Independent* even pointed out that Barber had to take the freight elevator up to his office in the segregated building where the paper was housed, questioning how he could fight Jim Crow when he was its victim.[6]

Washington hunted Barber even after he fled Atlanta in the wake of the 1906 race riot. Barber never again found steady work as a journalist, in part because Washington forwarded scathing letters to all of Barber's potential employers and undercut Barber's efforts to establish an independent journal. In desperation, Barber moved to Philadelphia and began to study dentistry, hoping that Washington had no designs against his pulling teeth. After establishing a career as a dentist, Barber had an opportunity, albeit diminished, to reenter race politics in the 1920s as a leader of the National Association for the Advancement of Colored People in Philadelphia. However, Barber's career had been shattered as a consequence of his valiant efforts to lead the streetcar boycott movement.[7]

Richmond race leader John Mitchell Jr. became one of the city's leading businessmen, heading the Mechanics Savings Bank, which fulfilled many of Mitchell's desires for African Americans to prosper through hard work and thrift.[8] But he continued to occupy the bully pulpit as editor of the *Richmond Planet*. Mitchell remained his own man, refusing to fall into any of the narrow categories such as "accommodationist" or "Washingtonian." While many other southern black newspaper editors paid a price for their independence, Mitchell continued to speak about the black political world on his own terms, fraught with contradictions and driven by his convictions. Mitchell remained a national voice in defense of full citizenship for all black Americans and a leader of the boycott movement, but each loss seemed to exact a price from his spirit.[9] Over time, he found it harder to believe that conditions could improve in the South.

The year 1906 was a turning point: the Virginia state legislature responded to the boycott by strengthening the law separating the races on the cars. In August of that year, Mitchell wrote an editorial in support of Du Bois and the Niagara Movement meeting in Harper's Ferry, West Virginia. His words regarding Niagara had a tone reminiscent of the struggle in Richmond that had foreshadowed his hopes and fears. Although he recognized that some southern blacks might identify the agitators of Niagara as dissenting "cranks," he reminded his readers that "every great revolution and every powerful reform movement [was] championed by . . . this kind" and that only after the struggle had ended would "conservative elements . . . come in and [enjoy] the benefits."[10] Mitchell remained hopeful that he and his fellow walking cranks would realize reform.

However, Mitchell was fearful as well. In one of his first admissions of intimidation, Mitchell commended the Niagara Movement's call for a radical reclamation of black citizenship rights: "Thousands of us down here will endorse its deliverances and pray for the success of its principles, but this will be done in our prayers." Mitchell admitted that he felt as though there was "but a step between me and death." Agitation in the South would surely put him at risk, but "cringing servility never secured the triumph of a cause." Mitchell concluded his endorsement of the movement's principles by saying that "the boldness" of the Niagara meeting had won the "admiration" of African Americans in Virginia; they were encouraged that "John Brown's soul is marching on." Protesters in Richmond thought of Niagara's march as they continued their own.[11]

Just one month later, in the wake of the Atlanta riot, as Washington begged targeted blacks to maintain "law and order," Mitchell reminded his readers about Du Bois's "timely address." Du Bois, an Atlanta resident, had warned blacks that the loss of "manhood rights" would result in lawlessness on the part of white southerners and "cringing servility" on the part of blacks who willingly relinquished their rights as citizens. Compromise would not suffice; Mitchell used the insult of the riot and the spirit of Niagara as an argument for continuing Richmond's streetcar boycotts.[12]

Despite Mitchell's resolve, Richmond's boycott crumbled as streetcar company officials remained willing to pay a high price for racial segregation. The failure of the protest does not suggest that the boycott was not a savvy political tactic. Avoiding the cars had been the best solution when the nation's courts refused to defend the public rights of black citizens. Their protests represented a radical approach to market forces: the recognition that as individuals, they were vulnerable to changes in the law but that collectively they could strike back at white business interests. Although already largely disfranchised, this young citizenry had learned well the lessons of the political arena. Their collective vote had swung elections in communities where the white vote was divided; their collective economic power could also make a dent. Through passive resistance—simply withdrawing themselves from the cars—they could mark their place on the city's terrain. Boycotts demonstrated to lawmakers and business leaders that even though the majority of blacks were the working poor, they were in fact significant.

Failure under these circumstances seemed inevitable. Boycotts depended on swaying public sentiment and reshaping legal opinions; over time, it became clear that neither change was possible in the Jim Crow South. And in spite of protesters' determination, streetcar boycotts were hard to wage, especially as cities grew larger and hope grew smaller. By 1906, Kelly Miller, a black professor at Howard University, was completely pessimistic about the outlook for the boycott movement, writing, "The jim crow car is universal—practically all Southern cities have separated the races in street car traffic." Miller argued that while protest had at first been popular, "two years ago, it was worth a colored man's standing to be seen on the cars," riding in segregated conditions eventually became simply "a matter of course." To Miller, the failure of the boycott movement was inevitable: giving way was "a plain law of social psychology." He believed that "the popular mind will not hold to one line of feeling for an indefinite length of time." Streetcar companies could simply wait for protesters' will to break: "Companies expect some hesitancy at first, but they feel sure that the colored people cannot hold out in the long run."[13] Mitchell, however, never returned to the cars and never reported in the *Richmond Planet* that the streetcar boycott had ended. Mitchell's walks through the city, his buggies, and eventually his fancy Stanley Steamer automobile represented his highly visible resistance.

Over time, even as Mitchell's investments in property and finance grew, he maintained a radical streak. His risk taking and bold spirit would mark his downfall. In 1921, Mitchell led efforts to challenge lily-white Republicanism in Virginia by running for governor at the top of an all-black ticket that included Maggie Lena Walker. The following summer, Mitchell hosted a visit by black nationalist agitator Marcus Garvey. One month later, Democratic state authorities launched an investigation of Mitchell's bank and investments. After his sloppy and perhaps illegal banking practices were revealed, Mitchell was convicted of fraud. Released on appeal following a few weeks in jail, he was determined to save his bank, his press, and his reputation but never regained his footing. He died in December 1929 at age sixty-six.

Walker met with much greater long-term success and is now a well-remembered figure in Richmond's African American history. Walker continued to lead the Independent Order of St. Luke and wage her campaign to lead Richmond's black women to greater success through independent businesses. Building from within the black community, St. Luke's Savings Bank proved to be the most solid of the city's numerous black banks, surviving a race-based investigation and the Great Depression. Walker's bank remains in business today. The National Park Service has preserved her lavish home in what was once Jackson Ward. The boycott does not figure prominently in the collective memory of Walker; it was one of few failures in an illustrious career.

However, the effects of the boycott in Richmond may reach farther than the defeats of 1906 and Mitchell's personal refusal to ride the cars. In 1917, an

African American real estate developer, S. P. B. Steward, who had purchased land on the outskirts of the city, wrote to the streetcar company. Steward was building a development for black residents on his land, and he asked Virginia Railway and Power to extend some lines to his new neighborhood, thereby enabling people to travel to their jobs, schools, and churches. Although the company's response has not survived, Steward wrote again to explain that he knew the motto among blacks was "stay off the cars" to avoid trouble and that he was aware that most black people tried to avoid riding streetcars. But, he insisted, he would actively campaign to get African Americans back into the habit of riding. More than a decade after the 1904 boycott began, black Richmond still had a reputation for resistance.[14] The nadir generation was neither silent nor accommodating and was not cowed by Jim Crow. The proponents of these protests were willing to band together to resist the humiliation of second-class citizenship. Both the prosperous and the poor sought to preserve their citizenship. Thousands like Homer Plessy, who lived in obscurity, continued to defend their communities, pay poll taxes, and avoided segregated trains and streetcars in the effort to retain their dignity.

The majority of African Americans were not able to continue the daily fight against the inequities of segregation. To travel the rails, they sat in segregated smokers. To travel through the cities, they sat in the backs of streetcars. Their efforts did not stop segregation, disfranchisement, or racial violence. But the history of the *Plessy* era reminds us that their failures planted seeds of resistance. Protest mattered even when it fell short. The failure of this generation would help to feed the consciousness of the next. The nadir generation may have been forced to tolerate a segregated world, but these protests remind us that toleration was not consent.[15]

NOTES

INTRODUCTION

1 Meier and Rudwick's groundbreaking article, "Boycott Movement," also begins with a mention of King and the Montgomery Bus Boycott movement. This introduction, like the project as a whole, builds on their research applying a range of new questions gleaned from legal, social, and gender history to the story of black dissent against segregated transportation. Although this project expands beyond their subject matter and draws very different conclusions than these early articles, it has been a pleasure to tread in the footsteps of giants.

2 Although historians of the Montgomery Bus Boycott of 1955–57 such as Taylor Branch and Randall Kennedy cite the 1921 or 1923 text of the law, the 1921 law was a revision of a 1903 law targeting the streetcar boycotts in Montgomery (1900) and Mobile (1902). The language of the 1921 law, which was designed to address the United Mine Workers of America's ongoing efforts to organize an interracial mining union, mirrors the 1903 law in language, character, and intent but expanded the existing law to target workers who might damage machinery and union organizers who would circulate materials; "advocate, advise or teach"; "organize or help to organize"; or "give aid or comfort to the protests." For the evolution of the law, see *General Laws of the Legislature of Alabama*, Act 329, H. 518; *Code of Alabama*, Chap. 176; Tompkins General and Local Laws, No. 23 H. 26; Branch, *Parting the Waters*, 168; Kennedy, "Martin Luther King's Constitution," 1036.

3 *General Laws of the Legislature of Alabama*, Act 329, H 518.

4 Rev. A. N. McEwen of the *Southern Watchman* reported that "a letter from the president of the Montgomery Street Railway Co. . . . said: The law has been

enforced only twenty-five days and we have realized a new los[s] of $1400, which is due from the fact that Negroes refuse to ride on the cars" ("Editorial," *Southern Watchman*, 15 September 1900, 2).

5 A. N. McEwen, "Editorial—The City Council of Montgomery Makes a Bad Break . . . ," *Southern Watchman*, 18 August 1900, 2.

6 Alsobrook, "Alabama's Port City," 411.

7 Mobile blacks forged a successful boycott very quickly in the fall of 1902. The largest white newspaper, the *Daily Register*, advocated the passage of the segregation law, arguing that the law would benefit both white and black passengers, making the false claim that the Montgomery boycott had failed, and arguing that segregation sought only to "protect the whites from those negroes who have no respect for others and very little for themselves." Despite insisting that the boycott was ill-advised, even the *Register* reported "the only thing noticeable was the absence of negroes from the cars . . . nearly all of them [were] walking." After a few weeks of the Mobile boycott, difficulties on the cars and a significant drop in revenues had resulted in a temporary victory. Although J. H. Wilson, president of Mobile Light and Railroad Company, insisted that the problem on the cars came mostly from whites who "would not obey the law," his comments also hinted at the impact of the black riders' boycott, insisting that if the protest continued, he would be forced to "take off cars or cut the pay of his men." The *Register* reported, "The company's receipts have fallen off. [Wilson] resolves to ignore the law." Pressed by their financial losses, streetcar company officials hoped "to test the constitutionality" of the streetcar ordinance ("Race Separation in the Streetcars," *Mobile Daily Register*, 5 November 1902, 2; "Separation Law Ignored," *Mobile Daily Register*, 2 December 1902, 2; "Editorial Notes," *Mobile Daily Register*, 3 December 1902, 4; "Ignoring the Separation Ordinance," *Mobile Daily Register*, 2 December 1902, 2).

8 Between November and December 1902, the *Southern Watchman* shifted from publishing regular accounts of the boycott to silence.

9 Anonymous postcard sent to John H. Holmes, a Unitarian minister who spoke out against lynching, quoted in Litwack, "Hellhounds," 11.

10 W. E. B. Du Bois, "The Parting of the Ways," *World Today*, April 1904, 521–23, rpt. in *Writings*, 200–202.

11 For local histories that provide a brief but multidimensional look at the streetcar boycott movement, see Dittmer, *Black Georgia*; Ortiz, *Emancipation Betrayed*; Ann Field Alexander, *Race Man*.

12 The notable exceptions are the works of legal, business, and economic historians Barbara Welke, Walter E. Campbell, and Jennifer Roback. But none of the existing studies connect an examination of African American life and political culture in the age of segregation to transportation protest. As Robin D. G. Kelley has noted in his study of black resistance on segregated buses during World War II, "While the primary project of civil rights scholarship has been to examine desegregation, the study of black resistance to segregated public

space remains one of the least developed areas of inquiry" (*Race Rebels*, 56). See Meier and Rudwick, "Boycott Movement"; Meier and Rudwick, "Negro Boycotts"; Welke, *All the Women Are White*; Campbell, "Corporate Hand"; Campbell, "Profit, Prejudice, and Protest"; Roback, "Political Economy"; Kelley, *Race Rebels*, 55–75.

13 In the 1880s, Washington believed that the black middle class would succeed in winning full rights on southern trains, writing that "by a quite persistent demand of [black riders'] rights on business principles, even this damnable and dishonest practice is beginning to give way before this class of young people." Despite his hopes, by the turn of the century, conditions had worsened. See Booker T. Washington, "To the Editor of the *Montgomery Advertiser*," in *Booker T. Washington Papers*, 2:270; Booker T. Washington, "A Speech before the Boston Unitarian Club, Boston 1888," in *Booker T. Washington Papers*, 2:501–2, "An Item in the *Boston Transcript*," in *Booker T. Washington Papers*, 5:403–5; Harlan, "Secret Life."

14 Washington redoubled his efforts between 1912 and 1914 to request improved conditions for black riders within a segregated system, penning editorials, pamphlets, and creating an event called Railroad Days. However, none of these efforts sought to end segregation (Harlan, *Booker T. Washington: The Wizard of Tuskegee*, 417–22). For more on Washington in the age of Jim Crow, see Harlan, *Booker T. Washington: The Making of a Black Leader*; Harlan, *Booker T. Washington: The Wizard of Tuskegee*. For recent scholarship that chronicles Washington's behind-the-scenes efforts to subvert segregation, see Shawn Lee Alexander, "We Know Our Rights"; West, *Education*.

15 Du Bois, *Autobiography*, 234–35.

16 David Levering Lewis, *W. E. B. Du Bois*, 244–45.

17 During his 1897–1910 tenure at Atlanta University, the professor did not comment in his publications or correspondence on the 1906–7 streetcar boycott in nearby Savannah. For a close account of Du Bois's Atlanta years, see David Levering Lewis, *W. E. B. Du Bois*; Capeci and Knight, "Reckoning with Violence."

18 Earl Lewis, *In Their Own Interests*.

19 This project draws on a rich and diverse body of literature that considers the ways that black organizational life, labor, urban space, gender, leadership, and ideas about uplift shaped African American life in the age of segregation. Influential works include Brown, "Womanist Consciousness"; Dorsey, *To Build Our Lives*; Gaines, *Uplifting the Race*; Gavins, *Perils and Prospects*; Gilmore, *Gender and Jim Crow*; Higginbotham, *Righteous Discontent*; Hunter, *To 'Joy My Freedom*; Kelley, *Hammer and Hoe*; Kelley, *Race Rebels*; Litwack, *Trouble in Mind*; Ortiz, *Emancipation Betrayed*; Shaw, *What a Woman Ought to Be*; Deborah Gray White, *Too Heavy a Load*; Chafe, Gavins, and Korstad, *Remembering Jim Crow*.

20 All of the cities that experienced long-term boycotts—Savannah, Georgia; Jackson, Mississippi; Richmond, Virginia; Jacksonville, Florida; and Nashville and Memphis, Tennessee—had established black banks by the 1900s (Report of

the Seventh Annual Convention of the National Negro Business League, Records of the National Negro Business League, Manuscript Division, Library of Congress, Washington, D.C.).

21 Meier and Rudwick "Boycott Movement," characterized the boycotts as a reflection of the black-middle-class desire to be included in the larger society. The authors noted that in contrast to the Montgomery boycott, all of the protests were short-lived and failed to stop segregation. Subsequent generations of historians studying this period have taken these assumptions at face value. While the leadership did seek control, the language suggests a tension within the community between middle-class leaders and working participants. While Meier and Rudwick correctly noted that leadership was drawn from the middle class, new evidence from the archives of streetcar companies suggests that the boycotts had a financial impact on companies in Richmond, Virginia, and Savannah, Georgia. Only broad popular participation from the working class would make possible such numbers. The tiny black middle class would not have made a dent in the bottom line of any urban streetcar company. Failure did not suggest a lack of broad participation. See Savannah Electric Company Records, George Johnson Baldwin Papers, Folders 2190–2202, Southern Historical Collection, University of North Carolina at Chapel Hill; Virginia Passenger and Power Records, in Virginia Electric and Power Company Records, 1849–1995, Vols. 433–39, Folders 518–27, Library of Virginia, Richmond.

22 John Mitchell Jr., "'Jim Crow' Street-Cars," *Richmond Planet*, 9 April 1904, 1.

23 *St. Luke Herald*, rpt. in *Colored American*, 16 April 1904. For more on women's resistance on trains, see Sumler-Edmond, "Quest for Justice"; Welke, *Recasting American Liberty*.

CHAPTER ONE

1 This view of the *Jennings* case is a revision of the history of segregation in New York. Although previous histories have mentioned Jennings's suit or the suit of James Pennington, no account has connected the two events or highlighted the flurry of sit-in protests that followed the *Jennings* case. But the evidence clearly indicates that *Jennings* sparked the formation of a new organization and protest on the part of supporters throughout the city.

2 Lhamon writes, "Jim Crow moved like a free man . . . enjoyed the liberty of every public conveyance from steamship to bus and train, sitting where he wished. He took occupation of the public sphere" (*Jump Jim Crow*, 37). The rhyme is verse 78 from a transcription of the song "Jim Crow, Still Alive!!!" (113).

3 Accounts of black travelers' difficulties filled abolitionist papers. For more on the abolitionist campaign to end segregation, see Litwack, *North of Slavery*, 106–9.

4 Douglass, *My Bondage and My Freedom*, 294–95.

5 Ruchames, "Jim Crow Railroads"; Litwack, *North of Slavery*, 104–8.

6 "Outrage upon Colored Persons," *Frederick Douglass' Paper*, 28 July 1854.

7 See "Brutality of Negrophobia," *Frederick Douglass' Paper*, 27 May 1853.

8 In 1850, New York had 13,815 free "colored" people, 10,749 blacks, and 3,066 mulattos. Although free people of color accounted for just over 2.5 percent of city's total population of 515,547, New York City was still home to one of the largest urban free African American populations. Just 9,961 blacks and mulattoes resided in New Orleans, a city famous for it large population of *gens de couleur libres* (free people of color) during the same year (U.S. Bureau of the Census, *Compendium*, table 69).

9 Ibid.; "Legal Rights Vindicated," *Frederick Douglass' Paper*, 2 March 1855.

10 "Outrage upon Colored Persons," *Frederick Douglass' Paper*, 28 July 1854.

11 "Legal Rights Vindicated," *Frederick Douglass' Paper*, 2 March 1855.

12 Ibid.

13 *Frederick Douglass' Paper*, 22 September 1854.

14 *New York Daily Tribune*, 23 February 1854, rpt. in "The Right of Colored Persons to Ride in the Railway Cars," *Pacific Appeal*, 16 May 1863.

15 "Colored Passengers in Railroad Cars," *New York Daily Times*, 30 May 1855.

16 "Outrage upon Colored Persons," *Frederick Douglass' Paper*, 28 July 1854.

17 Ibid.

18 "For Frederick Douglass' Paper," *Frederick Douglass' Paper*, 22 September 1854.

19 Thomas L. Jennings, "Appeal to the Citizens of Color," rpt. in "The Right of Colored Persons to Ride in the Railway Cars," *Pacific Appeal*, 16 May 1863.

20 Hewitt, *Protest and Progress*, 101.

21 "The Right of Colored Persons to Ride in the Railway Cars," *Pacific Appeal*, 16 May 1863.

22 "Legal Rights Vindicated," *Frederick Douglass' Paper*, 2 March 1855.

23 Ibid.

24 "Another Outrage," *Frederick Douglass' Paper*, 2 March 1855.

25 Hewitt, *Protest and Progress*, 103.

26 A full and astute account of Pennington's life appears in Blackett, *Beating*, chap. 1.

27 Ibid., 42–45, 49, 57–59.

28 For a broad discussion of "living-proof refutations" of pseudoscientific assertions of black inferiority, see Rael, "Common Nature."

29 *Colored American*, 8 April 1838, cited in Blackett, *Beating*, 13.

30 "Colored Persons in Public Conveyances," *Frederick Douglass' Paper*, 3 December 1852.

31 "Colored Persons on the Fulton Ferry-Boats," *New York Daily Times*, 10 August 1854.

32 J. W. C. Pennington, "The Fulton-Ferry Company and Rev. Dr. Pennington," *New York Daily Times*, 11 August 1854.

33 Blackett, *Beating*, 60–61.

34 "Jamaica Convention," *Colored American*, 9 May 1840.

35 "Notice," *Frederick Douglass' Paper*, 11 May 1855.

36 "Rights of Colored People," *Frederick Douglass' Paper*, 18 May 1855.

37 "The Sixth-Avenue Railroad vs. Colored Passengers," *New York Daily Times*, 12 May 1855.

38 "Colored People in City Cars," *New York Daily Times*, 29 May 1855.

39 Ibid.; "Dr. Pennington," *Frederick Douglass' Paper*, 1 June 1855; "The Case of Rev. Dr. Pennington," *Frederick Douglass' Paper*, 8 June 1855.

40 "Colored People in City Cars," *New York Daily Times*, 29 May 1855.

41 Ibid.

42 "Another Outrage," *New York Tribune*, rpt. in *Frederick Douglass' Paper*, 2 March 1855.

43 "The Rev. Dr. Pennington," *New York Tribune*, rpt. in *Frederick Douglass' Paper*, 8 June 1855.

44 "The Legal Rights Association," *Frederick Douglass' Paper*, 7 September 1855; "Meeting of Colored Citizens," *New York Daily Times*, 27 September 1855.

45 Sit-ins on the Sixth Avenue cars continued in October. The most discussed case was that of Thomas Downing, "a well known colored citizen," an oysterman, and owner of a refectory near Wall Street "frequented daily by throngs of principal bankers and merchants." His refusal to leave the car was cheered on by white passengers, who prevented the conductor from ousting Downing, and was assisted by a white male passenger who foiled the conductor's plan not to stop the car when Downing arrived at his stop. See "Colorphobia on City Railroad," *Frederick Douglass' Paper*, 5 October 1855; "The War of Colors," *New York Daily Times*, 5 October 1855.

46 "The War of Colors," *New York Daily Times*, 5 October 1855; "The Negroes and Sixth-Avenue Cars," *New York Daily Tribune*, 2 October 1855.

47 "Dr. Pennington: To the Stockholders of the Sixth-Avenue Railroad," *New York Daily Times*, 16 October 1855.

48 "Another Outrage upon the Eighth Avenue Railroad," *New York Daily Tribune*, 17 December 1856; Leslie M. Alexander, *African or American?*, 128–29.

49 "Important and Interesting Trial—Can Colored People Ride in the City Cars?," *New York Daily Times*, 18 December 1856.

50 "Superior Court," *New York Daily Times*, 20 December 1856.

51 Leslie M. Alexander, *African or American?*, 129. A black passenger, Maria Jenkins, sued a Sixth Avenue conductor who violently ejected her from a car "with the assistance of some of the passengers." The jury found against Jenkins "after having been out a few moments" ("Law Intelligence," *New York Times*, 16 April 1858).

52 See "Gradual Abolition Act, 1799," in *Jim Crow New York*, edited by Gellman and Quigley, 52–55; "Act Declaring 1827 as the End of Slavery in New York, 1817," in *Jim Crow New York*, edited by Gellman and Quigley, 67–72.

53 Blackett, *Beating*, 80–82.

CHAPTER TWO

1 John H. White Jr., *American Railroad Passenger Car*; Arnesen, *Brotherhoods*, 16.

2 Alvarez, *Travel*, ix.

3 Ayers, *Promise*, 9–11.

4 Alvarez, *Travel*, 15.

5 Stanton, Anthony, and Gage, *History*, 926–28.

6 Cohen, *At Freedom's Edge*, 217; McPherson "Abolitionists and the Civil Rights Act."

7 McPherson, "Abolitionists and the Civil Rights Act."

8 Wells-Barnett, *Crusade*, 18.

9 Wells Diary, 1885–87, 183, Ida B. Wells Papers, Box 9, Folder 8, Joseph Regenstein Library, University of Chicago.

10 The case law demonstrates that northern blacks sued against segregation and exclusion from ships, trains, and streetcars from 1855 to the mid-1870s, while southern blacks began to press suits against segregation on railroads in the late 1870s, with the number of cases increasing dramatically in the 1880s. For a closer examination, see Welke, *All the Women Are White*; Mack, "Law, Society, Identity"; Minter, "Freedom."

11 Brutal racial separations sometimes extended to train stations. Rebecca Smith, a native of South Carolina, sued the South Carolina Railway company after she was attacked and violently ejected from the "ladies' waiting room" when she tried to purchase a ticket to travel from Graniteville to Aiken, South Carolina. The railroad sales agent insisted that because she was a black woman, she would have to purchase her ticket on the side designated for male passengers, where "smoking and chewing or cursing" traditionally took place. When charging the jury, the Aiken county circuit court judge implied that perhaps Smith deserved to be removed from the ladies' waiting room not only on the basis of her race but also because she had been disorderly and unladylike. He ruled that "the agent would have had no right to force her out, and eject her, if she was conducting herself properly while there." Despite her elegant dress and behavior, the judge still asserted that she was disreputable simply because of her color (*Smith et al. v. Chamberlain*).

12 Welke, *All the Women Are White*, 16.

13 George Washington Cable, "The Silent South, 1885," in *Negro Question*, 113.

14 Railroad companies complained about the cost but on the whole did little to aid the campaigns of black passengers for equal accommodations. Poor treatment often went hand in hand with railroad officials' complaints. Booker T. Washington wrote privately to the general counsel of the Southern Pacific Railroad to inquire why black passengers were allowed to board and land on the connecting ferry run by the railroad only after whites and "buggies, wagons, carts and cattle" had boarded and disembarked. The railroad's attorney, Charles Harrison Tweed, offered no apology and instead responded that Washington was mistaken about the ferry that crossed the Mississippi to con-

nect the railroad route. Tweed also complained about the costs of the Jim Crow system: "Of course you are aware that the separated accommodations laws in force in most of the Southern States have entailed quite a heavy expense upon all the railroad companies in those States, but we should not be held responsible for regulations which we are powerless to prevent or control and which involve a constant expense to us which we would be very glad to avoid" ("From Charles Harrison Tweed," 30 September, 7 October 1901, in *Booker T. Washington Papers*, 6:220–21, 234–35).

15 Such claims were used to bar black women even without evidence that they were of "questionable" character. An African American woman from Memphis was denied seating in the first-class car even though she had purchased a first-class ticket and was "ejected" by "brutal violence" on grounds that she was "a notorious courtesan, addicted to lascivious and profane conversation and immodest deportment in public places." She was blocked from the ladies' car, which "was set apart to be exclusively used and occupied by persons of good character, and genteel and modest deportment" because the conductor believed she was of "improper character." Although there was no outside evidence that she was a prostitute, the conductor defamed her character in the effort to prevent her from sitting in the first-class car. So when black women and their gentlemen companions were asked to leave ladies' cars because of their race, such actions not only carried the stigma of racial segregation but also marked them and all black women as immoral or improper. African American women litigants sued not only to defend their right to first-class seating but also to defend their character (*Brown v. Memphis and C.R. Co.*).

16 Welke, *All the Women Are White*, 8.

17 George Washington Cable, "The Freedmen's Case in Equity, 1884," in *Negro Question*, 74.

18 Wilmington and Raleigh Railroad officials found that "the class of white men secured was less reliable than the slaves" (quoted in Arnesen, *Brotherhoods*, 8).

19 Ibid., 9–10. For more on convict labor on railroads, see Oshinsky, *Worse Than Slavery*.

20 Arnesen writes that Pullman "quickly became the since largest employer of African-American labor in the United States, carrying roughly 6,000 blacks on its payroll in 1914" (*Brotherhoods*, 17).

21 Ibid.

22 *Heard v. Georgia R.R. Co.*

23 James Weldon Johnson, *Along This Way*, 87.

24 Ibid., 84–86.

25 Ibid.

26 *Council v. Western and Atlantic R.R. Co.*

27 Welke, *All the Women Are White*, 181.

28 Ibid., 9–10.

29 "Lynch Law in the United States," *Ladies Pictorial*, Wells Papers, Box 8, Folder 10.

30 Cable, "Freedmen's Case in Equity," 71, 74–75.

31 Terrell, *Colored Woman*, 15–16.

32 As theorist Saidiya Hartman asserts, for white women, "citizenship did not imply or confer an equality of political rights": it offered protection instead of citizenship rights (*Scenes of Subjection*, 200).

33 Cooper, *Voice*, 90–91. Black women received neither citizenship nor protection. As Hall states, black women "shared with black men all the burdens of subordination; in addition, they were denied the deference granted women as compensation for powerlessness" (Hall, *Revolt against Chivalry*, 78). For more on black women's unique burden, see Hartman, *Scenes of Subjection*, 200.

34 Wells, "Model Woman," 188.

35 Hine, "Rape and the Inner Lives of Black Women," in *Hine Sight*, 37.

36 Testimony of G. H. Flowers, *Chesapeake, Ohio, and Southwestern R.R. v. Wells*, in Welke, *All the Women Are White*, 6.

37 *Williams et al. v. Jacksonville, T & K.W. Ry. Co.*

38 African Americans often employed what historian Joel Williamson terms "part-time" passing to benefit from first-class treatment (*New People*).

39 *Houck v. Southern Pacific Railway Company*. For a comparative perspective on the *Houck* case, see Sumler-Edmond, "Quest for Justice."

40 For studies that outline black women's attempts at protection from sexual attacks, see Hunter, *To 'Joy My Freedom*; Mann, "Slavery, Sharecropping, and Sexual Inequality"; Shaw, *What a Woman Ought to Be*.

41 *Southwestern Christian Advocate*, 7 August 1890, 4.

42 A. E. P. Albert, "Editorial Notes," *Southwestern Christian Advocate*, 31 July 1890, 1. Brown and Kimball have argued that class biases may have tainted perceptions of excursions: "A middle class that heralded public displays of material consumption, as in the construction of larger homes 'suitable for race advancement,' could at the same time denounce as wasteful working-class displays such as popular excursion trips. Many working-class families may have seen the ability to travel together on the one-day trips as important signs of their standing rather than as extravagance" ("Mapping the Terrain," 332).

43 For studies that explore excursions, see Blassingame, *Black New Orleans*, 144–45; Hunter, *To 'Joy My Freedom*, 150–51; Rabinowitz, *Race Relations*, 229; Dittmer, *Black Georgia*, 66.

44 For a comparable theory about black politics and public space on public transportation, see Kelley, *Race Rebels*, 55–76.

CHAPTER THREE

1 Reed, "Race Legislation."

2 Blassingame, *Black New Orleans*, 189–92; Fischer, *Segregation Struggle*, 30–41.

3 Blassingame points out that black legislators in Louisiana were at the cutting edge of African American attempts to stop segregationist practices on the

rails: "The attempts Negroes made to prohibit segregation on the railroads were far more sophisticated than any of their other campaigns" (*Black New Orleans*, 189–92).

4 For more on the politics of Creole and Black efforts to push for full suffrage and citizenship, see Logsdon and Bell, "Americanization."

5 I have employed the terms "Afro-Creole" and "Creole of color" to describe the French-speaking, Catholic, mixed-race descendents of free people of color in New Orleans to distinguish them from non-Creole African Americans. I have employed the terms "black American" and "black" to mean non-Creole populations in New Orleans. I have used the term "African Americans" as an overarching identity to describe both communities. The descriptive terms available to describe the complexities of community are limited; however, I have adopted this language as a way of better outlining the distinctions of identity in post-Emancipation New Orleans.

6 Bell, *Revolution*; Rousseve, *Negro in Louisiana*.

7 Fischer, "Racial Segregation"; Desdunes, *Our People and Our History*.

8 Blassingame, *Black New Orleans*.

9 For more on the legacy of Creoles of color, see Desdunes, *Our People and Our History*.

10 For a closer look at passing in New Orleans, see Anthony, "'Lost Boundaries.'"

11 Justice to Cable, 24 February 1887, in Somers, "Black and White," 29.

12 Thompson outlines the role of folklore and law in her discussion of the case of "Toucoutou," an Afro-Creole woman who attempted to be legally designated white. The futility of her failed case was memorialized in a Creole song. See Thompson, "'Ah Toucoutou.'"

13 George Washington Cable, "The Silent South, 1885," in *Negro Question*, 98.

14 George Washington Cable, "The Freedmen's Case in Equity, 1884," in ibid., 71–72.

15 Anthony, "Negro Creole Community"; Medley, "Sad Story," 106–7; *Soard's City Directory, New Orleans, 1900*, in *U.S. City Directories, 1882–1901* (microfilm); Keith Weldon Medley, "The Life and Times of Homer Plessy and John Ferguson," *New Orleans Times-Picayune*, 18 May 1996.

16 Desdunes, *Our People and Our History*, 144; Tourgée Papers (microfilm).

17 Medley, "Life and Times."

18 Miller, "Urban Blacks," 189, 192; Hair, *Carnival of Fury*, 69–71.

19 Jacobs, "Benevolent Societies," 21.

20 Olsen, "Reflections," 167.

21 Jacobs, "Benevolent Societies," 21–24; Somers, "Black and White," 32; Arnesen, *Waterfront Workers*.

22 Somers, "Black and White," 32; Bennett, *Religion*, 20–27; Arnesen, *Waterfront Workers*; Meier, "Negro Class Structure," 261.

23 "Editorial Notes," *Southwestern Christian Advocate*, 13 March 1890, 1; "Colored Schools of New Orleans," *Southwestern Christian Advocate*, 20 March 1890, 4; "Editorial Notes," *Southwestern Christian Advocate*, 27 February 1890, 1.

24 Because the extensive legal and historical literature on New Orleans in this era focuses almost exclusively on the Creole of color community or ignores distinctions in African American identity, little has been written about the non-Creole black community. The *Southwestern Christian Advocate* is a source that helps to outline the contours of identity within New Orleans's African American population. For more on Albert and the *Advocate*, see Penn, *Afro-American Press*, 223–27; Bennett, *Religion*.

25 Albert, *House of Bondage*, v.

26 *Daily Crusader*, 22 June 1895, 1; *Crusader*, 16 July 1891, 1, Crusader Clippings, R. L. Desdunes Papers, Xavier University Library, New Orleans.

27 Rousseve, *Negro in Louisiana*, 157; Anthony, "Negro Creole Community," 51. Although I believe Anthony goes too far in categorizing Creole efforts to break away from the non-Creole community, the work does highlight Afro-Creoles' distinct approach to the question of segregation. See also the foreword to Desdunes, *Our People, Our History*, xvii; Medley, "Sad Story," 109–10.

28 "Separating the Races on the Cars," *Southwestern Christian Advocate*, 13 March 1890, 4.

29 Ibid.

30 Ibid.

31 P. B. S. Pinchback, "Speech of Senator Pinchback—On Taking the Chair of the National Equal Rights Convention," Clippings File, P. B. S. Pinchback Papers, Moorland-Spingarn Library, Howard University, Washington, D.C.

32 ACERA grew out of the National Colored Convention held in Washington, D.C., in 1890. Men of both Creole and non-Creole descent were elected to represent Louisiana's districts, and Pinchback was the most prominent of the state's representatives Pinchback assumed a leadership position in the four-hundred-delegate national convention and spearheaded the organization of Louisiana blacks. For more on the convention, see J. W. Smith, "Our Washington Letter, Topical Talk about Persons and Things, The Convention— Bishop Jones," *Star of Zion*, 13 February 1890, 2. For more on Pinchback's background and career, see Haskins, *Pinkney Benton Stewart Pinchback*, 253–56.

33 Masthead, *Daily Crusader*, 22 June 1895, 2.

34 The one-drop rule meant that anyone with a traceable African ancestor, no matter how phenotypically white he or she might appear, would still by law be designated a Negro.

35 "The State Convention of Colored Men," *Southwestern Christian Advocate*, 23 January 1890, 5; "American Citizens' Equal Rights Association," *Southwestern Christian Advocate*, 13 March 1890, 4.

36 For more on Cruikshank and voting rights, see Goldman, *Reconstruction and Black Suffrage*.

37 "A Great National Movement," *Southwestern Christian Advocate*, 20 March 1890, 4; "Another Negro Butchered," *Southwestern Christian Advocate*, 29 May 1890, 1; "An Infamous Fabrication," *Southwestern Christian Advocate*, 12 June 1890, 4.

38 "Editorial Notes," *Southwestern Christian Advocate*, 3 April 1890, 1.

39 Pinchback, "Speech of Senator Pinchback."

40 Olsen, "Reflections."

41 "American Citizens' Equal Rights Association," *Southwestern Christian Advocate*, 29 May 1890, 5.

42 Ibid.

43 American Citizens' Equal Rights Association to Members, February 12, 1890, Pinchback Papers.

44 "Protest of the American Citizens' Equal Rights Association of Louisiana, against Class Legislation," *Southwestern Christian Advocate*, 5 June 1890, 4.

45 Ibid.

46 "Pleas against Class Legislation by Rev. A. E. P. Albert, D.D.," *Southwestern Christian Advocate*, 19 June 1890, 1.

47 Ibid.

48 Ibid.

49 Ibid.

50 Pinchback, "Speech of Senator Pinchback"; Desdunes, *Our People and Our History*, 145; "Political Review," *Southwestern Christian Advocate*, 17 July 1890, 4.

51 "A Convention," *Southwestern Christian Advocate*, 17 July 1890, 4.

52 Afro-American Council, "An Appeal to Officers of Southern States," Pinchback Papers.

53 Bennett, *Religion*, 92–94.

54 R. L. Desdunes to A. Tourgée, 28 February 1892, Tourgée Papers (microfilm). Desdunes's pride in ACERA's unique history may have been short-lived; he neglected to mention the organization in *Our People and Our History*, an omission that obscures this brief moment of cross-cultural alliance.

55 L. A. Martinet to A. Tourgée, 5 October 1891, Tourgée Papers (microfilm).

56 Medley, *We as Freemen*, 107.

57 Rabinowitz, *Race Relations*, 194.

58 L. A. Martinet to A. Tourgée, 5, 25 October 1891, Tourgée Papers (microfilm).

59 Nearly every member of the committee had a French surname and/or had his residence and place of business in the French Quarter, which affirms his status as an elite Creole of color. See *Soard's City Directory, New Orleans, 1900*, in *U.S. City Directories, 1882–1901* (microfilm).

60 Medley, *We as Freemen*, 117–18.

61 Foreword to Desdunes, *Our People, Our History*, xvii. Pinchback had attended Howard Law School and supported institutions of higher learning for black students but fervently opposed segregating public primary schools, believing that such distinctions would mark black children as inherently inferior (P. B. S. Pinchback, "On the Need for Equality in Education," n.d., Pinchback Papers).

62 L. A. Martinet to A. Tourgée, 5 October 1891, Tourgée Papers (microfilm).

63 "Report of Proceedings of the Citizens' Committee for the Annulment of Act

no. 111 Commonly Known as the Separate Car Law," *Plessy v. Ferguson* Records, Amistad Research Center, Tulane University, New Orleans.

64 *Crusader*, 28 May 1892, Desdunes Papers. The Supreme Court had done little to enforce the Reconstruction amendments and had struck down the Civil Rights Act of 1875, which gave black access to public accommodations, including trains, nine years earlier. Test cases for black rights would not succeed until after the turn of the twentieth century with Booker T. Washington's campaign to end peonage laws.

65 Ibid.

66 Wright, *Life behind a Veil*, 62–65.

67 *Acts of the General Assembly of the Commonwealth of Kentucky*, chap. 40.

68 S. E. Smith, *History*, 8.

69 *Anderson v. Louisville and N.R. Co.*; Wright, *Life behind a Veil*, 65.

70 *Civil Rights Cases.*

71 L. A. Martinet to A. Tourgée, 11, 5 October 1891, Tourgée Papers (microfilm); Desdunes, *Our People and Our History*, 29–30.

72 Logsdon and Powell, "Rodolphe Lucien Desdunes," 54; L. A. Martinet to A. Tourgée, 11, 5 October 1891, Tourgée Papers (microfilm). For an account of Tourgée's career as a race advocate, see Elliot, *Color-Blind Justice.*

73 L. A. Martinet to A. Tourgée, 11, 5 October 1891, Tourgée Papers (microfilm).

74 Ibid.

75 *May v. Shreveport Traction Co.*

76 L. A. Martinet to A. Tourgée, 7 December 1891, Tourgée Papers (microfilm).

77 Ibid., 28 December 1891, *Plessy v. Ferguson* Records.

78 Ibid., 5 October 1891, Tourgée Papers (microfilm).

79 Ibid., 5 October 1891, 26 May 1892.

80 Olsen, "Reflections," 174.

81 A 1785 Virginia statute defined Negroes as those who had an African ancestor as a parent or grandparent and allowed those who had a more distant ancestor to pass as legally but not socially white. Other states in the Upper South had similar protections. But as pressures on populations of free people of color increased in the 1850s, whites began to complain about the mixed-blood law and argued that such allowances blurred racial distinctions in dangerous ways. See Berlin, *Slaves without Masters*, 98–99, 365–66; Davis, *Who Is Black?*, 34.

82 L. A. Martinet to A. Tourgée, 5 October 1891, Tourgée Papers (microfilm).

83 Ibid., 7 December 1891.

84 Ibid., 11 October 1891.

85 Ibid., 7 December 1891.

86 Because prior arrangements had been made, Plessy was arrested by a private detective before the train left the station for its short journey.

87 For an edited account of the legal battle over *Plessy v. Ferguson*, see Brook Thomas, *Plessy v. Ferguson*. For a close analysis of the case law, the best account available appears in Lofgren, *Plessy Case.*

88 L. A. Martinet to A. W. Tourgée, May 20, 1893, Tourgée Papers (microfilm).

89 Klarman, *From Jim Crow to Civil Rights*, 10.

90 Booker T. Washington, "An Article in *Our Day*," in *Booker T. Washington Papers*, 4:186–87.

91 Booker T. Washington "Atlanta Exposition Address," in ibid., 1:73–76.

92 Frederick Douglass, "The Negro Exodus from the Gulf States: A Paper Read in Saratoga, New York on 12 September 1879," in *Frederick Douglass Papers*.

93 For more on Louisiana's connection to Cuba and the Spanish-American War, see Scott, *Degrees of Freedom*.

94 Washington, *Up from Slavery*, 69.

CHAPTER FOUR

1 The population of New Orleans, the largest city in the Deep South, included 339,075 people of color, just over 26 percent of the total (U.S. Bureau of the Census, *Negro Population*, 229).

2 E. Charles Charlton, *Street Railways of New Orleans, Interurbans Special no. 17*, 1955, Historic New Orleans Collection, Williams Research Center, New Orleans; U.S. Bureau of the Census, *Special Reports*, 24; Mitzell, *Streetcar Stories*. The Crescent City's streetcar system was characterized at the time as winding, chaotic, crowded, poorly administered, and heavily used. Five companies ran streetcars and maintained tracks, whereas many cities had streetcar systems run by a single company.

3 "The New Orleans Creole," *Southwestern Christian Advocate*, 19 October 1899, 8; Charlton, *Street Railways*.

4 Charlton, *Street Railways*; Louis C. Hennick and E. Harper Charlton, *The Streetcars of New Orleans*, 28–29, Historic New Orleans Collection; "The Carrollton Road Transferred," *New Orleans Daily Picayune*, 18 July 1902; "The Street Railroads," *New Orleans Daily Picayune*, 20 July 1902.

5 Grady, *Life and Labors*, 111–12.

6 The literature on the Progressive movement generally frames segregation as a stopgap for racial violence. See McGerr, *Fierce Discontent*, 182–84. McGerr writes, "Segregation was a complicated social phenomenon, and it served a complicated purpose for the progressives. . . . True to their mission to create a safe society for themselves and their children, the progressives turned to segregation as a way to halt dangerous social conflict that could not otherwise be stopped. . . . Progressives fairly readily accepted the inequitable arrangement of segregation. They did so because usually there were worse alternatives" (183). However, a close inquiry into the passage of segregation laws demonstrates that segregation did little to end racial violence in the cities where laws were passed. The Atlanta race riot happened six years after the city passed a law segregating the streetcars. Three years after Mobile's streetcars were segregated, they transported onlookers to the site of a multiple-victim lynching.

Progressives may have employed ending racial violence as an argument, but it was a thin argument at best. See "Race Separation in the Cars," *Mobile Daily Register*, 31 October 1902, 2; "While in Mobile" (rpt. from *Eutaw Mirror and Observer*), *Mobile Daily Register*, 3 June 1902, 4.

7 "The Street Railroads," *New Orleans Daily Picayune*, 20 July 1902.

8 Although Hair, *Carnival of Fury*, claims that New Orleans "trolleys served a predominantly white clientele even without segregation" and asserts that "most black New Orleanians could not afford to ride on a regular basis" (139), the history of protest against segregated streetcars beginning in the 1860s and continuing though the turn of the century, as well as innumerable accounts of black riders, suggests quite the opposite. Black riders in New Orleans and throughout the South constituted a large portion of the streetcar traffic. This heavy ridership alone implies that nearly all segments of the city rode the cars. See "The Street Railroads," *New Orleans Daily Picayune*, 20 July 1902; "The Strike of Electric Railway Employees," *Southwestern Christian Advocate*, 9 October 1902, 8.

9 "Editorial Notes," *Southwestern Christian Advocate*, 3 July 1902, 1; A. R. Holcombe, "The Separate Street-Car Law in New Orleans," *Outlook*, 29 November 1902.

10 U.S. Bureau of the Census, *Special Reports*, 30.

11 "Negroes Take Action," *New Orleans Daily Picayune*, 31 July 1902; "New 'Jim Crow' Law Becomes Operative," *New Orleans Times-Democrat*, 4 November 1902.

12 Wade, *Slavery in the Cities*, 267; "North and South," *Frederick Douglass' Paper*, 18 March 1852; *Niles Register*, 24 August 1833.

13 For a more detailed account of early battles against segregated streetcars in New Orleans, see Fischer, "Pioneer Protest"; Fischer, *Segregation Struggle*, 32–41; Blassingame, *Black New Orleans*, 189–90; Scott, *Degrees of Freedom*, 44.

14 Meier and Rudwick, "Origins," 309–10; Litwack, *Been in the Storm*, 263.

15 Painter, *Sojourner Truth*, 210–11.

16 The bill required the separation only in cities with more than fifty thousand residents, a category that included solely New Orleans (Hair, *Carnival of Fury*, 139).

17 "Editorial Notes," *Southwestern Christian Advocate*, 14 June 1900, 1; "Separate Street Car Ordinance Defeated," *Southwestern Christian Advocate*, 1 November 1900, 1.

18 "Rev. I. B. Scott, D.D.," *Southwestern Christian Advocate*, 4 June 1896, 4; "Editorial Notes," *Southwestern Christian Advocate*, 28 June 1900, 1.

19 "Discrimination on Georgia Street Cars," *Southwestern Christian Advocate*, 5 July 1900, 8.

20 *Southwestern Christian Advocate*, 9 October 1902; "The City Schools Reduced in Grade," *Southwestern Christian Advocate*, 5 July 1900, 8. For how segregation and disfranchisement connected to segregation within the Methodist Episcopal Church, see Bennett, *Religion*.

21 "Race Identity in New Orleans," *Southwestern Christian Advocate*, 19 July 1900, 8.

22 Ibid.

23 Ibid.

24 In the memoir *Lemon Swamp*, Fields reported that fair-skinned African Americans would pass for white "around strangers" on the streetcars in Charleston, South Carolina. But people willing to pass for privilege were the "laughing stock" of other African Americans. She also reported that many people who could have passed for white did not: "Not all light-skinned people had the Jim Crow spirit. Some carried themselves like members of the community and proud of it" (Fields with Fields, *Lemon Swamp*, 64).

25 "Race Identity in New Orleans," *Southwestern Christian Advocate*, 19 July 1900, 8.

26 Hair, *Carnival of Fury*; "Dark Days in New Orleans," *Southwestern Christian Advocate*, 2 August 1900, 8.

27 Hair, *Carnival of Fury*, 152–55; Wells-Barnett, "Mob Rule," 191.

28 Wells-Barnett, "Mob Rule," 171; Hair, *Carnival of Fury*, 153; "Better Than the United States Flag," *Southwestern Christian Advocate*, 2 August 1900, 8.

29 Hair, *Carnival of Fury*; Wells-Barnett, "Mob Rule"; "Dark Days in New Orleans," *Southwestern Christian Advocate*, 2 August 1900, 8.

30 Ibid.

31 Hair, *Carnival of Fury*, 177–78; "Editorial Notes," *Southwestern Christian Advocate*, 20 September 1900, 1.

32 Arnesen, *Waterfront Workers*, 140.

33 "Crowds Gone North" and untitled, *Southwestern Christian Advocate*, 16 August 1900, 8.

34 "Will It Be So During Mardi Gras?," *Southwestern Christian Advocate*, 1 November 1900, 1, 8.

35 "Some Lessons from the Outbreak of Last Week," *Southwestern Christian Advocate*, 2 August 1900, 1; Wells-Barnett, "Mob Rule," 160, 194; Hair, *Carnival of Fury*, 154; "Editorial Notes," *Southwestern Christian Advocate*, 2 August 1900, 1.

36 "Some Lessons from the Outbreak of Last Week," *Southwestern Christian Advocate*, 2 August 1900, 1.

37 For more on racial violence as labor control in the Atlanta race riot, see Godshalk, *Veiled Visions*, 177.

38 "Some Lessons from the Outbreak of Last Week," *Southwestern Christian Advocate*, 2 August 1900, 1.

39 "Separate Street Car Ordinance Defeated," *Southwestern Christian Advocate*, 1 November 1900, 1.

40 "Editorial Notes," *Southwestern Christian Advocate*, 5 June 1902, 1; *Mobile Daily Register*, 5 June 1902.

41 "Editorial Notes," *Southwestern Christian Advocate*, 5 June 1902, 1; A. R. Holcombe, "The Separate Street-Car Law in New Orleans," *Outlook*, 29 November 1902.

42 J. Max Barber, "The Aggressiveness of Jim-Crowism," *Voice of the Negro*, June 1904, 216–17.

43 W. E. B. Du Bois, "The Negro South and North," *Bibliotheca Sacra*, July 1905, 500–513, rpt. in *Writings*, 250–56. Du Bois continued, "There is in Georgia permissive legislation which allows cities to separate the races on street-cars by giving the Negroes the rear end of the car, and the whites the front. This is, however, seldom enforced, as the self-interest of street-car companies forbids it. Recently, however, we have had a curious experience in Atlanta. The old street-car line which covered the main part of the city was thought to be getting rich, and the city council chartered a rival line. The rival line bid for public favor by announcing that it would follow the state law, and separate the races on its cars. The only effect of this at first was to drive the Negro patrons to the old line. Then the new line, which had meantime 'influenced' a few extra councilmen, put through a city ordinance compelling all street-cars to discriminate."

44 J. Max Barber, "Execute the Law," *Voice of the Negro*, February 1905, 126–27.

45 J. Max Barber, "A Progressive Little Town," *Voice of the Negro*, November 1905, 754.

46 Booker T. Washington, "To Robert Elijah Jones," 3 November 1913, in *Booker T. Washington Papers*, 12:327; Robert. E. Jones, "From Robert Elijah Jones," 29 December 1913, in *Booker T. Washington Papers*, 12:385–87.

47 Robert. E. Jones, "From Robert Elijah Jones," 29 December 1913, in *Booker T. Washington Papers*, 12:385–87; A. R. Holcombe, "The Separate Street-Car Law in New Orleans," *Outlook*, 29 November 1902). Although Jones's description was written slightly more than a decade following the passage of the law, it is consistent with the rules that governed black passengers in 1902.

48 Case law 266, *Louisiana Digest*.

49 Robert E. Jones, "From Robert Elijah Jones," 29 December 1913, in *Booker T. Washington Papers*, 12:385–87.

50 Ibid.; "Crescent City Notes," *Southwestern Christian Advocate*, 3 January 1901, 16; "Personal and General," *Southwestern Christian Advocate*, 8 May 1902, 9.

51 Robert E. Jones, "From Robert Elijah Jones," 29 December 1913, in *Booker T. Washington Papers*, 12:385–87.

52 Ibid.

53 "The Facts Misrepresented," *Southwestern Christian Advocate*, 25 December 1902, 1.

54 "Editorial Notes," *Southwestern Christian Advocate*, 3 July 1902, 1.

55 *Morrison v. State*; *Patterson v. Taylor*; *Crooms v. Schad*.

56 *Bowie v. Birmingham Railway & Electric Co.*

57 Although they were educated members of an exclusive organization, these women were not part of New Orleans's famed Creole of color community. Creoles of color maintained separate chapters of the Masons and Eastern Star; for example, many of their functions were conducted in French, effectively barring non-Creoles from membership. These leading women did not have French surnames and resided in the desirable but Americanized Garden District. Their names and residences, along with their civic memberships and their

political tactics, clearly suggest that they were not Creoles of color but instead were affiliated with the city's Americanized black middle class. The city's Afro-Creole leadership did not take prominent leadership positions in the 1902 streetcar protest; instead, the movement was led by black New Orleanians. The frequent use of initials rather than full names also reflects their desire for respectable treatment. Members of the black middle class frequently used initials to force whites to call them Mr., Mrs., or Miss rather than by their first names. Such practices sought to dodge some of the insults of Jim Crow etiquette. See *Soard's City Directory, New Orleans, 1902*, in *U.S. City Directories, 1882–1901* (microfilm); Records of the Prince Hall Masons, Amistad Research Center, Tulane University, New Orleans.

58 "Negroes Take Action," *New Orleans Daily Picayune*, 31 July 1902; Jacobs, "Strategies," 86.

59 "Women's Work in New Orleans," *Southwestern Christian Advocate*, 17 October 1901, 4; Jacobs, "Benevolent Societies"; "Woman's Clubs Federation," *Southwestern Christian Advocate*, 8 January 1903, 8–9.

60 "Negroes Take Action," *New Orleans Daily Picayune*, 31 July 1902.

61 Nannie H. Burroughs, "Not Color but Character," *Voice of the Negro*, July 1904, 277–79.

62 For more on how Burroughs and other black women leaders balanced the quest for respectability and leadership, see Higginbotham, *Righteous Discontent*.

63 Arnesen, *Waterfront Workers*, 187.

64 "Editorial Notes," *Southwestern Christian Advocate*, 6 November 1902, 1.

65 "Negro Entertainments," *New Orleans Daily Picayune*, 3 December 1902.

66 "Side Lights of the Congress," *Southwestern Christian Advocate*, 28 August 1902, 8.

67 "Negro Entertainments," *New Orleans Daily Picayune*, 3 December 1902.

68 *Southwestern Christian Advocate*, 1 January 1903, 8.

69 Ibid.; Arnesen, *Waterfront Workers*, 86.

70 "The Facts Misrepresented," *Southwestern Christian Advocate*, 25 December 1902, 1.

71 "Editorial Notes," *Southwestern Christian Advocate*, 12 June 1902, 1; "Editorial Notes," *Southwestern Christian Advocate*, 4 September 1902, 1.

72 "Editorial Notes," *Southwestern Christian Advocate*, 19 June 1902, 1.

73 *State v. Pearson*; *Southwestern Christian Advocate*, 20 November 1902, 8; "Suing Car Line Officers," *New York Times*, 9 November 1902, 1.

74 Campbell's study of corporate competition among streetcar companies in Savannah, Georgia, and Roback's assessment of the political economy of segregated streetcars outline some of the reasons why corporations hesitated to enforce segregation laws. See Campbell, "Profit, Prejudice, and Protest"; Roback, "Political Economy."

75 "Screens Separate the Races in Street Cars," *New Orleans Daily Picayune*, 4 November 1902; "The Separate Car Law," *New Orleans Daily Picayune*, 18 October 1902; "Negroes Take Action," *New Orleans Daily Picayune*, 31 July 1902.

76 Booker T. Washington, "To Charles William Eliot," 7 March 1906, in *Booker T. Washington Papers*, 13:512.

77 *Southwestern Christian Advocate*, 1 January 1903, 8.

78 "The Separate Street Car Law Sustained," *Southwestern Christian Advocate*, 26 March 1903, 1; "Editorial Notes," *Southwestern Christian Advocate*, 26 February 1903, 1.

79 "Editorial Notes," *Southwestern Christian Advocate*, 26 February 1903, 1; "The New Orleans Street Car Situation," *Southwestern Christian Advocate*, 23 April 1903, 8.

80 "The New Orleans Street Car Situation," *Southwestern Christian Advocate*, 23 April 1903, 8.

81 "The Company Could Help Us Dally," *Southwestern Christian Advocate*, 7 May 1903, 8; Arnesen, *Waterfront Workers*, 187; Booker T. Washington, "To Robert Elijah Jones," 3 November 1913, in *Booker T. Washington Papers*, 12:327; Robert E. Jones, "From Robert Elijah Jones," 29 December 1913, in *Booker T. Washington Papers*, 12:385–87.

CHAPTER FIVE

1 U.S. Bureau of the Census, *Negro Population*, 229.

2 Giles B. Jackson, "The Negro as Real Estate Dealer," 23 August 1900, W. P. Burrell, "The Colored People of Richmond, VA, 1901," both in Records of the National Negro Business League, Manuscript Division, Library of Congress, Washington, D.C.

3 For more on the history of black organizations in Richmond, see Gavins, "Urbanization and Segregation." Ann Field Alexander also includes an excellent chapter on the Knights of Pythias, the Independent Order of St. Luke, and the United Order of True Reformers in her biography of John Mitchell Jr. (*Race Man*, chap. 11) For good analyses of women's leadership in Richmond's black organizations, see Brown, "Womanist Consciousness"; Brown and Kimball, "Mapping the Terrain"; Brown, "Negotiating and Transforming."

4 For more on the history of racial violence, see Shapiro, *White Violence*.

5 Cable, *Negro Question*; Blair, *Southern Prophecy*.

6 Through an alliance with the Readjuster Party, whose more populist doctrine attracted black voters, African Americans in Jackson Ward gained their greatest political strength between 1871 and 1896, when voters elected thirty-three black city council members (Chesson, "Richmond's Black Councilmen," 192–94).

7 Anderson participated in a debate on the subject "The Woman's Place Is in the Home" in favor of the idea that the woman's place was in business. See "Debate a Success," *Richmond Reformer*, 28 January 1905, 1; John Mitchell Jr., " 'Jim Crow' Street-Cars," *Richmond Planet*, 16 April 1904, 1; "Citizens Protest," *Richmond Planet*, 23 April 1904, 1; *J. L. Hill Printing Company's Directory, Richmond and Manchester, Va., 1901*, in *U.S. City Directories, 1882–1901* (microfilm).

8 Brown, "Uncle Ned's Children," 428.

9 Gavins, "Urbanization and Segregation."

10 Meier and Rudwick, "Boycott Movement," characterized these protests as con-servative, middle-class dissent, and most historians who mention the streetcar boycotts have repeated these labels. Some leaders may have been conservative in language and outlook regarding how protesters should behave, but boy-cotts nevertheless posed a fundamental and broad challenge to Jim Crow segregation. Ann Field Alexander suggests that the conservative language of the protests was an attempt to turn the tables on whites who insisted with the passage of each new piece of oppressive legislation that the restriction of black rights would result in harmonious relations between black and white southerners. Mitchell's language calling for a peaceful boycott was an attempt to put protest in the terms of white segregationists. As Alexander states, "Now whites would find their language used against them" (*Race Man*, 137).

11 *Code of Virginia*, 1904 Virginia Code 1294d; John Mitchell Jr., "'Jim Crow' Street-Cars," *Richmond Planet*, 9 April 1904, 4; *Richmond News Leader*, 7 April 1904, 3.

12 "Citizens Protest," *Richmond Planet*, 23 April 1904, 1; John Mitchell Jr., "'Jim Crow' Street-Cars," *Richmond Planet*, 9 April 1904, 4.

13 "Colored Folks Yet Walking: More Trouble—The Rule Very Annoying," *Richmond Planet*, 7 May 1904, 1.

14 "Richmond Passenger and Power Co. Trolley," ca. 1900, Cook Photograph Collection, Valentine Richmond History Center, Richmond, Va.

15 U.S. Bureau of the Census, *Twelfth Census*, vol. 13; Meier and Rudwick, "Boycott Movement," 761–62; "No Discrimination against Negroes," *Richmond News Leader*, 8 April 1904, 6; "Citizens Protest," *Richmond Planet*, 23 April 1904, 1; "The Separate Cars and the Negro," *Richmond Planet*, 27 October 1900, 4.

16 Brown, "Negotiating and Transforming," 50–51; "Citizens Protest," *Richmond Planet*, 23 April 1904, 1.

17 Maggie Lena Walker, "Nothing but Leaves, 1909," cited in Marlowe, *Right Worthy Grand Mission*, 56; Brown, "Womanist Consciousness," 616–17.

18 Walker, "Nothing but Leaves," cited in Marlowe, *Right Worthy Grand Mission*, 56.

19 "Our Reply to the News-Leader," *St. Luke Herald*, 3 September 1904.

20 "Jimcrowism Spreads," *St. Luke Herald*, 3 September 1904.

21 Maggie Lena Walker, "An Address for Men Only," St. Luke Hall, 1 March 1906, Maggie Lena Walker Papers, Box 3, Folder 24, Maggie Lena Walker National Historic Site, Richmond, Virginia.

22 "Who Are the Lynchers?" and "Editorial Notes," *St. Luke Herald*, 3 September 1904.

23 Maggie Lena Walker, "Stumbling Blocks," cited in Marlowe, *Right Worthy Grand Mission*, 58.

24 Walker, "Address for Men Only."

25 Maggie Lena Walker, Speech, Negro Young People's Christian and Educational Congress, Convention Hall, Washington, D.C., 5 August 1906, Walker Papers.

26 Ibid.

27 Ibid.

28 Giddings, *Ida*, 153.

29 The story of Barnes and Abernathy is recounted in Brown, "Negotiating and Transforming"; Lebsock, *Murder in Virginia*. The *Planet* regularly featured accounts of race riots, lynchings, and murders of black citizens; see "Mobs in Oklahoma," *Richmond Planet*, 5 May 1900, 4; "Died a Martyr of Race Rights," *Richmond Planet*, 13 October 1900, 1; "The Reign of Lawlessness: Judge Lynch's Bloody Work," *Richmond Planet*, 7 January 1899, 4. For an excellent biography of Mitchell, see Ann Field Alexander, *Race Man*.

30 Mitchell was an esteemed leader in Jackson Ward and had served on the Richmond City Council for eight years. After he was pushed out of politics, he became a leader in banking as the president of the Mechanics' Savings Bank (Ann Field Alexander, "Black Protest," 79–125).

31 Ibid., 117.

32 Charles Chesnutt to W. E. B. Du Bois, 27 June 1903, Du Bois Papers (microfilm).

33 Chesson, "Richmond's Black Councilmen," 216.

34 "The Steamboat Trouble," *Richmond Planet*, 29 September 1900, 4.

35 "Editorial Notes," *Richmond Planet*, 9 April 1904, 4.

36 "The Separate Cars and the Negro," *Richmond Planet*, 27 October 1900, 4; Ann Field Alexander, "Black Protest."

37 "The Separate Cars and the Negro," *Richmond Planet*, 27 October 1900, 4; Ann Field Alexander, "Black Protest."

38 "A Word from 'The Genteel Negro,'" *Richmond Planet*, 20 January 1900, 4.

39 "Editorial Notes," *Richmond Planet*, 10 March 1900, 4.

40 Ibid.

41 Ibid.

42 Ibid., 2 June 1900, 4.

43 Ibid., 3 March 1900, 4.

44 Ibid., 14 April 1900, 4.

45 Ibid., 5 May 1900, 4.

46 Chesson, "Richmond's Black Councilmen," 216; Ann Field Alexander, "Black Protest," 203.

47 "Editorial Notes," *Richmond Planet*, 29 September 1900, 4.

48 Ibid., 27 January 1900, 4.

49 Ibid., 10 March 1900, 4.

50 Ibid., 29 September 1900, 4.

51 Ibid., 10 March 1900, 4.

52 Ibid., 5 May 1900, 4.

53 Ibid.

54 Ibid., 10 March 1900, 4.

55 Ibid., 3 March 1900, 4.

56 Ibid., 5 May 1900, 4.

57 Ibid., 3 March 1900, 4.

58 Ibid.

59 Ibid., 27 October 1900, 4.

60 Ibid., 27 October 1900, 4, 10 March 1900, 4.

CHAPTER SIX

1 In 1887, Frank Sprague and the Sprague Electric Railway and Motor Company were hired by a group of New York investors to build a streetcar system in Richmond twelve miles long with forty cars. For more on the development of urban streetcars, see Klein, *Power Makers*.

2 Richmond's streetcar system was very orderly, following a simple grid pattern and serving the needs of ward-based neighborhoods. The streetcar was important given the steep grades throughout the city limits. H. P. Beck, "Map of the City of Richmond, Va. Jan. 25, 1904," and Clyde W. Saunders, "Map of the City of Richmond-Va., Dec. 6, 1906," both in Manuscript Collections, Library of Virginia, Richmond; Sanford, *Century of Commerce*, 52.

3 The *Richmond Planet*, 25 April 1903, advertised lots for sale in "Happy Woodville," the "colored man's paradise," and boasted that the suburban community was "not far from streetcars and just outside the city limits." The black middle class also benefited from the building of "streetcar suburbs" that broadened the communities available to black residents.

4 Chesson, *Richmond*, 102.

5 The imbalance between men and women in Clay Ward, which reported the second-highest black population, may reflect that some of the residents dispersed in the city's other wards may have been women boarders employed in white homes. The Negro population of Clay Ward was disproportionately female, with 3,211 women and 1,929 men. Although approximately 3,500 more black women than black men resided in the city at large, the small population of Clay Ward accounted for a large part of the gender gap. This phenomenon seems to reflect black women domestics who "lived out"—that is, resided in the homes of white employers. The 1900 Census recorded where people slept for the majority of the week, which in the case of live-in domestic workers was not necessarily the place inhabitants considered their homes or the community where they resided. Blacks who resided in other black communities, such as Church Hill, and who lived in surrounding suburbs and rural areas may have maintained connections of family, faith, and fellowship with Jackson Ward (U.S. Bureau of the Census, *Twelfth Census*, vol. 1). For a closer examination of the dynamics of domestic work, see Clark-Lewis, *Living In, Living Out*.

6 J. Douglas Smith, *Managing White Supremacy*, 23–26.

7 Although Jackson Ward ended as an official district in 1903, I agree with historians Brown and Kimball that "Jackson Ward is a function of history,

collective memory, mythology, and power; it is also a function of legislation, politics, and inequality" ("Mapping the Terrain," 316–17).

8 Meier and Rudwick, "Origins," 309–10; Litwack, *Been in the Storm*, 263.

9 Chesson, *Richmond*, 102; Brown, "Uncle Ned's Children," 467–71; Rachleff, *Black Labor*, 42.

10 Works Progress Administration, *Negro in Virginia*, 241; Wynes, "Evolution," 417; Ann Field Alexander, "Black Protest."

11 See *Supplement to the Code of Virginia*, Chaps. 226, 312.

12 "A Plea for Separation," *Richmond Planet*, 13 January 1900, 4.

13 "The 'Jim Crow' Car," *Richmond Planet*, 7 July 1900, 4.

14 "Jackson Ward Forgeries," *Richmond Planet*, 12 May 1900, 1; "To Meet to Disfranchise Us," *Richmond Planet*, 21 July 1900, 4; "The 'Jim Crow' Car," *Richmond Planet*, 7 July 1900, 4; "Editorial Notes," *Richmond Planet*, 20 January 1900, 4.

15 Earlier attempts to segregate public conveyances through the city council had been tempered by the presence of black councilmen representing Jackson Ward, who checked the city's ability to pass sweeping segregation ordinances. See Chesson, "Richmond's Black Councilmen"; Ann Field Alexander, "Black Protest."

16 Although Booker T. Washington privately opposed the segregation of public conveyances and sometimes funded efforts to challenge these laws, he made no public efforts to protest. Jackson sought Washington's financial backing and public endorsement for the Constitutional Rights Association, but Washington was unwilling to lend his support. Jackson's private negotiations with the Richmond City Council were the conciliatory style of protest both men preferred (Giles Beecher Jackson, "From Giles Beecher Jackson," in *Booker T. Washington Papers*, 5:649–51; Works Progress Administration, *Negro in Virginia*, 297).

17 Brundage, *Lynching*, 263.

18 Murray, *States' Laws*, 484–85; Guild, *Black Laws of Virginia*, 146–47.

19 John Mitchell Jr., "'Jim Crow' Street-Cars," *Richmond Planet*, 9 April 1904, 4.

20 Ibid.

21 "Trouble at Newport News," *Richmond Planet*, 13 January 1906, 4.

22 Ibid.

23 Gavins, "Urbanization and Segregation," 259–60; "The Streetcar Company's Troubles," *Richmond Planet*, 2 July 1904, 4; "'Jim Crow' Streetcars—Citizens Act," *Richmond Planet*, 16 April 1904, 1. Although Clay Street and some of the city's most important African American institutions lay outside of the voting boundaries of Jackson Ward, they were part of what contemporary black citizens considered the ward.

24 J. Max Barber, "The Aggressiveness of Jim-Crowism," *Voice of the Negro*, June 1904, 217.

25 "Walking Everywhere," *Appreciator*, rpt. in *Richmond Planet*, 30 April 1904, 4.

26 Ann Field Alexander, "Black Protest," 79, 113; Miller, "Urban Blacks," 192; "'Jim Crow' Streetcars—Citizens Act," *Richmond Planet*, 16 April 1904, 1.

27 "'Jim Crow' Streetcars—Citizens Act," *Richmond Planet*, 16 April 1904, 1.

28 "Major-General Jackson Pledges Support," *Richmond Planet*, 21 May 1904, 1.

29 Chesson, *Richmond*, 103–5.

30 "Citizens Protest," *Richmond Planet*, 23 April 1904, 1; "The New Knighthood in Flower," *Voice of the Negro*, March 1906, 167–68; Hunter, *To 'Joy My Freedom*, 128.

31 "Ask Fair Play on Trolleys," *Richmond News Leader*, 5 April 1904, 1, 7; Virginia Passenger and Power Company to Ferguson et al., copy, Richmond, Va., 7 April 1904, Maggie Lena Walker Papers, Box 3, Folder 23, Maggie Lena Walker National Historic Site, Richmond, Virginia; Meier and Rudwick, "Boycott Movement," 767–68, 770, 772–73; "Negro Split over Trolley," *Richmond News Leader*, 20 April 1904, 1, 2, 7.

32 "Negro Split over Trolley" and "Aunt Jemimy's Point of View," *Richmond News Leader*, 20 April 1904, 1, 2, 7.

33 "Pious Colored Folks Use Shank's Mare," *Richmond News Leader*, 2 May 1904, 3; "Colored Sunday-School Workers Walk in Sun," *Richmond Planet*, 11 June 1904, 1; "The Aggressiveness of Jim-Crowism," *Voice of the Negro*, June 1904, 216–17; "Emancipation Celebration," *Richmond Planet*, 8 April 1905, 1.

34 "Street-Car Situation Here," *Richmond Planet*, 21 May 1904, 1.

35 "Trouble on a Car—Conductor and Passenger Get into Strenuous Fist Argument," *Richmond Times-Dispatch*, 24 April 1904; "The Streetcar Trouble," *Richmond Planet*, 28 May 1904, 1.

36 The Montgomery Bus Boycott of the 1950s is historically distant, but experiences at that time suggest that African Americans who were willing to provide alternate forms of transportation to boycotters may have met resistance from white authorities.

37 L. B. Vaughn, "Letter to the Editor: A White Gentleman Speaks," *Richmond Planet*, 28 May 1904, 1.

38 Kellogg, "Negro Urban Clusters"; Miller, "Urban Blacks," 185–87.

39 "The Jim Crow Street-Car," *Richmond Planet*, 23 April 1904, 1, "A Street-Car Crash: Walking Colored Folks Not Injured," *Richmond Planet*, 14 May 1904, 1.

40 "Street-Car Situation," *Richmond Planet*, 30 April 1904, 1.

41 Hunter, *To 'Joy My Freedom*, 56.

42 "Negroes Boycott White Man," *New York Times*, 18 March 1904, 1.

43 U.S. Bureau of the Census, *Twelfth Census*, vol. 13.

44 Hunter, *To 'Joy My Freedom*, 57.

45 Brown and Kimball, "Mapping the Terrain," 320.

46 In a description of 1898 protests in Wilmington, North Carolina, advocating that black women should be helped on and off streetcars, historian Glenda Gilmore employs explicitly classed terms. Because "evidence is fragmentary," she is forced to "imagine the individual occurrences: a well-dressed middle-class black woman, heading home from shopping, attempting to juggle her burdens and mind her skirts as she jumped up on the car's high step" ("Murder, Memory," 82). Gilmore reduces black women's protests against streetcar conductors to an

individual and petty issue of middle-class inconvenience rather than a collective response to systematic acts of inequity. It is an assumption that poor women did not carry burdens or need help on and off the public conveyances. A revisioning of these individual acts of resistance and small demonstrations of protest against inequitable treatment is necessary in light of the evidence to the contrary concerning the streetcar boycotts of 1900–1906.

47 "The Street-Car Situation," *Richmond Planet*, 14 May 1904, 1.

48 Maggie Lena Walker, "An Address for Men Only," St. Luke Hall, 1 March 1906, Walker Papers, Box 3, Folder 24.

49 "Street-Car Situation," *Richmond Planet*, 30 April 1904, 1; "The Street-Car Situation Now," *Richmond Planet*, 18 June 1904.

50 "She Wanted Air, but It Cost $10," *Richmond Planet*, 23 July 1904, 1.

51 "A Rebuke to Jimcrowism," *Voice of the Negro*, August 1904, 302.

52 "Virginia Passenger and Power—Annual Report of the President to the Board of Directors and the Stockholders, 1903," in Virginia Passenger and Power Company, Board of Directors' and Stockholders' Minute Book, 1903–4, Virginia Electric and Power Company Records, 1849–1995, vol. 435, Library of Virginia, Richmond; U.S. Bureau of the Census, *Special Reports*, 236–74.

53 William Northrop and H. T. Wickham were appointed receivers of the Virginia Passenger and Power Company on 16 July 1904 by Edmund Waddill Jr., judge in the Circuit Court of the United States for the Eastern District of Virginia, in *Bowling Green Trust Co. v. Virginia Passenger and Power Co.*, Virginia Passenger and Power Company, Board of Directors' and Stockholders' Minute Book, 1903–4, Virginia Electric and Power Company Records, vol. 435.

54 "The Street Car Co. Here 'Busted,'" *Richmond Planet*, 23 July 1904, 1.

55 The decision that made Northrop's receivership permanent outlined that "upon his coming in, and through the instrumentality of those who caused him to be connected with the company, large pecuniary assistance was rendered the company, by reason whereof its financial disaster was for a considerable time averted" (*Bowling Green Trust Co. v. Virginia Passenger and Power Co.*).

56 "Trouble at Newport News," *Richmond Planet*, 13 January 1906, 4.

57 "Jim Crow Streetcars," *Richmond Planet*, 16 April 1904, 1; "Trouble on the Street-Cars," *Richmond Planet*, 4 June 1904, 1; "Colored Sunday-School Workers Walk in Sun," *Richmond Planet*, 11 June 1904, 1; "The Street Car Co. Here 'Busted,'" *Richmond Planet*, 23 July 1904, 1; Brown, "Uncle Ned's Children," 483–84.

58 "Notes" and "Angry about the Opera Parsifal," *Richmond Reformer*, 28 January 1905, 1.

59 "Notes," *Richmond Planet*, 13 January 1906, 4.

60 "Trouble at Newport News," *Richmond Planet*, 13 January 1906, 4.

61 Ibid.

62 Ibid.

63 "Fighting the Jim Crow Street Cars," *Richmond Planet*, 13 January 1906, 1, 8; "Negroes to Ride in Autos," *New York Times*, 15 September 1905, 2.

64 *Florida v. Patterson; Patterson v. Taylor; Crooms v. Schad*; "Florida Jim Crow Law Void," *New York Times*, 30 July 1905, 2; "Supreme Court—State or National—Which?," *Richmond Planet*, 3 February 1906, 4; Cassanello, "Avoiding 'Jim Crow,'" 450–52; Ortiz, *Emancipation Betrayed*, 119–24.

65 "Jim Crow Cars at Washington," *Richmond Planet*, 14 April 1906, 4–5; "Congressman Shot Negro in Street Car," *New York Times*, 28 March 1908, 1; "Praise Congressman Who Shot a Negro," *New York Times*, 29 March 1908, 16; "Topics of the Times," *New York Times*, 5 April 1908, 10.

66 "Notes," *Richmond Planet*, 24 March 1906, 4.

67 Ibid., 7 July 1906, 4.

68 Ibid., 26 May 1906, 4.

69 Ibid., 18 August 1906, 4.

70 "A Motorman's Blunder," *Richmond Planet*, 2 June 1906, 4.

71 "Jim Crow Law," *Richmond Planet*, 7 July 1906, 4.

72 "A Word about the Streetcars," *Richmond Planet*, 21 July 1906, 4.

73 Ibid.

74 "Other Facts Cited," *Richmond Planet*, 28 July 1906, 4.

75 "Our Worst Enemies," *Richmond Planet*, 25 August 1906, 4.

76 "The Present Outlook," *Richmond Planet*, 10 November 1906, 4.

CHAPTER SEVEN

1 For an account of Savannah's 1900 Emancipation Day, see Dittmer, *Black Georgia*, 1–2. For more on the African American Emancipation Days, see Wiggins, *O Freedom!*; Kachun, *Festivals of Freedom*.

2 Matthews, "Black Newspapermen," 362.

3 "Savannah Negroes Riotous," *New York Times*, 2 January 1906, 1.

4 U.S. Bureau of the Census, *Negro Population*.

5 Matthews, "Black Newspapermen."

6 "Editorial Notes," *Savannah Tribune*, 14 January 1899, 2; *Savannah Tribune*, 16 September 1899, 2.

7 "Editorial Notes," *Savannah Tribune*, 16 September 1899, 2.

8 Ibid.

9 Ibid.

10 Deveaux helped to organize the First Battalion Infantry of the Colored Georgia State Troops in Savannah in 1878. Military service took on profound meanings for this generation of African Americans, symbolizing not only freedom but also participatory citizenship. Although the state hesitated to call out the Colored Troops, they served important symbolic function in Savannah's public rituals, such as the annual Emancipation Day celebrations. For more on colored troops and their relevance to the public culture of African American communities in the urban South, see Brown and Kimball, "Mapping the Terrain"; Matthews, "Black Newspapermen"; Diamond and Baylen, "Demise";

Sholes' Directory of the City of Savannah, 1898 and *Goette's Savannah City Directory, 1901*, both in *U.S. City Directories, 1882–1901* (microfilm); "Minister's Meeting," *Savannah Tribune*, 2 December 1899, 3; "Editorial Notes," *Savannah Tribune*, 9 December 1899, 2.

11 "Editorial Notes," *Savannah Tribune*, 30 September 1899, 2; "Editorial Notes," 7 October 1899, 2.

12 "Keep Off Jim Crow Cars," *Savannah Tribune*, 23 September 1899, 3; "Only the Lower Class Went," *Savannah Tribune*, 30 September 1899, 2.

13 "Editorial Notes," *Savannah Tribune*, 23 September 1899, 2.

14 "Minister's Meeting," *Savannah Tribune*, 2 December 1899, 3; "Editorial Notes," *Savannah Tribune*, 9 December 1899, 2.

15 "Editorial Notes," *Savannah Tribune*, 16 December 1899, 2; "Editorial Notes," *Savannah Tribune*, 26 July 1902, 2.

16 U.S. Bureau of the Census, *Twelfth Census*, vol. 13; U.S. Bureau of the Census, *Negro Population*.

17 *Goette's Savannah City Directory, 1901*, in *U.S. City Directories, 1882–1901* (microfilm).

18 Baldwin to Nagle, 8 July 1902, George Johnson Baldwin Papers, Box 45, Folder 2090, Southern Historical Collection, University of North Carolina at Chapel Hill.

19 "Editorial Notes," *Savannah Tribune*, 19 July 1902, 2.

20 Wilson to Baldwin, 24 July 1906, Baldwin Papers, Box 47, Folder 2198.

21 Nash to Baldwin, 6 August 1906, Baldwin to Wilson, 10 November 1906, both in ibid., Box 47, Folder 2199.

22 Owens to Baldwin, 8 January 1907, Nash to Baldwin, 15 January 1907, both in ibid., Box 47, Folder 2203.

23 Campbell's study of Savannah Electric Company asserts that the Savannah City Council passed the resolution enforcing segregation in the effort to put the streetcar company out of business. For more on the machinations of the Savannah City Council, see Campbell, "Profit, Prejudice, and Protest."

24 "Editorial Notes," "'Jim Crow' or Not," and "Liberty for Each, for All, and Forever," *Savannah Tribune*, 1 September 1906, 4.

25 "Protest against Jim Crow," *Savannah Tribune*, 8 September 1906, 4; "Editorial Notes," *Savannah Tribune*, 15 September 1906, 4.

26 "Protest against Jim Crow," *Savannah Tribune*, 8 September 1906, 4; "St. Philip's Dots," *Savannah Tribune*, 13 October 1906, 4; Johnson et al. to Baldwin, 14 January 1902, Baldwin Papers, Box 45, Folder 2076; "Many Citizens Met: Well Attended Mass Meeting at St. Philip's," *Savannah Tribune*, 29 September 1906, 4.

27 "F.A.B. Church" and "Ministers Unions," *Savannah Tribune*, 15 December 1906, 4; "Liberty for Each, for All, and Forever," *Savannah Tribune*, 1 September 1906, 4.

28 *Georgia Equal Rights Convention* (pamphlet), 1906, Du Bois Papers (microfilm).

29 "Protest against Jim Crow," *Savannah Tribune*, 8 September 1906, 4.

30 *Goette's Savannah City Directory, 1901*, in *U.S. City Directories, 1882–1901* (micro-

film); "Ministerial Dots," *Savannah Tribune*, 17 November 1906, 4; "Emancipation Meeting," *Savannah Tribune*, 24 November 1906, 5.

31 "Second Baptist Church," *Savannah Tribune*, 1 September 1906, 4; *Sholes' Directory of the City of Savannah, 1898* and *Goette's Savannah City Directory, 1901*, both in *U.S. City Directories* (microfilm); "Minister's Meeting," *Savannah Tribune*, 2 December 1899, 3; "Editorial Notes," *Savannah Tribune*, 9 December 1899, 2.

32 "Second Baptist Church," *Savannah Tribune*, 1 September 1906, 4.

33 *Goette's Savannah City Directory, 1901*, in *U.S. City Directories, 1882–1901* (microfilm); "Candidates Nominated," *Savannah Tribune*, 29 September 1906, 4; "Masonic Column," *Savannah Tribune*, 14 January 1899, 2; Matthews, "Black Newspapermen."

34 A. L. Tucker, Attorney and Counselor-at-Law (advertisement), *Savannah Tribune*, 14 January 1899, 3; *Goette's Savannah City Directory, 1901*, in *U.S. City Directories, 1882–1901* (microfilm).

35 *Goette's Savannah City Directory, 1901*, in *U.S. City Directories, 1882–1901* (microfilm); "City Dots," *Savannah Tribune*, 2; Blassingame, "Before the Ghetto," 463–86; Charles Elmore, "An Historical Guide to Laurel Grove Cemetery South," Vertical Clippings File, African Americans, Georgia Historical Society, Savannah.

36 *Goette's Savannah City Directory, 1901*, *U.S. City Directories, 1882–1901* (microfilm); "Knights of Pythias," *Savannah Tribune*, 14 January 1899, 3.

37 *Goette's Savannah City Directory, 1901*, in *U.S. City Directories, 1882–1901* (microfilm); Metropolitan Mercantile and Realty Company (advertisement), *Savannah Tribune*, 15 September 1906, 4; Metropolitan Mutual Benefit Association (advertisement), *Savannah Tribune*, 13 October 1906, 5; "Candidates Nominated," *Savannah Tribune*, 29 September 1906, 4.

38 In 1902, some seventy-seven men signed a petition regarding the administration of Lincoln Park, the streetcar park designated for black patrons. Of the thirty-eight with occupations listed in the 1901 city directory, sixteen were barbers (Johnson et al. to Baldwin, 14 January 1902, Baldwin Papers, Box 45, Folder 2076; U.S. Bureau of the Census, *Twelfth Census*, vol. 13; *Goette's Savannah City Directory, 1901*, in *U.S. City Directories, 1882–1901* [microfilm]).

39 "Editorial Notes," *Savannah Tribune*, 22 September 1906, 4; "Editorial Notes," *Savannah Tribune*, 8 September 1906, 4.

40 "Editorial Notes," *Savannah Tribune*, 22 September 1906, 4; "Editorial Notes," *Savannah Tribune*, 8 September 1906, 4.

41 For an account of the passage of the 1891 Georgia separate car law, see Bacote, "Negro Proscriptions."

42 "Jim Crow Effective," *Savannah Tribune*, 15 September 1906, 4.

43 *Code of the State of Georgia*, 2718, emphasis added; Nash to Baldwin, 25 June 1906, Baldwin Papers, Box 47, Folder 2197. The city's narrow and orderly layout bounded by the banks of the Savannah River made Savannah a walking city with streetcars following a simple square pattern. African American residents were able to stage a formidable boycott of Savannah Electric's streetcars given their large population and walkable city on an even grade.

44 "Editorial Notes," *Savannah Tribune*, 15 September 1906, 4.

45 "Held Mass Meeting," *Savannah Tribune*, 15 September 1906, 4; Nash to Baldwin, 14 November 1906, Baldwin Papers, Box 47, Folder 2199; "'Jim Crow' Effective," *Savannah Tribune*, 15 September 1906, 4.

46 U.S. Bureau of the Census, *Twelfth Census*, vol. 13.

47 "Held Mass Meeting," *Savannah Tribune*, 15 September 1906, 4.

48 "'Jim Crow' Effective," *Savannah Tribune*, 15 September 1906, 4; Nash to Baldwin, 14 November 1906, Baldwin Papers, Box 47, Folder 2199.

49 Adelphia Club had a middle-class membership that included two postal carriers, a bookkeeper, a carpenter, a wagon driver, a porter, a carpenter, and a barber ("Outing Called Off," *Savannah Tribune*, 22 September 1906, 5; *Goette's Savannah City Directory, 1901*, in *U.S. City Directories, 1882–1901* [microfilm]).

50 Johnson et al. to Baldwin, 14 January 1902, Baldwin Papers, Box 45, Folder 2076.

51 Whittington Bernard Johnson, *Black Savannah*, 121; "Report of L. L. Reed, President of the Union Saving Bank," Seventh Annual Convention, Records of the National Negro Business League, Manuscript Division, Library of Congress, Washington, D.C.; "Organizing in Time," *Savannah Tribune*, 13 October 1906, 5; Nash to Baldwin, 14 November 1906, Baldwin Papers, Box 47, Folder 2199.

52 McMurray, "Black Intellectual"; Nash to Baldwin, 14 November 1906, Baldwin Papers, Box 47, Folder 2199.

53 W. E. B. Du Bois, "The Negro South and North," *Bibliotheca Sacra*, July 1905, 500–513, rpt. in *Writings*, 250–56.

54 "Editorial Notes," *Savannah Tribune*, 22 September 1906, 4. The streetcar company estimated that black riders fell from 24 percent to 3 percent of the total, an 87.5 percent drop in the number of black passengers (Nash to Baldwin, 14 November 1906, Baldwin Papers, Box 47, Folder 2199).

55 "Editorial Notes," *Savannah Tribune*, 22 September 1906, 4; Litwack, *Trouble in Mind*, xiv; Cade, "Out of the Mouths."

56 Matthews, "Black Newspapermen," 376.

57 "Editorial Notes," *Savannah Tribune*, 22 September 1906, 4.

58 "Race Riot in Atlanta," *Savannah Tribune*, 29 September 1906, 1; Dittmer, *Black Georgia*, 124–29. For accounts of the Atlanta race riot, see Hunter, *To 'Joy My Freedom*; Dittmer, *Black Georgia*; Godshalk, *Veiled Visions*.

59 "Negroes Use Guns," *Savannah Tribune*, 29 September 1906, 7; Dittmer, *Black Georgia*, 128–29; Gaines, *Uplifting the Race*, 60.

60 "Race Riot in Atlanta," *Savannah Tribune*, 29 September 1906, 1.

61 J. Max Barber, "Where Are Our Friends?" *Voice of the Negro*, October 1906, 437–39.

62 Ibid.

63 Ibid.

64 "Race Riot in Atlanta," *Savannah Tribune*, 29 September 1906, 1; "Editorial Notes," *Savannah Tribune*, 6 October 1906, 4; "Editorial Notes," *Savannah Tri-*

bune, 29 September 1906, 4; "Atlanta Cross," *St. Luke Herald*, rpt. in *Savannah Tribune*, 6 October 1906, 4.

65 "Many Citizens Met," *Savannah Tribune*, 29 September 1906, 4.

66 "Editorial Notes," *Savannah Tribune*, 29 September 1906, 4; "Editorial Notes," *Savannah Tribune*, 1 December 1906, 4; "Editorial Notes," *Savannah Tribune*, 13 October 1906, 4.

67 "Savannah Jim Crow Cars," *Savannah Tribune*, 29 September 1906, 4; "Editorial Notes," *Savannah Tribune*, 6 October 1906, 4.

68 "Why Should Gov. Terrell Utter Deliberate Falsehoods?," *New York Age*, rpt. in *Savannah Tribune*, 26 January 1907, 4.

69 "Editorial Notes," *Savannah Tribune*, 6 October 1906, 4; "Editorial Notes," *Savannah Tribune*, 15 December 1906, 4.

70 "Editorial Notes," *Savannah Tribune*, 22 September 1906, 4; "Editorial Notes," *Savannah Tribune*, 15 September 1906, 4.

71 Baldwin to Stone and Webster, 21 November 1906, Baldwin Papers, Box 47, Folder 2200.

72 Stone and Webster to Baldwin, 24 November 1906, in ibid., Box 47, Folder 2200.

73 Nash to Hunt, 26 November 1906, in ibid., Box 47, Folder 2202.

74 "Sparks, Live Coals, and Flames from St. James on Sunday and Monday Nights" and "Protest against Jim Crow," *Savannah Tribune*, 8 September 1906, 4; Nash to Hunt, 26 November 1906, Baldwin Papers, Box 47, Folder 2202.

75 Nash to Hunt, 26 November 1906, Baldwin Papers, Box 47, Folder 2202; Baldwin to Nash, 21 February 1907, Baldwin Papers, Box 47, Folder 2206.

76 "Editorial Notes," *Savannah Tribune*, 22 September 1906, 4.

77 Nelson to Baldwin, 15, 19 December 1906, *Savannah Press* clipping, all in Baldwin Papers, Box 47, Folder 2202; Nelson to Baldwin, 7 February 1907, Baldwin Papers, Box 47, Folder 2205.

78 Nelson to Baldwin, 19 December 1906, Baldwin Papers, Box 47, Folder 2202; Nelson to Baldwin, 7 February 1907, Baldwin Papers, Box 47, Folder 2205.

79 "Editorial Notes," *Savannah Tribune*, 16 March 1907, 4.

80 *Savannah Press* clipping, Baldwin Papers, Box 47, Folder 2202.

81 Nelson to Baldwin, 15 December 1906, in ibid.

82 Ibid.; Nelson to Baldwin, 19 December 1906, Baldwin Papers, Box 47, Folder 2202; Memo, Nelson to Baldwin, 12 February 1907, both in Baldwin Papers, Box 47, Folder 2205.

83 Memo, 28 February 1907, Nelson to Baldwin, 21 February 1907, both in Baldwin Papers, Box 47, Folder 2206.

84 Saltonstall to Stone and Webster, 7 January 1907, in ibid., Box 47, Folder 2203; Statement of the Advisory Committee, 30 January 1907, Baldwin Papers, Box 47, Folder 2205.

85 Advertisement, *Savannah Tribune*, 9 March 1907, 4; Baldwin to Nash, 21 February 1907, Baldwin Papers, Box 47, Folder 2206.

86 "Under the Present Jim Crow Law, 'Cut Out' Lincoln Park," *Savannah Tribune*, 9 March 1907, 4; "Jim Crow Protest," *Savannah Tribune*, 23 March 1907, 4; Nash to Baldwin, 17 May 1907, Baldwin Papers, Box 48, Folder 2215; "Editorial Notes," *Savannah Tribune*, 16 March 1907, 4.

87 "Editorial Notes," *Savannah Tribune*, 23 March 1907, 4.

88 Ibid., 1 June 1907, 4.

89 Ibid., 18 May 1907, 4; "Editorial Notes," *Savannah Tribune*, 20 April 1907, 4.

90 "Editorial Notes," *Savannah Tribune*, 8 June 1907, 4.

CHAPTER EIGHT

1 James Weldon Johnson, "Autobiography," 50, 92, 115.

2 Lewis, *W. E. B. Du Bois*, 319.

3 Harlan, "Booker T. Washington."

4 "Booker T. Washington and His Critics," *Atlanta Independent*, 26 March 1904.

5 "Editorial Notes," *Atlanta Independent*, 20 August 1904.

6 "The Niagara Movement May Be 'Headless,' but It Is Not Graftless," *Atlanta Independent*, 14 July 1906; "'The Voice of the Negro,'" *Atlanta Independent*, 8 April 1905.

7 Harlan, "Booker T. Washington," describes Barber's struggle to fight off Washington's campaign to silence him as journalist.

8 Mitchell frequently used the *Planet* to advertise his success and promote the interests of his bank; see, e.g., "The Mechanics Savings Bank of Richmond," an ad that appeared regularly in the *Richmond Planet* in 1904.

9 "Notes," *Richmond Planet*, 18 August 1906, 4.

10 "The Niagara Movement," *Richmond Planet*, 25 August 1906, 4.

11 Ibid. For another example of positive coverage of Niagara Movement events, see "Colored Folks Active," *Richmond Planet*, 10 February 1906, 4.

12 "Notes," *Richmond Planet*, 29 September 1906, 4.

13 Kelly Miller, "A Circuit of the South," *Voice of the Negro*, September 1906, 663–66.

14 Black Customers' Line Extension Request, Virginia Electric and Power Company Records, 1849–1995, Box 5, Folder 7, Library of Virginia, Richmond.

15 W. E. B. Du Bois, "The Parting of the Ways," *World Today*, April 1904, 521–23, rpt. in *Writings*, 200–202.

BIBLIOGRAPHY

MANUSCRIPT SOURCES
Chapel Hill, N.C.
  Southern Historical Collection, University of North Carolina
    George Johnson Baldwin Papers
Chicago, Ill.
  Joseph Regenstein Library, University of Chicago
    Ida B. Wells Papers
New Orleans, La.
  Amistad Research Center, Tulane University
    Nils R. Douglas Papers
    Plessy v. Ferguson Records
    Records of the Prince Hall Masons
  Manuscript Collections, Tulane University
    George Washington Cable Collection
    Thomas Dabney Collection
  Williams Research Center
    Historic New Orleans Collection
  Xavier University Library
    R. L. Desdunes Papers
Richmond, Va.
  Library of Virginia
    City of Richmond Records
    First African Baptist Church, Richmond, Va., Minute Books
    Virginia Electric and Power Company Records, 1849–1995,
        Business Records Collection

Maggie Lena Walker National Historic Site
   Maggie Lena Walker Papers
Valentine Museum, Richmond History Center
   Independent Order of St. Luke Papers
   George and Huestis Cook Photographic Collection
Savannah, Ga.
   First African Baptist Church
      Church Records
   Georgia Historical Society
      Vertical Clippings File, African Americans
Washington, D.C.
   Manuscript Division, Library of Congress
      Nannie Helen Burroughs Papers
      Records of the National Negro Business League
      Mary Church Terrell Papers
      Booker T. Washington Papers
   Moorland-Spingarn Research Collection, Howard University
      P. B. S. Pinchback Papers

MICROFILM COLLECTIONS

W. E. B. Du Bois Papers at the University of Massachusetts Library, Amherst.
Albion W. Tourgée Papers, 1801–1924. Westfield, N.Y.: Chautauqua County
   Historical Society.
J. L. Hill Printing Company's Directory, Richmond and Manchester, Va., 1901.
   New Haven, Conn.: Research Publications.
U.S. City Directories, 1882–1901. New Haven, Conn.: Research Publications.

LEGAL CASES

Anderson v. Louisville and N.R. Co., 62 F. 46 (1894).
Bowie v. Birmingham Railway and Electric Co., 27 So. 1016 (1900).
Bowling Green Trust Co. v. Virginia Passenger and Power Co., 133 F. 186 (1904).
Brown v. Memphis and C.R. Co., 4 F. 37 (1880).
Civil Rights Cases, 109 U.S. 3 (1883).
Council v. Western and Atlantic R.R. Co., 1 Interstate Com. Rep. 638,
   1 I.C.C. 339 (1887).
Crooms v. Schad, 51 Fla. 168, 40 So. 497 (1906).
Florida v. Patterson, Florida Reports 50 (1905).
Heard v. Georgia R.R. Co., 46 I.C.C. (1888).
Houck v. Southern Pacific Railway Company, 38 F. 226 (1888).
Louisville, New Orleans, and Texas R.R. v. Mississippi, 133 U.S. 587 (1890).
May v. Shreveport Traction Co., 53 So. 671, 127 La. 420, 32 LRA (NS) 206.

Morrison v. State, 95 S.W. 494 (1905).
Patterson v. Taylor, 51 Fla. 275, 40 So. 493 (1905).
Plessy v. Ferguson, 163 U.S. 537 (1896).
Smith et al. v. Chamberlain, 17 S.E.371 (1893).
State v. Pearson, 110 La. 387, 34 So. 575 (1903).
United States v. Cruikshank et al., 92 U.S. 542 (1876).
Williams et al. v. Jacksonville, T & K.W. Ry. Co., 26 Fla. 533, 8 So. 446 (1890).

CENSUS AND GOVERNMENT DOCUMENTS

Acts of the General Assembly of the Commonwealth of Kentucky. Frankfort, Ky.:
    Johnson, 1893.
Alabama General and Local Laws—Passed at the Special Session, 1921.
    Montgomery, Ala.: Brown, 1921.
Code of Alabama, vol. 3, *Criminal*. Nashville, Tenn.: Marshall and Bruce, 1907.
Code of the State of Georgia: Adopted August 15, 1910. Atlanta: Foote and Davies, 1911.
Code of Virginia. St. Paul, Minn.: West, 1904.
Digest . . . of Louisiana/Louisiana Reports . . . 1900 to 1910. New Orleans:
    Hansell, 1911.
General Laws of the Legislature of Alabama. Montgomery, Ala.: Brown, 1903.
Park's Annotated Code of the State of Georgia, 1914. Atlanta: Harrison, 1914.
Supplement to the Code of Virginia. Richmond, Va.: Waddley, 1899.
Tompkins General and Local Laws—Passed at the Special Session, 1921.
    Montgomery, Ala.: Brown, 1921.
U.S. Bureau of the Census. *Compendium of the Seventh Census, 1850*.
    Washington, D.C.: Tucker, 1854.
——. *Negro Population, 1790–1915*. Washington, D.C.: U.S. Government Printing
    Office, 1918.
——. *Special Reports: Street and Electric Railways, 1902*. Washington, D.C.:
    U.S. Government Printing Office, 1905.
——. *Twelfth Census of the United States, 1900*. Vol. 1, *Population*, part 1.
    Washington, D.C.: U.S. Government Printing Office, 1901.
——. *Twelfth Census of the United States, 1900*. Vol. 13, *Occupations*.
    Washington, D.C.: U.S. Government Printing Office, 1904.

NEWSPAPERS AND PERIODICALS

Atlanta Independent
Frederick Douglass' Paper
Mobile Daily Register
Mobile Southern Watchman
New Orleans Crusader
New Orleans Daily Picayune
New Orleans Times Democrat
New Orleans Times-Picayune
New York Colored American
New York Daily Times
New York Daily Tribune
New York Freeman

New York Outlook
Richmond Planet
Richmond News Leader
Richmond Reformer
Richmond St. Luke Herald
Richmond Times-Dispatch

San Francisco Pacific Appeal
Savannah Morning News
Savannah Tribune
Southwestern Christian Advocate
Star of Zion
Voice of the Negro

SECONDARY SOURCES

Albert, Octavia Victoria Rodgers. *The House of Bondage; or, Charlotte Brooks and Other Slaves.* New York: Hunt and Eaton, 1890.

Alexander, Adele Logan. *Ambiguous Lives: Free Women of Color in Rural Georgia, 1789–1879.* Fayetteville: University of Arkansas Press, 1991.

Alexander, Ann Field. "Black Protest in the New South: John Mitchell, Jr., (1863–1929) and *The Richmond Planet.*" Ph.D. diss., Duke University, 1973.

——. *Race Man: The Rise and Fall of the "Fighting Editor," John Mitchell, Jr.* Charlottesville: University of Virginia Press, 2002.

Alexander, Leslie M. *African or American?: Black Identity and Political Activism in New York City, 1784–1861.* Urbana: University of Illinois Press, 2008.

Alexander, Shawn Leigh. "'We Know Our Rights and Have the Courage to Defend Them': The Spirit of Agitation in the Age of Accommodation, 1883–1909." Ph.D. diss., University of Massachusetts, 2004.

Alsobrook, David Ernest. "Alabama's Port City: Mobile during the Progressive Era, 1896–1917." Ph.D. diss., Auburn University, 1983.

Alvarez, Eugene. *Travel on Southern Antebellum Railroads, 1828–1860.* University: University of Alabama Press, 1974.

Anthony, Arthe A. "'Lost Boundaries': Racial Passing and Poverty in Segregated New Orleans." In *Visions and Revisions: Perspectives on Louisiana Society and Culture*, edited by Vaughan Burdin Baker, 125–41. Lafayette: Center for Louisiana Studies, University of Louisiana at Lafayette, 2000.

——. "The Negro Creole Community in New Orleans, 1880–1920: An Oral History." Ph.D. diss., University of California, Irvine, 1978.

Arnesen, Eric. *Brotherhoods of Color: Black Railroad Workers and the Struggle for Equality.* Cambridge: Harvard University Press, 2001.

——. *Waterfront Workers of New Orleans: Race, Class, and Politics, 1863–1923.* New York: Oxford University Press, 1991.

Ayers, Edward L. *The Promise of the New South: Life after Reconstruction.* New York: Oxford University Press, 1992.

Bacote, Clarence A. "Negro Proscriptions, Protest, and Proposed Solutions in Georgia, 1880–1908." *Journal of Southern History* 25 (November 1959): 471–98.

Baker, Ray Stannard. *Following the Color Line: American Negro Citizenship in the Progressive Era.* New York: Harper and Row, 1964.

Barnes, Catherine A. *Journey from Jim Crow: The Desegregation of Southern Transit.*
New York: Columbia University Press, 1983.

Bell, Caryn Cosse. *Revolution, Romanticism, and the Afro-Creole Protest Tradition in
Louisiana, 1718–1868.* Baton Rouge: Louisiana State University Press, 1997.

Bennett, James B. *Religion and the Rise of Jim Crow in New Orleans.* Princeton:
Princeton University Press, 2005.

Berlin, Ira. *Slaves without Masters: The Free Negro in the Antebellum South.* New York:
Pantheon, 1974.

Blackett, R. J. M. *Beating against the Barriers: The Lives of Six Nineteenth-Century
Afro-Americans.* Ithaca: Cornell University Press, 1986.

Blair, Lewis H. *A Southern Prophecy: The Prosperity of the South Dependent on the
Elevation of the Negro.* Edited and introduction by C. Vann Woodward. Boston:
Little, Brown, 1964.

Blassingame, John W. "Before the Ghetto: The Making of the Black Community
in Savannah, Georgia, 1865–1880." *Journal of Social History* 6 (Summer 1973):
463–88.

——. *Black New Orleans, 1860–1880.* Chicago: University of Chicago Press, 1973.

Branch, Taylor. *Parting the Waters: America in the King Years, 1954–63.* New York:
Simon and Schuster, 1988.

Brooks, Maxwell R. *The Negro Press Re-Examined.* Boston: Christopher, 1959.

Brown, Elsa Barkley. "Negotiating and Transforming the Public Sphere: African
American Political Life in the Transition from Slavery to Freedom." In *Jumpin'
Jim Crow: Southern Politics from Civil War to Civil Rights,* edited by Jane Dailey,
Glenda Elizabeth Gilmore, and Bryant Simon, 28–66. Princeton: Princeton
University Press, 2000.

——. "Uncle Ned's Children: Negotiating Community and Freedom in
Postemancipation Richmond, Virginia." Ph.D. diss., Kent State University, 1994.

——. "Womanist Consciousness: Maggie Lena Walker and the Independent Order
of Saint Luke." *Signs* 14 (Spring 1989): 610–33.

Brown, Elsa Barkley, and Gregg D. Kimball. "Mapping the Terrain of Black
Richmond." *Journal of Urban History* 21 (March 1995): 296–346.

Brundage, W. Fitzhugh. *Lynching in the New South: Georgia and Virginia, 1880–1930.*
Urbana: University of Illinois Press, 1993.

Cable, George Washington. *The Negro Question: A Selection of Writings on Civil
Rights in the South.* Edited by Arlin Turner. Garden City, N.Y.: Doubleday, 1958.

Cade, John B. "Out of the Mouths of Ex-Slaves." *Journal of Negro History* 20 (July
1935): 294–337.

Campbell, Walter Elijah. "The Corporate Hand in an Urban Jim Crow Journey."
Ph.D. diss., University of North Carolina at Chapel Hill, 1991.

——. "Profit, Prejudice, and Protest: Utility Competition and the Generation of
Jim Crow Streetcars in Savannah, 1905–1907." *Georgia Historical Quarterly* 70
(Summer 1986): 197–231.

Capeci, Dominic J., Jr., and Jack C. Knight. "Reckoning with Violence: W. E. B. Du Bois and the 1906 Atlanta Race Riot." *Journal of Southern History* 62 (November 1996): 727–66.

Cassanello, Robert. "Avoiding 'Jim Crow': Negotiating Separate and Equal on Florida's Railroads and Streetcars and the Progressive Era Origins of the Modern Civil Rights Movement." *Journal of Urban History* 34 (March 2008): 435–57.

Cell, John W. *The Highest Stage of White Supremacy: The Origins of Segregation in South Africa and the American South*. Cambridge: Cambridge University Press, 1982.

Chafe, William H., Raymond Gavins, and Robert Korstad, eds. *Remembering Jim Crow: African Americans Tell about Life in the Segregated South*. New York: New Press, 2001.

Chesson, Michael B. *Richmond after the War, 1865–1890*. Richmond: Virginia State Library, 1981.

———. "Richmond's Black Councilmen, 1871–96." In *Southern Black Leaders of the Reconstruction Era*, edited by Howard Rabinowitz, 191–222. Urbana: University of Illinois Press, 1982.

Clark-Lewis, Elizabeth. *Living In, Living Out: African American Domestics and the Great Migration*. New York: Kodansha, 1996.

Cohen, William. *At Freedom's Edge: Black Mobility and the Southern White Quest for Racial Control, 1861–1915*. Baton Rouge: Louisiana State University Press, 1991.

Cooper, Anna Julia. *A Voice from the South*. New York: Oxford University Press, 1988.

Davis, F. James. *Who Is Black?: One Nation's Definition*. University Park: Pennsylvania State University Press, 1991.

Delaney, David. *Race, Place, and the Law, 1836–1948*. Austin: University of Texas Press, 1998.

Desdunes, Rodolphe Lucien. *Our People and Our History: A Tribute to the Creole People of Color in Memory of the Great Men They Have Given Us and of the Good Works They Have Accomplished*. Translated and edited by Dorothea Olga McCants. 1911. Baton Rouge: Louisiana State University Press, 1973.

Dethloff, Henry C., and Robert R. Jones. "Race Relations in Louisiana, 1877–98." *Louisiana History* 9 (Winter 1968): 301–23.

Diamond, B. I., and J. O. Baylen. "The Demise of the Georgia Guard Colored, 1868–1914." *Phylon* 45 (December 1984): 311–13.

Dittmer, John. *Black Georgia in the Progressive Era, 1900–1920*. Urbana: University of Illinois Press, 1977.

Dollard, John. *Caste and Class in a Southern Town*. New Haven: Yale University Press, 1937.

Dorsey, Allison. *To Build Our Lives Together: Community Formation in Black Atlanta, 1875–1906*. Athens: University of Georgia Press, 2004.

Douglass, Frederick. *The Frederick Douglass Papers*. Series 1, *Speeches, Debates, and*

Interviews. 5 vols. Edited by John W. Blassingame and John R. McKivigan. New Haven: Yale University Press, 1979–92.

——. *Life and Times of Frederick Douglass*. New York: Gramercy, 1993.

——. *My Bondage and My Freedom*. New York: Penguin, 2003.

Du Bois, W. E. B. *The Autobiography of W. E. B. Du Bois: A Soliloquy on Viewing My Life from the Last Decade of Its First Century*. New York: International, 1968.

——. *Writings by W. E. B. Du Bois in Periodicals Edited by Others*. Edited by Herbert Aptheker. Millwood, N.Y.: Kraus-Thomson, 1982.

Elliot, Mark. *Color-Blind Justice: Albion Tourgée and the Quest for Racial Equality from the Civil War to Plessy v. Ferguson*. New York: Oxford University Press, 2006.

Fields, Mamie Garvin, with Karen Fields. *Lemon Swamp and Other Places: A Carolina Memoir*. New York: Free Press, 1983.

Fischer, Roger A. "A Pioneer Protest: The New Orleans Street Car Controversy of 1867." *Journal of Negro History* 53 (July 1968): 219–33.

——. "Racial Segregation in Ante Bellum New Orleans." *American Historical Review* 74 (February 1969): 926–37.

——. *The Segregation Struggle in Louisiana, 1862–77*. Urbana: University of Illinois Press, 1974.

Fultz, Michael. "'The Morning Cometh': African-American Periodicals, Education, and the Black Middle Class, 1900–1930." *Journal of Negro History* 80 (Summer 1995): 97–112.

Gaines, Kevin K. *Uplifting the Race: Black Leadership, Politics, and Culture in the Twentieth Century*. Chapel Hill: University of North Carolina Press, 1996.

Gatewood, Willard B. *Aristocrats of Color: The Black Elite, 1880–1920*. Bloomington: Indiana University Press, 1990.

Gavins, Raymond. *The Perils and Prospects of Southern Black Leadership: Gordon Blaine Hancock, 1884–1970*. Durham: Duke University Press, 1977.

——. "Urbanization and Segregation: Black Leadership Patterns in Richmond, Virginia, 1900–1920." *South Atlantic Quarterly* 79 (Summer 1980): 257–73.

Gayles, Gloria Wade. "Black Women Journalists in the South, 1880–1905: An Approach to the Study of Black Women's History." *Callaloo* 11/13 (February 1981): 138–52.

David N. Gellman and David Quigley, eds. *Jim Crow New York: A Documentary History of Race and Citizenship, 1777–1877*. New York: New York University Press, 2003.

Giddings, Paula J. *Ida: A Sword among Lions*. New York: Amistad, 2008.

Gilmore, Glenda E. *Gender and Jim Crow: Women and the Politics of White Supremacy in North Carolina, 1896–1920*. Chapel Hill: University of North Carolina Press, 1996.

——. "Murder, Memory, and the Flight of the Incubus." In *Democracy Betrayed: The Wilmington Race Riot of 1898 and Its Legacy*, edited by David S. Cecelski and Timothy B. Tyson, 73–93. Chapel Hill: University of North Carolina Press, 1998.

Godshalk, David Fort. *Veiled Visions: The 1906 Atlanta Race Riot and the Reshaping of American Race Relations*. Chapel Hill: University of North Carolina Press, 2005.

Goldman, Robert M. *Reconstruction and Black Suffrage: Losing the Vote in Reese and Cruikshank*. Lawrence: University Press of Kansas, 2001.

Gordon, Fon Louise. *Caste and Class: The Black Experience in Arkansas, 1880–1920*. Athens: University of Georgia Press, 1995.

Grady, Henry W. *Life and Labors of Henry W. Grady: His Speeches, Writings, Etc.* Atlanta: Huggins, 1890.

Griggs, Sutton E. *Imperium in Imperio*. 1899. New York: Arno, 1969.

Guild, June Purcell. *Black Laws of Virginia: A Summary of the Legislative Acts of Virginia Concerning Negroes from Earliest Times to the Present*. New York: Negro Universities Press, 1969.

Hair, William Ivy. *Carnival of Fury: Robert Charles and the New Orleans Race Riot of 1900*. Baton Rouge: Louisiana State University Press, 1976.

Hale, Grace Elizabeth. *Making Whiteness: The Culture of Segregation in the South, 1890–1940*. New York: Pantheon, 1998.

Hall, Jacquelyn Dowd. *Revolt against Chivalry: Jessie Daniel Ames and the Women's Campaign against Lynching*. New York: Columbia University Press, 1993.

Harlan, Louis R. "Booker T. Washington and the Voice of the Negro, 1904–1907." *Journal of Southern History* 45 (February 1979): 45–62.

———. *Booker T. Washington: The Making of a Black Leader, 1856–1901*. New York: Oxford University Press, 1975.

———. *Booker T. Washington: The Wizard of Tuskegee, 1901–1915*. New York: Oxford University Press, 1983.

———. "The Secret Life of Booker T. Washington." *Journal of Southern History* 37 (August 1971): 393–416.

Hartman, Saidiya V. *Scenes of Subjection: Terror, Slavery, and Self-Making in Nineteenth-Century America*. New York: Oxford University Press, 1997.

Haskins, James. *Pinkney Benton Stewart Pinchback*. New York: Macmillan, 1973.

Hewitt, John H., Jr. *Protest and Progress: New York's First Black Episcopal Church Fights Racism*. New York: Garland, 2000.

Higginbotham, Evelyn Brooks. *Righteous Discontent: The Women's Movement in the Black Baptist Church, 1880–1920*. Cambridge: Harvard University Press, 1993.

Hine, Darlene Clark. *Hine Sight: Black Women and the Re-Construction of American History*. Bloomington: Indiana University Press, 1994.

Hirsch, Arnold R., and Joseph Logsdon, eds. *Creole New Orleans: Race and Americanization*. Baton Rouge: Louisiana State University Press, 1992.

Horton, James Oliver. *Free People of Color: Inside the African American Community*. Washington, D.C.: Smithsonian Institution Press, 1993.

Hunter, Tera W. *To 'Joy My Freedom: Southern Black Women's Lives and Labors after the Civil War*. Cambridge: Harvard University Press, 1997.

Inscoe, John C., ed. *Georgia in Black and White: Explorations in the Race Relations of a Southern State, 1865–1950*. Athens: University of Georgia Press, 1994.

Jackson, Joy J. *New Orleans in the Gilded Age: Politics and Urban Progress, 1880–1896*. Baton Rouge: Louisiana State University Press, 1997.

Jacobs, Claude F. "Benevolent Societies of New Orleans Blacks during the Late Nineteenth and Early Twentieth Centuries." *Louisiana History* 29 (Winter 1988): 21–34.

———. "Strategies of Neighborhood Health-Care among New Orleans Blacks: From Voluntary Association to Public Policy." Ph.D. diss., Tulane University, 1980.

Johnson, Arthur, and Ronald M. Johnson. "Away from Accommodation: Radical Editors and Protest Journalism, 1900–1910." *Journal of Negro History* 62 (October 1977): 325–38.

Johnson, Charles S. *Patterns of Negro Segregation.* New York: Harper, 1943.

Johnson, James Weldon. *Along This Way: The Autobiography of James Weldon Johnson.* New York: Da Capo, 1973.

———. "The Autobiography of an Ex-Colored Man." In *James Weldon Johnson: Writings*, 1–127. New York: Library of America, 2004.

Johnson, Whittington Bernard. *Black Savannah, 1788–1864.* Fayetteville: University of Arkansas Press, 1996.

Kachun, Mitch. *Festivals of Freedom: Memory and Meaning in African American Emancipation Celebrations, 1808–1915.* Amherst: University of Massachusetts Press, 2003.

Kawash, Samira. *Dislocating the Color Line: Identity, Hybridity, and Singularity in African-American Literature.* Stanford, Calif.: Stanford University Press, 1997.

Kelley, Robin D. G. *Hammer and Hoe: Alabama Communists during the Great Depression.* Chapel Hill: University of North Carolina Press, 1990.

———. *Race Rebels: Culture, Politics, and the Black Working Class.* New York: Free Press, 1994.

Kellogg, John. "Negro Urban Clusters in the Postbellum South." *Geographical Review* 67 (July 1977): 310–21.

Kennedy, Randall. "Martin Luther King's Constitution: A Legal History of the Montgomery Bus Boycott." *Yale Law Journal* 98 (April 1989): 999–1067.

Klarman, Michael J. *From Jim Crow to Civil Rights: The Supreme Court and the Struggle for Racial Equality.* New York: Oxford University Press, 2004.

Klein, Maury. *The Power Makers: Steam, Electricity, and the Men Who Invented Modern America.* New York: Bloomsbury, 2008.

Lebsock, Suzanne. *A Murder in Virginia: Southern Justice on Trial.* New York: Norton, 2003.

Lewis, David Levering. *W. E. B. Du Bois: Biography of a Race.* New York: Holt, 1993.

Lewis, Earl. *In Their Own Interests: Race, Class, and Power in Twentieth-Century Norfolk, Virginia.* Berkeley: University of California Press, 1991.

Lhamon, W. T. *Jump Jim Crow: Lost Plays, Lyrics, and Street Prose of the First Atlantic Popular Culture.* Cambridge: Harvard University Press, 2003.

Litwack, Leon F. *Been in the Storm So Long: The Aftermath of Slavery.* New York: Vintage, 1980.

———. "Hellhounds." In *Without Sanctuary: Lynching Photography in America*, edited by James Allen, 8–37. Santa Fe, N.M.: Twin Palms, 2005.

————. *North of Slavery: The Negro in the Free States, 1790–1860*. Chicago: University of Chicago Press, 1961.

————. *Trouble in Mind: Black Southerners in the Age of Jim Crow*. New York: Knopf, 1998.

Lofgren, Charles A. *The Plessy Case: A Legal-Historical Interpretation*. New York: Oxford University Press, 1987.

Logsdon, Joseph, and Caryn Cosse Bell. "The Americanization of Black New Orleans, 1850–1900." In *Creole New Orleans: Race and Americanization*, edited by Arnold R. Hirsch and Joseph Logsdon, 201–61. Baton Rouge: Louisiana State University Press, 1992.

Logsdon, Joseph, and Lawrence Powell. "Rodolphe Lucien Desdunes: Forgotten Organizer of the Plessy Protest." In *Sunbelt Revolution: The Historical Progression of the Civil Rights Struggle in the Gulf South, 1866–2000*, edited by Samuel C. Hyde, Jr., 42–72. Gainesville: University Press of Florida, 2003.

Lynch, Hollis R. *The Black Urban Condition: A Documentary History, 1866–1971*. New York: Crowell, 1973.

Macdonald, Robert, ed. *Louisiana's Legal Heritage*. Baton Rouge: Louisiana State Museum, 1983.

Mack, Kenneth W. "Law, Society, Identity, and the Making of the Jim Crow South: Travel and Segregation on Tennessee Railroads, 1875–1905." *Law and Social Inquiry* 24 (Spring 1999): 377–404.

Mann, Susan A. "Slavery, Sharecropping, and Sexual Inequality." In *We Specialize in the Wholly Impossible: A Reader in Black Women's History*, edited by Darlene Clark Hine, Wilma King, and Linda Reed, 281–302. Brooklyn, N.Y.: Carlson, 1995.

Marlowe, Gertrude Woodruff. *A Right Worthy Grand Mission: Maggie Lena Walker and the Quest for Black Economic Empowerment*. Washington, D.C.: Howard University Press, 2003.

Matthews, John M. "Black Newspapermen and the Black Community in Georgia, 1890–1930." *Georgia Historical Quarterly* 68 (Fall 1984): 356–81.

McGerr, Michael. *A Fierce Discontent: The Rise and Fall of the Progressive Movement in America, 1870–1920*. New York: Oxford University Press, 2003.

McMurray, Linda O. "A Black Intellectual in the New South: Monroe Nathan Work, 1866–1945." *Phylon* 41 (Fall 1980): 333–44.

————. *To Keep the Waters Troubled: The Life of Ida B. Wells*. New York: Oxford University Press, 1998.

McPherson, James M. "Abolitionists and the Civil Rights Act of 1875." *Journal of American History* 52 (December 1965): 493–510.

Medley, Keith Weldon. "The Sad Story of How 'Separate but Equal' Was Born." *Smithsonian* 24 (February 1994): 104–16.

————. *We as Freemen: Plessy v. Ferguson*. Gretna, La.: Pelican, 2003.

Meier, August. "Booker T. Washington and the Negro Press: With Special Reference to the Colored American Magazine." *Journal of Negro History* 38 (January 1953): 67–90.

——. "Negro Class Structure and Ideology in the Age of Booker T. Washington." *Phylon* 23 (Fall 1962): 258–66.

Meier, August, and David Lewis. "History of the Negro Upper Class in Atlanta, Georgia, 1890–1958." *Journal of Negro Education* 28 (Spring 1959): 128–39.

Meier, August, and Elliott Rudwick. *Along the Color Line: Explorations in the Black Experience.* Urbana: University of Illinois Press, 1976.

——. "The Boycott Movement against Jim Crow Streetcars in the South, 1900–1906." *Journal of American History* 55 (March 1969): 756–75.

——. "Negro Boycotts of Jim Crow Streetcars in Tennessee." *American Quarterly* 21 (Winter 1969): 755–63.

——. "The Origins of Nonviolent Direct Action in Afro-American Protest: A Note on Historical Discontinuities." In *Along the Color Line: Explorations in the Black Experience*, 307–404. Urbana: University of Illinois Press, 1976.

Miller, Zane L. "Urban Blacks in the South, 1865–1920: The Richmond, Savannah, New Orleans, Louisville, and Birmingham Experience." In *The New Urban History: Quantitative Explorations by American Historians*, edited by Leo F. Schnore, 184–204. Princeton: Princeton University Press, 1975.

Minter, Patricia Hagler. "Freedom: Personal Liberty and Private Law: The Failure of Freedom: Class, Gender, and the Evolution of Segregated Transit Law in the Nineteenth-Century South." *Chicago-Kent Law Review* 70 (1995): 993–1009.

Mitzell, Michael, prod. *Streetcar Stories.* New Orleans, WYES, TV12. Video.

Morgan, Lynda J. *Emancipation in Virginia's Tobacco Belt, 1850–1870.* Athens: University of Georgia Press, 1992.

Murray, Pauli, ed. *States' Laws on Race and Color.* Athens: University of Georgia Press, 1997.

O'Kelly, Charlotte G. "Black Newspapers and the Black Protest Movement: Their Historical Relationship, 1827–1945." *Phylon* 43 (March 1982): 1–14.

Olsen, Otto H. "Reflections on the *Plessy v. Ferguson* Decision of 1896." In *Louisiana's Legal Heritage*, edited by Edward F. Haas, 163–87. Pensacola, Fla.: Perdido Bay, 1983.

Ortiz, Paul. *Emancipation Betrayed: The Hidden History of Black Organizing and White Violence in Florida from Reconstruction to the Bloody Election of 1920.* Berkeley: University of California Press, 2006.

Oshinsky, David M. *Worse Than Slavery: Parchman Farm and the Ordeal of Jim Crow Justice.* New York: Free Press, 1996.

Painter, Nell Irvin. *Sojourner Truth: A Life, a Symbol.* New York: Norton, 1996.

Penn, I. Garland. *The Afro-American Press and Its Editors.* New York: Arno, 1969.

Perdue, Robert E. *The Negro in Savannah, 1865–1900.* New York: Exposition, 1973.

Rabinowitz, Howard N. *Race Relations in the Urban South, 1865–1890.* New York: Oxford University Press, 1978.

Rachleff, Peter J. *Black Labor in the South: Richmond, Virginia, 1865–1890.* Philadelphia: Temple University Press, 1984.

Rael, Patrick. "A Common Nature, a United Destiny: African American Responses to Racial Science from the Revolution to the Civil War." In *Prophets of Protest: Reconsidering the History of American Abolitionism*, edited by Timothy Patrick McCarthy and John Stauffer, 183–99. New York: New Press, 2006.

Reed, Germaine A. "Race Legislation in Louisiana, 1864–1920." *Louisiana History* 6 (Winter 1965): 379–92.

Roback, Jennifer. "The Political Economy of Segregation: The Case of Segregated Streetcars." *Journal of Economic History* 46 (December 1986): 901–17.

Rousseve, Charles Barthelemy. *The Negro in Louisiana: Aspects of His History and His Literature*. New Orleans: Xavier University Press, 1937.

Ruchames, Louis. "Jim Crow Railroads in Massachusetts." *American Quarterly* 8 (Spring 1956): 61–75.

Sanford, James K. *A Century of Commerce, 1867–1967*. Richmond, Va.: Richmond Chamber of Commerce, 1967.

Scott, Rebecca J. *Degrees of Freedom: Louisiana and Cuba after Slavery*. Cambridge: Belknap Press of Harvard University Press, 2005.

Shapiro, Herbert. *White Violence and Black Response: From Reconstruction to Montgomery*. Amherst: University of Massachusetts Press, 1988.

Shaw, Stephanie. *What a Woman Ought to Be and to Do: Black Professional Women Workers*. Chicago: University of Chicago Press, 1996.

Smith, J. Douglas. *Managing White Supremacy: Race, Politics, and Citizenship in Jim Crow Virginia*. Chapel Hill: University of North Carolina Press, 2002.

Smith, S. E., ed. *The History of the Anti–Separate Coach Movement of Kentucky: Containing Half-Tone Cuts and Biographical Sketches*. Evansville, Ind.: National Afro-American Journal and Directory, 1895[?].

Somers, Dale A. "Black and White in New Orleans: A Study in Urban Race Relations." *Journal of Southern History* 40 (February 1974): 19–42.

Stanton, Elizabeth Cady, Susan B. Anthony, and Matilda Joslyn Gage. *History of Woman Suffrage*. Vol. 2, *1861–1876*. New York: Arno, 1969.

Suggs, Henry Lewis, ed. *The Black Press in the South, 1865–1979*. Westport, Conn.: Greenwood, 1983.

Sumler-Edmond, Janice. "The Quest for Justice: African American Women Litigants, 1867–1890." In *African American Women and the Vote*, edited by Ann D. Gordon with Bettye Collier Thomas, 100–119. Amherst: University of Massachusetts Press, 1997.

Terrell, Mary Church. *A Colored Woman in a White World*. New York: Hall, 1996.

Thomas, Brook, ed. *Plessy v. Ferguson: A Brief History with Documents*. Boston: Bedford, 1997.

Thomas, William G. *Lawyering for the Railroad: Business, Law, and Power in the New South*. Baton Rouge: Louisiana State University Press, 1999.

Thompson, Shirley. " 'Ah Toucoutou, Ye Conin Vous': History and Memory in Creole New Orleans." *American Quarterly* 53 (June 2001): 232–66.

Tunnell, Ted. *Crucible of Reconstruction: War, Radicalism, and Race in Louisiana, 1862–1877*. Baton Rouge: Louisiana State University Press, 1984.

Wade, Richard C. *Slavery in the Cities: The South, 1820–1860*. New York: Oxford University Press, 1964.

Warner, Sam B. *Streetcar Suburbs: The Process of Growth in Boston, 1870–1900*. Cambridge: Harvard University Press and MIT Press, 1962.

Washington, Booker T. *Booker T. Washington Papers*. Edited by Louis Harlan. 14 vols. Urbana: University of Illinois Press, 1972–89.

——. *Up from Slavery*. New York: Signet Classic, 2000.

Welke, Barbara Young. *All the Women Are White, All the Blacks are Men, or Are They?: Law and Segregation on Common Carriers, 1855 to 1914*. ABF Working Paper 9215. Chicago: American Bar Foundation, 1992.

——. *Recasting American Liberty: Gender, Race, Law, and the Railroad Revolution, 1865–1920*. New York: Cambridge University Press, 2001.

Wells-Barnett, Ida B. *Crusade for Justice: The Autobiography of Ida B. Wells*. Edited by Alfreda M. Duster. Chicago: University of Chicago Press, 1970.

——. "Iola on Discrimination." In *The Memphis Diary of Ida B. Wells*, edited by Miriam Decosta-Willis, 186–87. Boston: Beacon, 1995.

——. "Mob Rule in New Orleans: Robert Charles and His Fight to the Death." In *Southern Horrors and Other Writings: The Anti-Lynching Campaign of Ida B. Wells, 1892–1900*, edited by Jacqueline Jones Royster, 158–208. Boston: Bedford/St. Martin's, 1997.

——. "The Model Woman: A Pen Picture of the Typical Southern Girl." In *The Memphis Diary of Ida B. Wells*, edited by Miriam Decosta-Willis, 187–89. Boston: Beacon, 1995.

West, Michael Rudolph. *The Education of Booker T. Washington: American Democracy and the Idea of Race Relations*. New York: Columbia University Press, 2006.

White, Deborah Gray. *Too Heavy a Load: Black Women in Defense of Themselves, 1894–1994*. New York: Norton, 1999.

White, John H., Jr. *The American Railroad Passenger Car*. Baltimore: Johns Hopkins University Press, 1978.

Wiggins, William H. *O Freedom!: Afro-American Emancipation Celebrations*. Knoxville: University of Tennessee Press, 1987.

Williamson, Joel. *New People: Miscegenation and Mulattoes in the United States*. New York: Free Press, 1980.

Woodward, C. Vann. "The National Decision against Equality." In *American Counterpoint: Slavery and Racism in the North-South Dialogue*, 212–33. Boston: Little, Brown, 1971.

——. *The Strange Career of Jim Crow*. New York: Oxford University Press, 1955.

Works Projects Administration of Virginia. *The Negro in Virginia*. New York: Hastings House, 1940.

Wright, George C. *Life behind a Veil: Blacks in Louisville, Kentucky, 1865–1930*. Baton Rouge: Louisiana State University Press, 1985.

Wynes, Charles E. "The Evolution of Jim Crow Laws in Twentieth Century Virginia." *Phylon* 28 (Winter 1967): 416–25.

INDEX

Parks, Rosa, 1

Passing, 53, 213 (n. 81); case of Lola Houck, 46–47; and Creoles of color, 54–55, 79, 80, 210 (nn. 10, 12); and mistaken identity, 95–96, 155; in *Autobiography of an Ex-Colored Man*, 195–96; "part-time," 209 (n. 38), 216 (n. 24)

Pearson, H. H., Jr., 89, 112–13, 114. *See also* New Orleans Railway Company

Penn, William H., 110

Pennington, James W. C.: background, 22–23, 205 (n. 26); contesting segregation, 24–29, 30, 31–32, 204 (n. 1)

People's Grocery Company, 44

Phillips, W. B., 158–59

Pinchback, P. B. S.: contesting segregation, 52, 92; and ACERA, 62–63, 64, 68–69, 211 (n. 32); and black colleges, 70, 212 (n. 61)

Plessy, Homer. See *Plessy v. Ferguson*

Plessy v. Ferguson (1896), 5, 11, 51, 98; segregation policy before, 15–16, 35–37; case, 51, 79–80, 81–82, 213 (n. 87); Homer Plessy, 56–57, 76–77, 200; and place in legal history, 82; response to, 82–85, 87; and subsequent protest, 106, 113–14; as legal precedent, 125, 143

Politics of protection, 108

Porter, Peter S., 29–30, 31

Portsmouth, Va., 162

Powhatan Club, 142

Price, A. D., 121

Price, Kate, 107

Prince Hall Masons, 9, 107, 166, 174, 175, 192

Progressivism, 89–90, 95, 173, 214–15 (n. 6)

Pullman Company, 33, 38, 208 (n. 20); cars, 52, 76

Pullman porters, 38, 97

Race riots, 40, 87, 92, 119, 146; New Orleans (1900), 96–101; threats of, 148; Atlanta (1906), 162–63, 181–85, 197, 214–15 (n. 6), 216 (n. 37), 229 (n. 58)

Racial violence: ejection from streetcars, 15, 17–20, 25–26, 29–30, 52, 92, 106, 206 (n. 51); ejection from trains, 17, 35, 38–42, 43, 45–47, 73, 77, 79, 208 (n. 15); attacks on streetcars, 97, 161, 170–72, 181; random violence against African Americans, 99, 180–81; attacks against black workers during labor disputes, 98.*See also* Lynching; Race riots; Sexual assault against African American women

Railroads: segregation, 6–7, 34–41, 45–46, 51, 62, 64, 93, 142–44; suits, 6–8, 39, 40–46; descriptions of cars, 7–8, 34–42; gender divisions, 42–48, 66–68, 77; passing on board, 46–47, 75; class divisions, 47–49, 55. *See also* Excursions; Racial violence

Readjuster Party, 134, 219 (n. 6)

Reconstruction, 4, 9, 12, 67, 70, 71, 83, 120, 134, 141, 144, 148, 166, 211 (n. 36), 213 (n. 64); law, 16; northern black volunteers, 31–32; railroads, 33–37; excursions, 47; political alliances between Creoles of color and Americanized black leaders, 52; Afro-Creole leadership, 54; black migration to New Orleans, La., 57–58, 88; erosion of legal gains after, 62, 83, 89; protesting segregation and exclusion, 92–93, 140, 142; education during, 126

Republican Party, 12, 34, 58, 64, 69, 73–74, 121, 144, 171, 174, 183, 199

Rice, Thomas "Daddy," 16–17, 180

Richmond, Va., 8, 115, 185, 203 (n. 20), 219 (nn. 3, 6); antebellum segregation, 92; Reconstruction-era protest, 93, 125, 142; African American class